The Certified Quality Auditor's HACCP Handbook

Also available from ASQ Quality Press

After the Quality Audit: Closing the Loop on the Audit Process, Second Edition
J. P. Russell and Terry Regel

Internal Quality Auditing
Denise Pronovost

Puzzling Auditing Puzzles
J. P. Russell and Janice Russell

The Quality Audit Handbook, Second Edition
J. P. Russell, editing director

Fundamentals of Quality Auditing
B. Scott Parsowith

Food Processing Industry Quality System Guidelines
ASQ Food, Drug, and Cosmetic Division

To request a complimentary catalog of ASQ Quality Press publications, call 800-248-1946, or visit our Web site at www.qualitypress.asq.org .

The Certified Quality Auditor's HACCP Handbook

ASQ Food, Drug, and Cosmetic Division

ASQ Quality Press
Milwaukee, Wisconsin

The Certified Quality Auditor's HACCP Handbook
ASQ Food, Drug, and Cosmetic Division

Library of Congress Cataloging-in-Publication Data

The certified quality auditor's HACCP handbook / ASQ Food, Drug, and Cosmetic Division.
   p. cm.
  Includes bibliographical references and index.
  ISBN 0-87389-496-0 (alk. paper)
  1. Food adulteration and inspection—Handbooks, manuals, etc. 2. Food handling—Safety
measures—Handbooks, manuals, etc. 3. Food industry and trade—Safety measures—Handbooks,
manuals, etc. I. American Society for Quality. Food, Drug, and Cosmetic Division.

TX531 .C47 2002
363.19'26—dc21   2001004220

10 9 8 7 6 5 4 3 2 1

ISBN 0-87389-496-0

Acquisitions Editor: Annemieke Koudstaal
Project Editor: Craig S. Powell
Production Administrator: Gretchen Trautman
Special Marketing Representative: Denise M. Cawley

ASQ Mission: The American Society for Quality advances individual, organizational,
and community excellence worldwide through learning, quality improvement, and
knowledge exchange.

Attention Bookstores, Wholesalers, Schools and Corporations: ASQ Quality Press books,
videotapes, audiotapes, and software are available at quantity discounts with bulk purchases for
business, educational, or instructional use. For information, please contact ASQ Quality Press at
800-248-1946, or write to ASQ Quality Press, P.O. Box 3005, Milwaukee, WI 53201-3005.

To place orders or to request a free copy of the ASQ Quality Press Publications Catalog, including
ASQ membership information, call 800-248-1946. Visit our Web site at www.asq.org or
http://qualitypress.asq.org .

Printed in the United States of America

 Printed on acid-free paper

American Society for Quality

Quality Press
600 N. Plankinton Avenue
Milwaukee, Wisconsin 53203
Call toll free 800-248-1946
Fax 414-272-1734
www.asq.org
http://qualitypress.asq.org
http://standardsgroup.asq.org
E-mail: authors@asq.org

Table of Contents

Part IV   Applying HACCP to the Food Processing Industry

Part VI   Appendices

Foreword

The *Certified Quality Auditor's HACCP Handbook* is intended to serve as a baseline of hazard analysis critical control point (HACCP) knowledge for quality auditors. It provides a description of the HACCP principles and a discussion of how these principles are applied to various segments of the food industry and the medical device industry.

HACCP is more than failure mode effect analysis (FMEA) for food. It is a product safety management system that evolved and matured in the commercial food processing industry to allow food processors to take a proactive approach to prevent food borne diseases. Over the years, HACCP has been slowly accepted by the food processing industry. In 1973, the Food and Drug Administration (FDA) published Low Acid Canned Food Regulations. These regulations were developed using the principles of HACCP. Later the FDA developed and published the Pasteurized Milk Ordinance, another set of regulations based on HACCP. In 1985, The Food and Nutrition Board of the National Research Council published two books recommending that HACCP be used as a product safety system to ensure the production of safe food. Since these landmark publications, HACCP has been incorporated into food regulations and customer purchasing requirements. Both the FDA and United States Department of Agriculture (USDA) have embraced HACCP as the most effective method to ensure farm-to-table food safety in the United States. Furthermore, with the incorporation of the seven principles of HACCP into the Codex Alimentarius Commission Food Hygiene standard, HACCP has been embraced as the international standard for ensuring food safety. Recently, HACCP has expanded beyond the food processing industry and is being piloted in the medical device industry. The FDA is evaluating the pilot results to determine whether HACCP should be incorporated into medical device regulations.

This volume could not have been undertaken without the help of a cross-functional team. The contributors to this volume represent industry, regulatory, and academic sectors. They also represent a wealth of perspectives and experiences in processed foods, meat and poultry, seafood, dairy, food service, farming, and medical devices. The contributors have applied HACCP to both large and small manufacturing operations and many have extensive international experience in applying the HACCP principles in other cultural settings. I would like to give special thanks to three friends who helped edit this volume: Prosy Abarquez-Delacruz, Don Cripe, and Janice Smith. In addition, I would like to thank the following professionals (listed alphabetically) who wrote chapters for this volume:

Prosy Abarquez-Delacruz, J.D.	Jeff Kronenberg, Ph.D.
Bill Bennet	Michael Mihalic
Dana Coleman	Mary Ann Platt
Kathryn Cooper	Irwin Plonk
Nate Geary	Jim Rushing, Ph.D.
Kelly Karr Getty, Ph.D.	Marianne Smukowski
Bruce Haggar	Len Steed
Michael Hernandez	John Surak, Ph.D.
Masaaki J. Hori	Steve Wilson

I would also like to thank Robert Diaz, Suchart Choven, Michelle Iannucci, Andy Gould, Ed Nelson, Cliff Pappas, Ph.D., and John Rushing, Ph.D., for providing valuable input to this volume. This volume would not have been possible without the leadership of the 1999-2000 chair of the Food, Drug, and Cosmetic Division of the American Society for Quality (ASQ), Ed Nelson. Ed utilized the division's chair award to fund this project.

The Food, Drug, and Cosmetic Division of ASQ has taken leadership in providing services to assist companies verifying HACCP programs. In 1999, the Division led the development of the ASQ Certified Quality Auditor's (CQA)-HACCP examination. The Division's 2001 vision of resources for quality systems and leadership development in FDA–regulated industries inspired the undertaking of this book. As quality professionals, it is the Division membership's intent also to be part of the leadership efforts to implement safety in conjunction with quality and operational excellence in all industries, such that each manufacturing and distribution firm has a *house of safety and quality* anchored in HACCP (hazard analysis critical control points), *good manufacturing practices* (GMPs), *quality management systems*, and *sanitation standard operating procedures* (SSOPs). By institutionalizing these efforts, quality and safety will be sustained for generations to come.

John G. Surak, Ph.D.
Senior Editor and Project Leader
Clemson, SC, USA

Part I

An Introduction to HACCP

1

History and Overview of HACCP: Primitive and Modern Food Preservation Methods

Humans have been concerned with the availability of food from the dawn of their existence. Prehistoric humans were hunters and gatherers who needed to find and catch food. As time passed humans began to grow and preserve their own food. And still later in history, humans became concerned with preparing, conserving, and maintaining a steady supply of food. Advances in social organization from small group to large group living, and from nomadic hunting and gathering to communal life in a fixed place paralleled the need for a reliable source of food.

The methods for saving food for the proverbial rainy day may have begun with air drying, salting, and the use of spices and herbs; and then advanced to more sophisticated technologies such as canning and freezing. Advances in technology took thousands of years, and many occurred by accident. Transfer of technology occurred slowly because of lack of communication and commerce among geographically dispersed societal groups.

However, as trade and communications increased, primitive food preservation technologies were transferred from one culture to another. Two examples of this are (1) the drying of grain and the storage of those grains in large granaries in the Middle East and Africa; and (2) the bringing of pasta, a different form of preserved grain, from China to Europe by the explorer Marco Polo. As commerce became more important, laws were developed to control the quantity and quality of traded goods, including food, as well as services. The first comprehensive written code was set down by Hammurabi, circa 2500 B.C. Later, laws were set forth in the Torah and the Holy Bible (see Leviticus, chapter 11 and Deuteronomy, chapter 7). Since all of the advances in food preservation technology are impossible to chronicle here, only some of the more important advances that have influenced modern techniques for making safe food available to all are discussed below. All modern methods are not new: primitive preservation methods such as drying, salting, and smoking are still used. Other currently used methods for preserving foods include heat preservation by canning in hermetically sealed containers, pasteurization, freezing, freeze-drying, and air drying. The use of these preservation methods was the first documented preventive response to anticipated hazards. The anticipatory and preventive methodology that became known as HACCP began here.

HACCP PREDECESSORS

At some point, scientists discovered that microscopic organisms could cause food spoilage. This led to the theory that food could be preserved if the spoilage organisms could be destroyed and kept from reentering the food product. For this to occur, the temperature and water content of food had to be reduced to levels that would not support the growth of spoilage organisms. Pasteur and Clarence Birdseye were leaders in food processing technology. Additionally, research in industrial areas unrelated to the production of food by quality gurus such as Walter A. Shewhart, J. M. Juran, and W. Edwards Deming was adapted by others and applied to the control of quality in the production and preservation of food.

One of the earliest collaborative efforts of industry and government addressed the problems of milk borne disease. In the 1920s, two industry associations and one professional association developed uniform standards for fittings used in dairy and food handling equipment. The standards for fittings became known as 3-A Standards. "Since 1944, the 3-A Program has included representation from suppliers and equipment fabricators, all national dairy processing associations, the U.S. Department of Agriculture (USDA), the U.S. Public Health Service (USPHS) and state regulatory agencies."[1]

Milk safety was accomplished by controlling the following factors, which are elements of what is known today as the hazard analysis and critical control point (HACCP)[2] approach to product safety:

- the health and sanitation of the dairy herd

- the times of collection and temperatures of milk from collection to processing

- the use of a terminal heat treatment to reduce microbial content

- the standardization of equipment

- the scrupulous cleaning of processing plant and equipment

- the control of the temperature of the processed product after pasteurization and while in transit and in storage

As the populace of the United States shifted from agrarian to urban living, there was an increasing need to process foods for mass transport and consumption in cities. The early emphasis on raw agricultural products later shifted to processed products.

---

[1]More information about the 3-A Program is available online at: www.3-a.org/main.html.

[2]Hazard analysis and critical control points. The terms "hazard analysis and critical control points system" or "hazards analysis and critical control points concept" are used interchangeably.

Currently, food is prepared outside of the home for consumption in homes, restaurants, hospitals, nursing homes, and prisons; aboard airplanes, ships, and trains; during camping or wartime; and even in space vehicles. These new modes of consumption required the development of new methods for use in the preparation, packaging, and storage of foods to ensure the availability of food that is safe, nutritious, and wholesome.

HACCP AND THE SPACE PROGRAM

In the late 1950s, the National Aeronautics and Space Administration (NASA) saw the need for special foods for space travel.[2] The early space vehicles were small, and there was neither room for standard kitchen appliances—refrigerator, stove, freezer—nor for the pantry, cupboards, and countertops commonly used for the storage and preparation of foods. In addition, concerns existed about the kinds of food that an astronaut could take on a space journey to provide proper nutritional, gustatory, and safety properties. It was also important that the space vehicle and its contents not introduce harmful microorganisms into space.

Before the dawn of the space age, food quality and safety were controlled mainly by inspection after the fact. But NASA wanted assurances that safety was built into the design of the food. In the early 1960s, the Pillsbury Company was asked to develop the first space foods, as well as to design a system for controlling the safety of space foods, used first for the *Mercury* flights, and later for the *Gemini* and *Apollo* flights. NASA was also concerned about food crumbs floating in the cabin and fouling the instruments of the space vehicles. Pillsbury easily solved the crumb problem by coating bite-sized pieces of food to prevent crumbling. But they had a more daunting task in ensuring the bacterial quality of space foods.

To ensure that foods used in the space program were safe, Pillsbury developed the hazard analysis and critical control point (HACCP) system outlined in Figure 1.1. HACCP was designed to prevent safety hazards. By systematically evaluating the ingredients, environs, and processes used to fabricate a food; identifying areas of potential risk; and determining the critical control points (that is, those points in the process that must be controlled to prevent an unacceptable risk), the manufacturer would have assurance of process and product integrity.

As the NASA flights became longer, additional logistical requirements challenged Pillsbury to refine the HACCP system. Pillsbury collaborated with NASA and the U.S. Army's Natick Laboratories to develop HACCP as a proactive system for manufacturing and supplying safe foods for space travelers. By the time the Eagle landed and man set foot on the moon in 1969, Pillsbury had developed HACCP as we know it today.

However, in 1967 the U.S. Food and Drug Administration (FDA) and the food industry began a pilot self-certification program that was designed to incorporate HACCP concepts into the food manufacturing process. In addition, participants in the

---

[3]More information about the U.S. space program is available online at: www.spaceflight.nasa.gov/history.

HACCP involves seven principles:

- Analyze hazards. Potential hazards associated with a food and measures to control those hazards are identified. The hazards could be biological, such as a microbe; chemical, such as a toxin; or physical, such as ground glass or metal fragments.

- Identify critical control points. These are points in a food's production—from its raw state through processing and shipping to consumption by the consumer—at which the potential hazard can be controlled or eliminated. Examples are cooking, cooling, packaging, and metal detection.

- Establish preventive measures with critical limits for each control point. For a cooked food, for example, this might include setting the minimum cooking temperature and time required to ensure the elimination of any harmful microbes.

- Establish procedures to monitor the critical control points. Such procedures might include determining how and by whom cooking time and temperature should be monitored.

- Establish corrective action to be taken when monitoring shows that a critical limit has not been met—for example, reprocessing or disposing of food if the minimum cooking temperature is not met.

- Establish procedures to verify that the system is working properly—for example, testing time-and-temperature recording devices to verify that a cooking unit is working properly.

- Establish effective record keeping to document the HACCP system. This would include records of hazards and their control methods, the monitoring of safety requirements, and action taken to correct potential problems. Each of these principles must be backed by sound scientific knowledge: for example, published microbiological studies on time and temperature factors for controlling food borne pathogens.

Figure 1.1   What is HACCP?

Source: U.S. Food and Drug Administration. "A State-of-the-Art Approach to Food Safety." FDA Backgrounder (August 1999).

pilot program were required to share information about their products and processes and quality control, including planned changes, with the FDA. The overall objectives were (1) to have the industry participants exercise more control over their operations, and (2) to give the FDA a better view of the controls exercised by the industry participants than a random inspection would allow. This program was ahead of its time. It was not politically correct then, so it felt the wrath of Congress and the consumer, neither of whom believed that industry was capable of "self-certifying." The FDA altered the program and eliminated the name "self-certification," calling it instead, the "cooperative quality assurance program." However, the revamped program (later discontinued) retained HACCP at its core.

APPLICATION OF HACCP TO OTHER INDUSTRIES

In the early 1970s, Pillsbury transferred the HACCP concept from the space program to production in its commercial food plants. This technology was also transferred to the FDA in a contract for training FDA personnel in HACCP concepts. In the early 1960s, the State of California's Department of Health pioneered the application of HACCP in its canning industry. It became the prototype for a regulation—21 Code of Federal Regulations, Part 113—promulgated by the FDA in the mid-1970s in response to an industry petition. This regulation, more commonly known as 21 CFR Part 113, incorporates HACCP concepts to govern the production of low-acid canned foods in hermetically sealed containers. HACCP is now mandatory in the FDA program for food safety for fish and shellfish (21 CFR Part 123) and other products.[4]

What made HACCP so popular after languishing for so long? After all, HACCP had been used in food processing plants since the late 1960s but had not been adopted on a large scale. Perhaps the climate was right: public health officials were concerned about emerging pathogens, and consumers and industry were concerned about food safety. These sectors with converging interests knew there had to be a better way to ensure the safety of foods. Similarly, the economy had become globalized and food safety had become an international, rather than simply a national, concern.

A succession of reports by three prestigious groups opened the door to HACCP on a global basis:

- The National Academy of Sciences report *Microbiological Criteria for Foods and Food Ingredients,* 1985

- Report of The International Commission for the Microbiological Specifications for Food (ICMFS), 1988

- The Codex Commission on Food Hygiene's *Guidelines for the Application of the Hazard Analysis and Critical Control Point (HACCP) System,* 1991, adopted by the Joint FAO/WHO Codex Commission, 20th Session, 1993.

Today, technology from the space meals systems has been transferred to the private sector and is being used in meal systems for the elderly.[5] Regulators now require manufacturers of certain foods to use HACCP systems, and will probably require HACCP systems for additional foods in areas where food safety problems become

---

[4]More information about the National Food Safety Initiative and HACCP in the federal government is available online at: vm.cfsan.fda.gov/list.html.

[5]More information on meal systems for the elderly is available online at: www.jsc.nasa.gov/pao/spinoffs/mealsys.html.

apparent. U.S. Congressional committees with oversight of federal agency programs will watch closely as HACCP's proactive system of hazard identification and prevention is integrated into these agencies' industry requirements. Over time these actions at the federal level may lead to the adoption of HACCP by the entire food industry. In anticipation of this, some sectors of the food industry have adopted HACCP voluntarily as they gain a greater appreciation of its advantages in preventing food safety problems. HACCP has proven to be an effective system for preventing food borne diseases and increasing the safety of foods. This knowledge has influenced other industries regulated by the FDA. Currently the seven principles of HACCP are being applied on a pilot scale to the medical device industry to increase the safety of their products.

2

Tasks for HACCP
Plan Development

ASSESSING THE NEED FOR A HACCP PLAN

The information contained in a HACCP plan will vary since unique cultural issues and many different processes exist within individual companies. Normally a HACCP plan is product- and process-specific, but some plans use a *unit operations* or *recipe* approach. For example, in a retail setup, a HACCP plan could be developed for a specific clam chowder recipe or for heat-processed foods in general.

Assessing the need for the implementation of a HACCP plan is the responsibility of the executive management group. External pressures to implement a HACCP system are exerted on industry from two primary sources: government regulations and customer requirements. In industries where HACCP is mandated by government (regulatory HACCP), the choice to implement and maintain a viable HACCP system is a foregone conclusion because it is a requirement of doing business for both large and small organizations. Although less prescriptive, customer-motivated HACCP requirements typically are viewed as being market driven or as offering a strategic advantage in a competitive market place. The following list suggests common reasons for implementing a HACCP program.

- The company's internal nonconforming product is responsible for the loss of a significant sum of money.

- Competitors making similar products have experienced marketplace failures that have resulted in costly product recalls, loss of customers, and loss of market share.

- National and international government agencies and standards-setting groups require all processors, distributors, and retailers to participate in a regulated HACCP program.

- A large customer mandates that all suppliers must implement a verifiable HACCP program to remain a preferred supplier.

- Even when a HACCP program is not required, many companies voluntarily choose to implement one because they think it is the right thing to do and believe it may provide a marketing advantage.[1]

PRELIMINARY TASKS FOR HACCP DEVELOPMENT

In the development of a HACCP plan, five preliminary tasks need to be completed before the HACCP principles are applied to a specific product and/or process: (1) assemble the HACCP team, (2) describe the product and its distribution, (3) describe the intended use and consumers of the product, (4) develop a flow diagram that describes the process, and (5) verify the accuracy of the flow diagram.

Assembling the HACCP Team

The executive management group is responsible for providing the necessary budget and resource planning to ensure effective implementation and maintenance of the HACCP system. When communicating the need for HACCP and expressing the desire to make it part of the organization's culture, management should clearly define the goals of the program and when the program is expected to be fully operational. Some companies include their product safety goals in policy statements that are easily understood by all company personnel. An example of a typical policy statement would be "To produce safe product worldwide."

An upper-level manager often signs the HACCP plan as a record of official endorsement. The executive management group is responsible for communicating the direction of the organization and the need to change for regulatory compliance and customer satisfaction.

Regardless of the size of the organization, an individual employee's knowledge of product safety issues in the raw materials, the process, the product use, and distribution requirements will be influenced by diverse circumstances and a unique corporate culture. Regulated HACCP systems specifically require that personnel involved in the planning, implementation, and maintenance of a HACCP system receive documented training. In order to analyze and develop the resources available within the organization, it is recommended that the HACCP team be multidisciplinary. This helps to ensure that primary and shared responsibilities are not overlooked or heavily loaded onto one department, for example the quality department.

Table 2.1 may be helpful in deciding what departments have primary or shared responsibilities for the steps required for HACCP plan implementation. Table 2.1 could be useful for audit planning since it indicates the department and personnel responsible for individual components of the HACCP system.

Table 2.1 Establishing company accountabilities and audit responsibilities for HACCP.

HACCP requirement	Executive group	R&D	QA	Process and packaging	Purchasing	Sales and marketing	Distribution
HACCP team members	S	S	P	S	S	S	S
Product type and distribution	S	P	S	S		S	S
Intended use and customers	S	P				S	
Develop flow diagram		S	S	P			S
Verify flow diagram		S	S	P			S
1. Conduct hazard analysis		S	P	S			
2. Identify CCPs		S	P	S			S
3. Establish critical limits		P	S	S			
4. Establish monitoring procedures		S	S	P			S
5. Establish corrective actions		S	S	P			
6. Establish record keeping procedures			P	S			
7. Establish verification procedures	S	S	P	S			

P = Primary   S = Shared
The company needs to establish which departments and personnel are responsible for the individual HACCP requirements.
The independent HACCP auditors need to establish which departments and personnel are responsible for the individual components of the HACCP system.

The task of assembling and maintaining a HACCP team is an auditable activity. A HACCP auditor must allow for differences in approach and company culture when reviewing the structure and participants in an organization's HACCP system. Auditors reviewing a program controlled by a HACCP plan must be open-minded and focused on scientific suitability and effective execution of the product safety plan. Competent auditors exclude personal preferences while conducting audits and report on positive and negative aspects of the program in an objective manner. A typical audit review of the development of the HACCP team may include the following questions.

1. *Why did the organization start HACCP and what consultants or company departments were included on the project?* The HACCP team should include balanced representation from all plant departments to ensure that personnel with appropriate expertise

have participated in the development of the HACCP system. It is not unusual for the HACCP team to include outside facilitators such as consultants, academics, or the corporate quality group when internal resources are inadequate or unavailable to construct a scientifically valid HACCP plan. During the course of the audit, the knowledge level and expertise of HACCP participants should be evaluated by reviewing qualifications, assessing the logic used to construct the HACCP plan, and interviewing employees. The purpose of this review is to evaluate if the auditee has demonstrated enough cross-functional expertise to adequately analyze the significant biological, chemical, and physical hazards in its product and process. As a group, the ideal HACCP team would include employees with technical and practical knowledge of raw materials, process equipment, packaging, and distribution requirements. The inclusion of manufacturing staff on the HACCP team is encouraged because these employees are the ones who typically monitor *critical control points* (CCPs). Access to personnel records may be governed by regulatory or company guidelines, so auditors reviewing qualifications should take great care to ensure that the auditee is comfortable with this process.

2. *Have the HACCP team and the team leader or coordinator been suitably identified in the company's documentation system?* The auditor should be able to easily identify the members of the HACCP team, as well as the team leader, or coordinator. The HACCP team's responsibilities should be clearly defined in the quality system procedures, work instructions, or forms contained in the HACCP system documentation. The auditor must be able to identify the person(s) responsible for the five preliminary requirements for HACCP plan implementation, as well as those responsible for the application of the seven principles of HACCP: conducting a hazard analysis (chapter 3), determining critical control points, or CCPs (chapter 4), establishing critical limits (chapter 5), establishing monitoring procedures (chapter 6), establishing procedures for corrective actions and product disposition (chapter 7), establishing verification procedures (chapter 8), and identifying records that will be retained as evidence that the HACCP system is effectively implemented (chapter 9). Well-defined responsibilities for specified requirements, activities, and records to be audited will help the auditors complete their evaluations in an efficient manner. The HACCP team leader has the responsibility of communicating the overall effectiveness of the HACCP system, resolving internal conflict, and communicating resource needs to executive management.

3. *Have the HACCP team and other appropriate personnel received HACCP training?* Personnel responsible for implementing and maintaining the HACCP system should receive initial and ongoing training from an accredited HACCP course provider. If the plant, corporate group, or customer has provided in-house HACCP training, the auditor should review the content of the course to ensure that it complies with recognized HACCP guidelines. The auditor should access training records for the HACCP team members, the personnel performing CCP monitoring, and those administering the program to ensure that HACCP training is current.

Potential areas of weakness may be found in companies with high personnel turnover rates or where HACCP systems have been written and implemented with little or no involvement of plant personnel. Where appropriate, an auditor may correlate

HACCP system deficiencies to the effectiveness of the training or to availability of resources provided by executive management.

Auditors should not serve as consultants while performing a third-party audit. However, ISO 10011, *Guidelines for Auditing Quality Systems*, allows an auditor to offer nonbinding recommendations termed "opportunities for improvement." These guidelines permit an auditor to inform the auditee where further information, guidance materials, or technical literature can be obtained without compromising impartiality during the audit process. Additionally, the scope of an audit should be communicated prior to the on-site visit and confirmed during the opening meeting to ensure that there is agreement as to which products and process lines are to be audited for compliance with the company's HACCP system.

Describing the Product and Its Distribution

The company must have a clear description of the products produced and distribution requirements, as well as descriptions of any intermediate products or by-products sold as raw materials to other processing plants. This permits the proper identification of hazards and allows the team to reasonably limit the scope of the hazards analysis to events that can occur from manufacturing to the marketplace. The audit team might consider the following questions.

1. *What product(s) does the plant make at this site and what product line(s) is included in the HACCP system audit?* This simple question will help clarify which areas of the plant and what records are to be assessed during the audit. Once the scope of the audit is confirmed, the audit team can plan the HACCP system audit by assigning areas or criteria to be assessed to individual auditors. It is the auditee's responsibility to provide plant contacts for assisting in the review of HACCP activities and records. The lead auditor will typically make the team auditor assignments, check on the progress of the audit, confirm nonconformances, and report on the overall effectiveness of the HACCP system at the closing meeting.

2. *What HACCP system standard is to be applied?* Regulated HACCP systems typically have a defined performance standard, and forms issued by the relevant government agency for documenting HACCP plans. The auditors should be familiar with the required forms and have a checklist for the HACCP standard used during the audit. It is common practice for the auditing group to send a copy of the blank audit checklist to the auditee so that the audit criteria can be reviewed prior to the actual on-site audit. The auditing group often includes a list naming the auditors who will be performing the audit and stating their qualifications. This enables the auditee to feel secure that the auditors are qualified to review their product and process.

In unregulated HACCP systems, emphasis and structure may vary because of company and customer influence. It is important to note that the HACCP system standard used should apply only to product safety, not quality issues. The HACCP standard used by the company to formulate its program should be clearly established to explain HACCP system exclusions and potentially conflicting requirements. A reference copy of the HACCP standard should be available for review to define interpretations when differences of opinion occur during the audit. Examples of recognized HACCP systems include, but are not limited to, the U.S. National Advisory Committee on Microbiological Criteria for Foods (NACMCF), the WHO/FAO Codex Alimentarius Commission for HACCP, the U.S. Food and Drug Administration's Seafood HACCP Regulation, and the U.S. Department of Agriculture's HACCP Regulation (USDA/FSIS) for meat and poultry.

3. *What is the common name of your product(s), processing methods, and the distribution requirements?* The common name for the product produced typically will be stated in the introduction section of the HACCP system manual, product specification sheet, quality plan, or product form. The auditor should obtain a list of all products produced on-site at the plant. This information can be obtained from multiple sources at the plant, such as the sales, quality, or production departments. The information from each source should be compared to evaluate whether the list of products produced is up-to-date and to verify that new and existing product or process modifications have been effectively communicated to the appropriate personnel. For example, the marketing, product development, and production departments usually are responsible for new products, new processes, process changes, and raw material changes. Has the company effectively reviewed HACCP requirements with regards to new raw materials and the plant's capability to make the product safely on the existing or new equipment? How are changes communicated to the affected departments and what group reviews the impact on existing HACCP systems? Although changes in raw materials, the process, or product can be viewed as reassessment activities, the organization should explain how these activities are achieved relative to their HACCP system requirements.

The list of products produced can be used to sample the processing methods and testing methods contained in the HACCP plan or the quality plan. The distribution requirements are contained in the quality plan and should include the requirements for safe handling of the product to ensure product integrity throughout the distribution chain. Examples of safe handling instructions include labeling the product for shelf life, temperature, and humidity requirements. The testing data and technical information used to determine product handling, storage, and distribution requirements should be available for review to clarify the logic used when establishing requirements for product safety.

Describing the Intended Use and End User

The normal intended use of the product and likely end user of the product must be clearly defined in the HACCP system documentation. Even though many companies state that their product is to be used by the general public, certain population groups may have unique risk factors that preclude safe use of the product. Some potential users of the product may have special needs and considerations due to their age group or the condition of their health. Typically, infants, young children, the elderly, and the immunocompromised present the largest concern because people in these age groups or conditions may not be able to withstand the stress of treatment with or consumption of the product, resulting in severe health consequences.

Another avenue for reviewing appropriate, or in some cases inappropriate, customer use would be during the review of the prerequisite programs for HACCP (see pages 17–19 of this chapter for a general overview of prerequisite programs and chapter 12 for an in-depth discussion of prerequisite areas pertaining to food safety). Serious safety issues associated with the use of a product should be recorded in the customer complaint program. The auditor should sample the product-safety-related customer complaints and look for recorded instances where consumption or usage has led to significant illness or injury. If controllable hazards have been identified as a result of consumer complaints, the company needs to institute corrective action and verify the effectiveness of the actions taken.

Developing a Process Flow Diagram

Next, a process flow diagram should be developed to evaluate each process step, from receiving of raw materials to shipping of product, to ensure that significant product safety hazards have not been overlooked or underestimated. The flow diagram should represent all process steps under the control of the company and may include steps prior to and after the plant's operation. The auditor should ask who or what group has the primary responsibility for each HACCP step. Typically, the personnel responsible for developing a flow diagram are members of the HACCP team. Often, the best results are achieved by including personnel from the engineering, maintenance, quality, and production departments. These employees' practical and technical knowledge of the process and equipment makes them valuable team members.

During initial development, the flow diagram should be very detailed. Each step in the process or movement of product through the manufacturing process should be noted. All steps from receiving to shipping must be identified so that the members of the HACCP team can use their combined knowledge to analyze potential product safety hazards. Biological, chemical, and physical hazards that are deemed significant and reasonably likely to occur, or that are inherent in the raw materials, must be reviewed for appropriate controls during the hazard analysis assessment. After hazard analysis assessment has been completed, the flow diagram may be simplified to make it easier to understand and to clearly represent the placement of the CCPs.

For simplicity and ease of understanding, process flow diagrams are usually represented in block formation. The auditor should be flexible and accept any reasonable format for flow diagrams as long as the content is accurate and understandable. Both handwritten flow diagrams and computer-generated models are acceptable since the method used often depends on the resources available within the organization.

Verifying the Accuracy of the Process Flow Diagram

The process and responsibility for verifying the accuracy of a process flow diagram should be clearly stated in the organization's HACCP quality system procedures. The company may elect to have the HACCP team physically "walk through" the entire process from receiving to shipping to gain consensus as to whether the flow diagram clearly depicts the process. The company should have a valid reason for the manner in which it has chosen to construct the flow diagram. Where there are considerable amounts of raw materials, processing equipment such as receiving stations or conveyors, or inspection and testing prior to processing, the company may elect to break out receiving into a separate flow diagram for clarity and accuracy in hazard analysis review. This approach, if appropriate, will allow for a thorough review of the company's existing product safety procedures, generally referred to as prerequisite programs for HACCP.

Failing to include a process step in the HACCP plan will result in an inaccurate representation of the process and could lead to disastrous consequences. The omission of a processing step could mean that the step was not subjected to the required scientific hazard analysis review for biological, chemical, and physical hazards. A HACCP auditor should physically review the flow diagrams during the plant audit and understand how they were constructed.

In regulated HACCP, process flow diagrams usually are signed and dated to serve as a record that they were officially reviewed. The HACCP auditor should review all flow diagrams to ensure that they were reviewed and accepted as accurate within the site being audited. The following question should be asked when reviewing process flow diagrams: "What group or person is responsible for verifying the accuracy of the flow diagrams and how are the diagrams kept up-to-date?"

The HACCP auditor should allow enough time to actually walk through the plant to sample the accuracy and content of the flow diagrams. If process steps are omitted or bundled (grouped together) on the flow diagram, the auditor should ask the HACCP team to explain why this choice was made. For example, most flow diagrams state that receiving is the first step. However, the auditor may note that several bulk raw materials are received at the facility in addition to palletized raw materials. The bulk systems may contain sieving or other control systems designed to protect product safety or integrity. The auditor should assess each situation individually by asking questions and requesting more documentation that proves that product safety systems are in effect.

Another potential area of weakness is the handling of rework product. Most processes generate some type of rework. If the auditor notes that rework is being placed back into the process flow the question should be asked: How and by what activities are product safety controls being applied? In most cases, the application of the prerequisite programs will allow for effective preventive controls, but the significance of omissions noted on a process flow diagram must be investigated and evaluated by the audit team.

The organization should have documented procedures that address how a change in manufacturing prompts a review or modification of the original process flow diagram. The quality system procedures should state what group is responsible for reacting to process changes that could affect the HACCP product safety systems, and explain how that information should be communicated throughout the company. At a minimum, the process flow diagrams should be reviewed annually to ensure that any changes in the manufacturing process have been reviewed for their impact on the HACCP product safety systems. Examples of process changes may include equipment replacement, equipment additions, line relocation, or significant equipment modifications. The HACCP auditor should ask about changes to the manufacturing process and look for evidence that the process flow diagram is still technically accurate. Figure 2.1 is a verified process flow diagram with the CCPs noted.

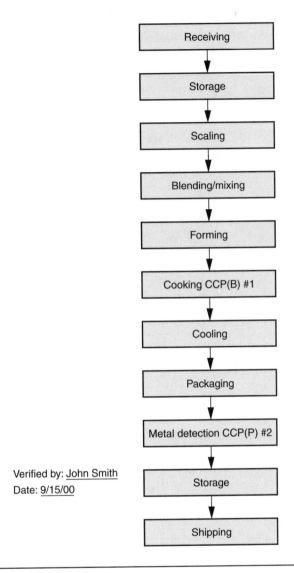

Figure 2.1 Verified process flow diagram.

ESTABLISHING THE PREREQUISITE PROGRAM

An important part of the establishment of a successful HACCP system is the prior or simultaneous implementation of a prerequisite product safety program. Elements of a prerequisite program are the building blocks or foundation to the "House of Product Safety" (see Figure 2.2). The National Advisory Committee on Microbiological Criteria for Foods (NACMCF) specifies in its guidelines for application of HACCP principles[2] (1997) that a food HACCP system should be built on a solid foundation of prerequisite programs. Prerequisites are procedures, including good manufacturing practices (GMPs), which address adequate and sufficient operational conditions to protect public

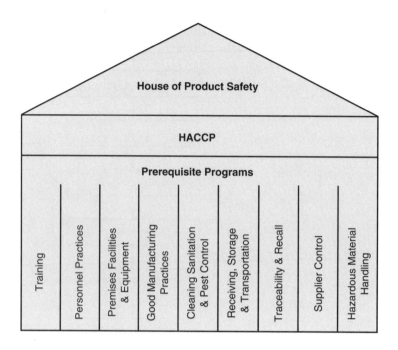

Figure 2.2   House of Product Safety.

health. These procedures include personnel hygiene practices; employee training; cleaning and sanitation procedures; product recall programs; design, operation, and maintenance of equipment, grounds, and facilities; water safety; and handling of product throughout manufacturing and distribution.

An effective HACCP system cannot be built without the underpinning prerequisite programs. Prerequisite programs typically are not part of a HACCP system, and items covered in prerequisites rarely are designated as CCPs. This concept has been well-defined when applying HACCP in the food processing industry. The primary difference between CCPs and prerequisite controls is that prerequisites ensure that food products are wholesome and do not contain objectionable contaminants, whereas CCPs are established solely for the purpose of controlling significant, life- or health-threatening food hazards. Prerequisite programs address these types of food hazards only in instances where the hazard analysis for ingredients/raw materials and for process steps indicates that such a hazard has a low likelihood for occurrence. For example, even though broken glass from overhead light fixtures can be a significant food hazard, glass control and shielding of glass in overhead lighting usually is designated as a prerequisite program. This is because typically there is a very low likelihood or frequency of breakage incidents in food plants. Thus, CCPs address food safety only, while prerequisites overlap into product quality and may involve other types of controls, such as quality or "control" points and operational steps. Finally, since CCPs apply to food hazards at specific points or steps in production or the process flow, they are specific to individual products and production lines. Prerequisites such as employee hand washing and sanitizing typically are implemented across an entire facility.

Food hazards are biological, chemical, or physical contaminants that could cause illness or injury if ingested, including *Listeria*, aflatoxin, glass, and metal. Contaminants that are non-injurious but are objectionable to the consumer are not hazards. Examples include burned product, hair, yeast, non-mycotoxin-forming molds, and food grade lubricants.

Many ways exist to describe and categorize prerequisite product safety programs, depending on the regulatory perspective and industry sector. In some industry segments a certain prerequisite may be of minor importance, while in others it may be essential and could even be designated as a CCP. Chapter 12 includes a more in-depth discussion of specific prerequisite food safety programs.

REFERENCES

1. Donald A. Corlett, Jr., *HACCP User's Manual* (Gaithersburg, MD: Aspen, 1998): 23.
2. U.S. National Advisory Committee on Microbiological Criteria for Foods, *Hazard Analysis and Critical Control Point Principles and Application Guidelines.* (Washington, DC: U.S. Food and Drug Administration, 14 August 1997).

Part II

Principles of HACCP

3

Principle #1—Conduct
Hazard Analysis

PURPOSE OF HAZARD ANALYSIS

Once the five preliminary tasks in the development of a HACCP plan have been completed, the HACCP team should undertake the first principle of HACCP: conducting a hazard analysis. Considered by many to be the foundation of a HACCP plan, the hazard analysis attempts to identify all potential hazards of a product, their sources, and the probability of their occurrence. Only then can appropriate control measures (product factors or processes that reduce or eliminate the hazard potential) be employed.

TYPES OF HAZARDS

A hazard is anything that could cause harm to the consumer using a product. All hazards must be identified scientifically so that the potential risks can be assessed. Could a particular food or medical device hazard cause an illness, an allergic reaction, or a physical injury? If so, what can be done to prevent or minimize the possibility of the risk occurring?

Food Hazards

The HACCP system for food processing has identified three types of hazards that can occur in food products. Classified by source, these hazards can be microbiological, chemical, or physical.

Microbiological Hazards. Pathogens and microbial toxins such as those listed in Table A.1 in Appendix A are significant hazards in many foods. Some individual ingredients and/or finished products have the potential to contain pathogens or allow development of microbial toxins which can cause mild to severe illness, and which have even been associated with deaths. Additionally, permanent, lifelong debilitations can result from microbiological hazards.

There are two types of pathogenic microorganisms: non-spore-forming and spore-forming. A non-spore-forming pathogen is a food borne microorganism recognized as a public health hazard that can cause illness or death in humans. Non-spore-forming pathogens include viruses, parasites, and bacteria. A spore-forming pathogen, on the other hand, is an organism capable of producing chemical- or heat-resistant spores. Upon outgrowth of the spores, the vegetative cells may produce toxins of public health significance that can cause illness or death in humans.

Chemical Hazards. As shown in Table A.3 in Appendix A, chemical contaminants in food may be naturally occurring or may be added during the processing of food. High levels of harmful chemicals have been associated with acute cases of food borne illnesses, while lower levels can be responsible for chronic illness.

Potential chemical hazards include mycotoxins, antibiotics, pesticides, and sulfites. In most cases, due to the low likelihood of occurrence and/or the nature of the hazard, prerequisite programs are the best method of control. However, in certain instances a chemical hazard may be recognized as a CCP and controlled as such. For example, many chemical substances, and nearly every food or food ingredient, can potentially cause an adverse reaction in at least one individual. However, a small group of substances, called allergens, are known to cause severe life-threatening reactions that affect larger population groups. A substance is classified as an allergen if one or more of the following criteria exist: documented cases (published in scientific or medical journals) of severe, life-threatening reactions; several independent reported cases of these reactions; or clear scientific evidence or validation of the reaction by an expert experienced in the area of allergic reactions.

Physical Hazards. In general, physical hazards are any objects or materials that (1) are part of the product but are to be removed (such as bones in meat), or (2) are not designed to be part of the product but may be inadvertently introduced into the product during the production process (such as pieces of glass, metal, hard plastic, and so on).

Extraneous matter does not usually present a significant risk of a severe adverse health effect. Minor or moderate injuries such as those described in Table A.2 in Appendix A are more common when physical hazards are encountered. While control of extraneous matter inherent to product raw materials (for example, bones, cherry pits, nut shells) is important for quality, the risks associated with these materials generally are less severe. Detection/removal devices for these objects are not necessarily managed as critical control points (CCPs). Prerequisite programs such as supplier selection and approval, preventive maintenance, and so forth, are usually the best controls for the elimination or reduction of extraneous matter in products. However, in some cases, the characteristics (size, shape, and type) of the extraneous matter may potentially cause serious harm such as internal injury or choking. On that basis, some physical hazards must be managed as CCPs and controlled through appropriate measures such as detection/removal devices.

Codex Alimentarius recognizes that many life-threatening reactions to food substances can be avoided if the allergic person is aware that the substance is present. Latex in gloves, peanuts in a cookie, and penicillin in a prescription of antibiotics are all potentially allergenic substances that can be avoided if their presence is communicated through proper product labeling, and so on.

For guidance on the list of allergenic materials that will meet the above criteria, consult with authorities on the topic. The list of materials will be different depending on the industry and how the material will come in contact with or be ingested by the consumer. Allergens and the prerequisite programs used to offset the risk of contact with them are discussed in detail in chapter 12.

Medical Device Hazards

The medical device industry has identified ten hazards that can occur in medical devices: physical, biological, chemical, electrical, radiation, explosion, environmental, performance quality, misdiagnosis, and delayed treatment.[1] The medical device industry has classified these hazards either by the source of the hazard or by the types of injuries that patients may experience as a result of nonperformance, misuse, or erroneous results (for example, pregnancy test kits) of the device. Table B.1 in Appendix B lists examples of hazards in medical devices.

Physical Hazards. Physical hazards can cause physical trauma to the patient. They can result from material failure or the unintentional use of nonconforming material.

Biological Hazards. Biological hazards can be of microbiological or non-microbiological origin. Microbiological hazards include contamination of sterile products with microorganisms or pyrogens. Biological hazards also include materials that can cause bio-incompatibility and allergic reactions in sensitive individuals.

Chemical Hazards. Chemical hazards may originate from component material used to manufacture the device. These hazards include naturally occurring chemicals, as well as unintentionally or incidentally added chemicals.

Electrical Hazards. Several types of electrical hazards can occur in products, including electrical failure, interferences, and electrical shocks.

Radiation Hazards. Radiation can be a hazard if it is inappropriately used. It can cause injury to both the patient and the caregiver.

Explosion Hazards. An explosion hazard may occur if a medical device is used in an environment that contains inflammable gases, or if the device uses batteries that produce inflammable gases.

Environmental Hazards. Adverse environmental conditions during storage, shipment, or use may adversely affect medical devices.

Performance Quality Hazards. Performance quality hazards include malfunctions that result from manufacturing errors, inadequate directions, and software or hardware errors.

Misdiagnosis and Delayed Treatment Hazards. Misdiagnosis and delayed treatment hazards are the most common errors that occur with medical devices. The two major sources of these types of errors are (1) false negative results causing either no treatment or delayed treatment, and (2) false positive results causing inappropriate treatment of the patient.

PERFORMING A HAZARD ANALYSIS

Hazard analysis is a two-step process: hazard identification and hazard evaluation. Hazard identification involves analyzing each raw material, production process, and consumer use. It also includes identifying appropriate control measures to reduce or eliminate potential hazards. Hazard evaluation is the process of reviewing each hazard that is identified to determine the severity of the health risk to the consumer and the probability of occurrence.

There is no one way in which to complete a hazard analysis. It is imperative that a cross-functional team with appropriate technical experts is involved in the hazard analysis, and that the evaluation is performed on the actual product and process. As the team works during the hazard analysis it will identify and document hazards as well as control measures. Figure 3.1 gives examples of questions to be considered by the HACCP team when conducting a hazard analysis for a food product. Figure 3.2 gives examples of similar questions to be considered in the hazard analysis for a medical device.

Examples of Questions to be Considered When Conducting a Hazard Analysis

The hazard analysis consists of asking a series of questions that are appropriate to the process under consideration. The purpose of the questions is to assist in identifying potential hazards.

Ingredients

- Does the food contain any sensitive ingredients that may present microbiological hazards (e.g., *Salmonella*, *Staphylococcus aureus*); chemical hazards (e.g., aflatoxin, antibiotic or pesticide residues); or physical hazards (stones, glass, metal)?

- Are potable water, ice, and steam used in formulating or in handling the food?

- What are the sources (e.g., geographical region, specific supplier)?

Figure 3.1   Identification of hazards in foods.

Source: U. S. National Advisory Committee on Microbiological Criteria for Foods (NACMCF). *Guidelines for Application of HACCP Principles,* Appendix C. Washington, DC: U. S. Food and Drug Administration, 14 August 1997.

Intrinsic Factors

- What hazards may result if the food composition is not controlled?

- Does the food permit survival or multiplication of pathogens and/or toxin formation in the food during processing?

- Will the food permit survival or multiplication of pathogens and/or toxin formation during subsequent steps in the food chain?

- Are there other similar products in the marketplace? What has been the safety record for these products? What hazards have been associated with the products?

Procedures Used for Processing

- Does the process include a controllable processing step that destroys pathogens? If so, which pathogens? Consider both vegetative cells and spores.

- If the product is subject to recontamination between processing (e.g., cooking, pasteurizing) and packaging, which biological, chemical, or physical hazards are likely to occur?

Microbial Content of the Food

- What is the normal microbial content of the food?

- Does the food product change in such a way to allow for the growth of microorganisms?

- Does the microbial population change during the normal time the food is stored prior to consumption?

- Does the subsequent change in microbial population alter the safety of the food?

- Do the answers to the above questions indicate a high likelihood of certain biological hazards?

Facility Design

- Does the layout of the facility provide an adequate separation of raw materials from ready-to-eat (RTE) foods if this is important to food safety? If not, what hazards should be considered as possible contaminants of the RTE products?

- Is positive air pressure maintained in product packaging areas? Is this essential for product safety?

- Is the traffic pattern for people and moving equipment a significant source of contamination?

Figure 3.1 *Continued.*

Equipment Design and Use

- Will the equipment provide the time–temperature control that is necessary for safe food?

- Is the equipment properly sized for the volume of food that will be processed?

- Can the equipment be sufficiently controlled so that the variation in performance will be within the tolerances required to produce a safe food?

- Is the equipment reliable or is it prone to frequent breakdowns?

- Is the equipment designed so that it can be easily cleaned and sanitized?

- Is there a chance for product contamination with hazardous substances; e.g., glass?

- What product safety devices (e.g., metal detectors, magnets, sifters, filters, screens, thermometers, bone removal devices, dud detectors) are used to enhance consumer safety?

- To what degree will normal equipment wear affect the likely occurrence of a physical hazard (e.g., metal) in the product?

- Are allergen protocols needed in using equipment for different products?

Packaging

- Does the method of packaging affect the multiplication of microbial pathogens and/or the formation of toxins?

- Is the package clearly labeled "Keep Refrigerated" if this is required for safety?

- Does the package include instructions for the safe handling and preparation of the food by the end user?

- Is the packaging material resistant to damage thereby preventing the entrance of microbial contamination?

- Are tamper-evident packaging features used?

- Is each package and case legibly and accurately coded?

- Does each package contain the proper label?

- Are potential allergens in the ingredients included in the list of ingredients on the label?

Figure 3.1   *Continued.*

Sanitation

- Can sanitation have an impact upon the safety of the food that is being processed?
- Can the facility and equipment be easily cleaned and sanitized to permit the safe handling of food?
- Is it possible to provide sanitary conditions consistently and adequately to assure safe foods?

Employee Health, Hygiene, and Education

- Can employee health or personal hygiene practices impact upon the safety of the food being processed?
- Do the employees understand the process and the factors they must control to assure the preparation of safe foods?
- Will the employees inform management of a problem which could impact upon safety of food?

Conditions of Storage between Packaging and the End User

- What is the likelihood that the food will be improperly stored at the wrong temperature?
- Would improper storage lead to a microbiologically unsafe food?

Intended Use

- Will the food be heated by the consumer?
- Will there likely be leftovers?

Intended Consumer

- Is the food intended for the general public?
- Is the food intended for consumption by a population with increased susceptibility to illness (e.g., infants, the aged, the infirmed, immunocompromised individuals)?
- Is the food to be used for institutional feeding or the home?

Figure 3.1 *Continued.*

Materials and Components

- Does the product contain materials or components that may present a hazard?

- Have the significant specifications and special storage conditions been identified?

Intrinsic Factors

- What factors must be controlled to ensure safety?

- Does the device permit survival, growth, or the formation of toxins of microbiological origin during manufacturing?

- Has the safety of similar devices in the marketplace been determined?

Procedures Used for Manufacturing

- Is there a controllable manufacturing step that destroys microorganisms?

- Can recontamination of the device occur after sterilization?

- Does the process contain steps that remove all hazards?

- Has a risk analysis been conducted on all hazards?

- Have methods been determined to detect nonconformances or deviations in the process or product?

Bioburden of the Device

- Is the device commercially sterile?

- Is it likely that the device will contain microorganisms?

- What is the normal microbiological load for the device?

Facility Design

- Does the plant layout provide adequate separation of raw components/materials, from in-process devices, finished products, rework, and returned products?

- Is positive air pressure maintained in the product packaging area?

- Do traffic patterns provide a significant source of contamination?

- Have significant environmental controls been identified?

Figure 3.2   Hazard analysis of medical devices.

Source: Association of Food and Drug Officials. *Medical Device HACCP Training Curriculum.* Draft Edition. York, PA: AFDO, 1999.

Equipment Design

- Does the manufacturing equipment provide for proper controls of time and temperature?
- Is the equipment of proper size for production volumes?
- Can the equipment be controlled to meet the performance tolerances?
- Is the equipment reliable?
- Can the equipment be properly cleaned and sanitized?
- Have product safety devices such as metal detectors, magnets, and filters been incorporated into the manufacturing process?

Packaging

- Does the packaging method affect product safety?
- Do packages clearly label appropriate storage conditions that affect safety?
- Does the packaging material provide an appropriate barrier to prevent microbiological or other types of contamination?
- Is a tamper evident package used?
- Are the primary and secondary packages properly labeled and coded?

Sanitation

- Can sanitation affect the safety of the product?
- Can the facility and manufacturing equipment be properly and consistently cleaned and sanitized?

Employee Health, Hygiene, and Education

- Can employee health or personal hygiene affect the safety of the product being manufactured?
- Do employees understand the processes and factors that must be controlled to ensure product safety?
- Do employees inform management when problems occur that can affect product safety?

Figure 3.2 *Continued.*

Conditions for Storage

- What is the likelihood that the product will be improperly stored?
- What errors in storage could lead to hazards?

Intended Use

- Will the product be manipulated by the caregiver or the patient?
- Will there be reuse of the device?

Intended Customer

- Where will the product be used in the field?
- Will it be used by an at-risk or special needs population?

Record Keeping

- Is there an adequate and appropriate record keeping procedure for the manufacture of the product to ensure product quality?

Figure 3.2 *Continued.*

Hazard Identification

The HACCP team must examine all factors that have an impact on the safety of the final product, as well as characteristics of the product at each stage of production, through distribution and consumer use. The process of hazard identification is actually quite easy once the preliminary tasks discussed in chapter 2 have been performed. A good HACCP team, made up of the right technical experts, will be able to identify the potential hazards for most materials very quickly.

The preliminary tasks for development of a HACCP plan include describing the product and its distribution, as well as describing its intended use and consumers. This information can be used to evaluate any intrinsic factors of the product that could cause or prevent a risk to the consumer. For example, inherent characteristics of two types of beverages—carbonated soft drinks and milk—can be compared to show how risk of hazards differs due to the chemical makeup of these products.

Milk is from an animal, it is a neutral pH product, and it contains protein and sugars (lactose). These factors lend it to be easily contaminated by pathogenic microorganisms, as is evidenced by the history of the product. In addition, the environment of the milk provides an excellent growth medium for microorganisms. Without further treatment to kill the pathogenic microorganisms there is an increased probability that consumers who drink untreated milk will get food poisoning.

Carbonated soft drinks, on the other hand, generally are produced from refined chemicals or processed agricultural materials, highly purified waters, and may contain sugars. The pH of the finished product is between 2 and 3. Therefore limited opportunities exist for the product to become contaminated with pathogenic microorganisms, as supported by the product history.

Milk has an inherent microbial risk to it that must be controlled; the other carbonated beverage product has an inherent microbial safety. Soft drinks, in fact, have a low probability of causing food poisoning as long as the product meets the specified design. Other intrinsic factors that are part of a product evaluation include processes that make a product consumable, such as the baking of a cake, the frozen storage of ice cream, the dry nature of a vitamin pill, or the filtering of ground coffee. These factors contribute to making the product consumable, and thus safer, but such factors are often beyond the manufacturer's control. While evaluating intrinsic factors and examining how they are handled throughout processing can eliminate or reduce the occurrence of many hazards, to assure the safety of a product the HACCP team must also examine how the consumer may use the product. The intrinsic factors of a product's raw materials, the process, and consumer use become significant parts of the hazard analysis.

Raw Materials. Each material used to make a finished product must be evaluated for its potential to have physical, chemical, or microbiological hazards. All materials that can be incorporated into the finished product or that can be put into a consumer's mouth must be evaluated. This includes rework, recycle, reclaim, processing aids, packaging materials, (including shipping and storage containers), subcomponents, and water and steam sources.

As each material is evaluated, the identification of the potential for the hazard is based on the safety history of the material: scientific and/or historical evidence of the presence of the hazard. A *sensitive raw material* is any material that is likely to contain pathogens or toxins and/or that allows the growth of any pathogen. The definition is sometimes expanded to include raw materials that are historically known to contain physical or chemical hazards. The HACCP team must agree on the meaning being applied to "sensitive raw material" so that everyone understands what is meant by the term.

After all raw materials for a product have been identified they must be described in detail and documented. What is the material? What are its intrinsic factors? Who is the supplier? What is its function in the finished product? How is it manufactured, packaged, and distributed? All of these factors will have an impact on the safety or risk potential that a material may have on the finished product. These items should be described in enough detail so that anyone picking up the documentation would have a clear understanding of exactly what the material is even without the physical samples of the materials. This will ensure that HACCP team members have access to all of the information they need to provide an accurate assessment of the material during the hazard analysis.

Key pieces of information to identify about each material are its physical state and how it is handled. Physical state is the description of the material. Is the material wet or dry? What are the pH, water activity (A_w), types of acidulants? Does it contain fermentable carbohydrates or preservatives? What is the size and shape of the material? Is it alcohol or water based? Is it processed or direct from the field (raw commodity) type of material? Handling refers to how the material is processed, packaged, stored, and distributed. Is the material heat processed? Is it ground and sifted? Is it filtered? Is it shipped in tanker cars or bagged in low-density, polyethylene-lined, 45-pound bags? Is it stored refrigerated or at room temperature?

After the material has been defined, and the process by which it is made and handled is known, types of hazards that could be introduced into the finished product from the individual raw materials must be identified. It is not enough just to state that pathogenic microorganisms can be present in the material. The HACCP team must specify which organisms could be present, then describe the severity of the health consequences if the identified hazard is not controlled.

The likelihood of occurrence of the potential hazard needs to be determined based on documented historical or scientific evidence. Similar materials can be considered when determining the evidence of risk. There may be little or no documentation available on a particular material because it has not been widely studied or used. However, a lack of scientific evidence does not mean that no risk exists, especially when hazards have been associated with similar products already in use. Table 3.1 provides an example of documentation for the raw material hazard analysis.

One of the most difficult aspects of completing the raw material evaluation is understanding the supplier of the material. Research and actual site inspections may be required to get a clear and concise review. Not all raw materials will require the same degree of evaluation. For instance, some raw commodities will undergo processing steps specifically designed to eliminate hazards. Suppliers of these materials will be subject to less scrutiny than suppliers of other materials because it is expected that these unprocessed commodities will contain hazards. For this type of material, the degree of control (reduction of hazards) will often fall to the manufacturer of the finished good.

However, if the material is processed, the purchaser often expects that potential hazards will be eliminated or reduced to an acceptable level, and that there is a low probability of occurrence. The control of the hazard will then be the responsibility of the manufacturer of that material. In these cases, verification that the supplier has implemented an effective quality system is critical to assuring the safety of the final finished good.

ISO certification can provide verification that the company has a structured, documented, and implemented quality system. ISO certification alone, though, is not a guarantee of safe products. If the quality system has failed to identify key product safety activities, there is an increased potential of a product safety risk.

A site audit is the best method for gaining a complete understanding of the quality system of each supplier. All manufacturing sites that supply materials should be audited before entering into a contract with the supplier and receiving any materials. It is important to be assured that a supplier has effective good manufacturing practices (GMPs) and product safety programs in place. Ideally, all suppliers will also be using HACCP as a key part of their product safety program.

Table 3.1 Hazard analysis documentation of raw material.

Ingredient	Description	Storage	Determine potential hazards associated with material	Assess severity of health consequences if potential hazard is not properly controlled	Determine likelihood of occurrence of potential hazard if not properly controlled.
Pasteurized liquid whole egg	Liquid whole eggs are made up of both the yolk and the white from chicken eggs. The eggs are washed, checked for quality, and mechanically cracked. The liquid egg is then pumped into a large tank through a 60 mesh filter and held at 45°F until enough material is accumulated for pasteurization. It is then pasteurized at 191°F for 10 seconds and rapidly cooled to 40°F. It is shipped in tanker trucks that are held at <42°F. Material is liquid, with a neutral pH. It contains fermentable carbohydrates and is an excellent growth medium for microorganisms.	After pasteurization, eggs must be held at no greater than 45°F for no greater than 5 days.	Microbiological— Salmonella in finished product.	Salmonellosis is a food borne infection causing a moderate to severe illness that can be caused by ingestion of only a few cells of Salmonella.	Product is made with liquid eggs, which have been associated with past outbreaks of Salmonellosis. Recent problems with Salmonella serotype Enteritidis in eggs cause increased concern. Probability of Salmonella in raw eggs cannot be ruled out. If not effectively controlled, some consumers are likely to be exposed to Salmonella from this food.
			Chemical—Eggs are a known food allergen.	Egg allergic individuals can suffer health consequences from mild to severe. There have been documented cases of death caused from severe allergic reactions to eggs.	As an ingredient in the finished product, unless it is properly identified as in the ingredient statement, their is a probability of the product being consumed by a food allergic individual.
			Physical— Eggshells	There are no documented cases of severe injuries caused by eggshells. There are cases of minor mouth abrasions.	There is a low probability of any injury from eggshells as the liquid eggs are filtered through a 50 mesh screen and the shells are brittle.

Source: Modification of Appendix D, U.S. National Advisory Committee on Microbiological Criteria for Foods (NACMCF). *Guidelines for Application of HACCP Principles.* Washington, DC: U.S. Food and Drug Administration, 14 August 1997.

The purchaser should research the product quality performance history of each supplier. Information on product recalls is part of the public record, so information on a product type or a company history can be obtained by requesting the information through the Freedom of Information Act or by checking the appropriate Web sites. The U. S. Food and Drug Administration (FDA) publishes Enforcement Reports going back a number of years. If a product type or a company has a record of multiple product recalls in the recent past, the purchaser needs to take this information into account when identifying the potential risks and probability of the risk occurring. This information should be considered when completing the hazard analysis.

It is not in the best interest of a company to buy any material without a complete understanding of the supplier's organization. It is unwise to enter into any contract with an organization without knowledge of its financial stability. It is also important to make sure that the organization can supply the materials needed in a timely way while meeting all specifications.

The last step in the analysis of a supplier is to understand the supplier's (contract manufacturer, if applicable) practices. A common practice is to have a contract manufacturer make product. The purchasing company must be sure that the supplier understands that all approvals are contingent upon the manufacturing location that has been approved to supply the material. If the supplier uses contract manufacturing, the purchaser should be sure that the supplier has a good quality system for the approval and oversight of contract manufacturers. In the absence of such a program, the purchaser should retain the right to refuse material from a specific contract manufacturer.

Process Review. After all materials that are used to make the finished product have been evaluated and any potential hazards that they may contribute have been identified, the HACCP team should evaluate each step in the process (receiving to consumer use) and identify all potential points in the process where hazards can be introduced. Aspects of the processing environment to consider include facility design, traffic flows, equipment design, the function of a specific processing step, and whether the step could potentially introduce or eliminate a hazard. Process steps that are designed to reduce hazards also should be identified at this time.

A good, documented quality system includes an understanding of all the steps involved in the manufacturing of a product. What is done and by whom?, what training do they receive?, and what records are kept?, are just some of the questions that must be asked about each step in the process.

Consider, for example, the process of receiving dried whole egg into a facility. The specification for the material states that a Certificate of Analysis (COA) on the quality of the material must be received at the facility before or at the time of the shipment. One of the items tested for is a pathogen. The following paragraphs explain what is done and why for this step of the process.

Material arrives at the shipping and receiving dock of a facility and the driver provides the shipping clerk with the bill of lading. The shipping clerk checks the raw material against specification requirements. The specification states that a COA is required for each lot of material. Microbiological testing to be done includes tests for

Salmonella, fat, and moisture. If the COA has not been received prior to shipment, then it needs to be included in the documentation accompanying the delivery.

It is important for the HACCP team to understand why the specification requires pathogen testing to be performed and why the supplier does the testing rather than the receiving facility. Of the tests required, two are indicators for product safety: the test for *Salmonella* and the one for moisture level (if too high, the eggs could provide a media for growth of microorganisms). The supplier performs the tests to reduce the risk of introducing and potentially using a contaminated material by assuring that the microbiological hazard has been controlled even before the product is brought into the facility.

Now that it has been established why the COA is required, we understand why it is so important that the shipping clerk knows exactly what to do. The shipping clerk should compare all packages of the material to the lot numbers presented on the COA. If there is not a COA on file for a lot of material, then it must be rejected. The shipping clerk's work instructions must clearly state the steps to be followed when a deviation is found, such as the lack of a COA for a lot of material.

If the material were found to be acceptable, the shipping clerk would then file the information, including the COA, and make the material available to the operation for processing. This one step ensures that the microbiological hazard of the dried whole eggs is being controlled at the supplier by providing documentation via the COA that the hazard has been controlled.

This process of checking prevents the use of an untested and potentially contaminated material in the manufacture of the finished product. Whether this step of checking a shipment of products for the proper COA is a CCP or not is for the HACCP team to discuss. First the processing step and potential hazards must be identified, and then the specific mechanisms for controlling the hazards determined.

This same process needs to be completed for every step of the making, distributing, and use of a product. Every step must be regarded as potentially introducing and/or eliminating a hazard. Figure 3.1 and Table 3.1 can provide guidance on the type of questions to ask when completing this step of the hazard analysis. But it is impossible to make a complete list of questions, so remember to ask: Who is doing what, with what, when is it being done, where is being done, why is it done, how is it done?

Someone who actually does the task should be part of the HACCP team for this step of the analysis. Ideally, the discussion should include an observation of the process to verify that what is presumed to be happening is actually happening.

Allergen Review. One commonly forgotten step in the hazard analysis for processing steps is allergen review, which attempts to identify the risk of contamination by unlabeled allergens through equipment cross-contamination. It is possible for an allergenic material to be accidentally incorporated into a product simply because the product is made on the same production equipment as another product which contains the allergenic material. Therefore the HACCP team needs to analyze what is actually produced on a specific production line.

The first step is to establish what other products are produced on the same production line and to determine if any of these products contain an allergenic material. Once it is understood what allergenic materials are used on specific production equipment, the next question is: Do the product(s) that are covered by this specific HACCP plan contain the same allergenic materials? If the answer is "yes," then confirming that the product labeling has the allergen clearly identified is the control measure. If the answer is "no," the product in question does not have the same allergen profile as other products made on the same production equipment. This increases the potential for the introduction into the product of an allergenic material that is not identified on the label. The HACCP team needs to review the hazard and identify the control measure for it.

Consumer Use and Identification of Control Measures. When a hazard is identified, the control measure(s) for it must be identified. The HACCP team must ask the question: How is the consumer protected from this hazard? Not all control measures will be within a manufacturer's control; often it will be the consumer's responsibility to control the hazard. In such cases, it is the manufacturer's duty to inform the consumer of potential risks by including instructions for safe product use. Dosage restrictions on medications such as "Do not exceed six tablets in 24 hours" or directions such as "Keep refrigerated" on shell eggs are examples of statements provided by the manufacturer on product packaging to help ensure that products are used in the recommended amounts and stored properly. Sterile medical devices commonly have a statement declaring that the product must be used before a certain date, or that the contents are sterile only if the package has not been opened.

All control measures must have an identified scientific basis for being an effective means of control. For example, certain time/temperature applications have been proven to kill microorganisms. A dry material, or material with low water activity (A_w), will not promote the growth of microorganisms. These control measures for microorganisms have scientific bases.

If it is found that a processing step or a material actually introduces a hazard into the product, the hazard should be designed out of the process when possible. For example, if eggs are added to a product solely for flavor, why not add a flavor that is not microbiologically sensitive to perform the same function? This replacement would eliminate the potential for the introduction of *Salmonella* into the finished product.

At times a hazard may be identified and no known control measures for it are in place. In those cases it will be necessary to design a control measure, with a scientific basis, into the process or product.

Hazard Evaluation

After hazards and their appropriate control measures have been identified, each hazard should be evaluated for severity and probability of risk. This needs to be done before establishing whether the control measure is a CCP or is part of a prerequisite program.

Severity of Risk. The severity of a risk is a difficult thing to assess. Severity often is judged based on a scale of high, moderate, or low, with high being life-threatening reactions or those causing irreversible organ damage or failure, and low being minor reactions or reversible and treatable medical conditions. The most common reaction to a hazard may be low to moderate; however, in certain individuals or population groups (the aged, infirm, immunocompromised, or infants) the health consequences may be life threatening.

Obviously the most severe risk of any hazard is death. No ethical company would knowingly create a product that would harm or kill anyone. However, historical evidence exists of products that have hurt and killed people. In some cases, the cause was ignorance of the risk. In other cases, changes in the environment brought the hazard to light. Either way, the manufacturer is obligated to eliminate or reduce the risk of harm.

A number of factors must be considered to assess the potential health and safety risk to the consumer if a hazard is not controlled. The HACCP system is not as effective for controlling hazards with consequences that tend to manifest themselves over the long term and cannot be directly correlated to the ingestion or use of a specific product. HACCP is most effective with health consequences that are immediate and that can be traced to the actual product ingested or used. For example, compare the potential for liver cancer caused by the consumption of mycotoxins in grain versus the potential for *Salmonella* food borne disease from eating a raw egg. It is easy to directly correlate the eating of a raw egg to a case of food borne disease that manifests itself within 24 hours from consumption. On the other hand, it is much more difficult to identify whether a specific lot of grain eaten 30 years prior could have had an elevated mycotoxin level that may have caused liver cancer, especially if the person was exposed to other chemicals that can cause liver cancer.

When considering the severity of a hazard the following questions need to be asked: What are the health consequences (mild to severe) if exposed to the hazard? What is the potential duration of the illness or injury? If the HACCP team does not know the answers to these questions, it should seek professional advice. Often state and federal regulatory agencies publish epidemiological summaries or morbidity/mortality reports that establish the hazard profiles of different products. The severity of a risk is not lower just because the HACCP team is unfamiliar with its health consequences.

Probability of Risk. The final and most difficult part of the hazard analysis is the assessment of the probability of risk. While difficult, the decisions made on probability can make the difference between a focused, effective HACCP system and one with so many CCPs in it that it is ineffective, difficult to manage, and overly burdensome to the organization.

One of the factors to consider when trying to establish the probability of a hazard is the product history. Has the hazard been found in this product/material before? If possible, identify the source of contamination and determine whether patterns exist or if the problem appears to be random. The frequency of occurrence should also be identified: How many times has it happened in the past?

Another factor is the control measure. Does the control measure rely on undependable methods for control, such as people, weather, or microorganism growth? Or is the control measure highly dependable and in statistical control within very specific limits such as heat treatment or pH? These will affect the probability of occurrence. The greater the predictability of the action, the better the understanding of the probability.

If the product that the HACCP plan is being designed for is either a new product or a product with no clear history, the HACCP team should look at other similar products. Have hazards been found in similar products? Products undergoing similar manufacturing processes (for example, dry mix) and products containing common raw materials (such as egg-containing products) should be examined.

One way to determine whether the hazard is common and the risk is severe is to look at the regulations, both domestic and worldwide, for the industry. In general, if a regulatory body has addressed the hazard and prescribed a specific control measure, then it has been done with forethought and is, in most cases, based on scientific evidence. Another source of information is product safety actions taken by companies or regulatory agencies. A product recall is also validation of the probability of occurrence, especially if it happens more than once and to more than one company. The FDA regularly publishes notices of food and medical device recalls. A review of those recalls can indicate if similar products have been recalled and may help to establish a probability of occurrence. Sterility problems always underlie a large number of the total recalls of medical devices. While the methods for sterility assurance have high confidence values, recalls for inadequate sterilization based on related problems, including packaging, are common.

Many industry trade associations and regulatory bodies are developing model HACCP plans to assist companies. Since many smaller organizations do not have the internal resources to perform a HACCP analysis, model plans provide a good starting point for information on what type of hazards can be expected on a product. There is, however, a significant risk to the direct adoption of any model HACCP plan. Every HACCP plan is product- and production-line specific. They are one of a kind and must be reviewed with each change in raw material or the process. One minor change in the product or process can introduce a significant hazard that may not be controlled. Model HACCP plans are developed to be generic; they do not and cannot take into account the specifics that make up any finished product. It is impossible for a model plan to identify hazards that are the result of a supplier's history, allergen cross-contamination, or even the intrinsic factors for any specific finished product.

Not all potentially random, accidental occurrences can be protected against. What is the probability of an employee's reading glasses accidentally falling into a mixer and going unnoticed? It has happened, but how many times? In all the millions of packages of products over decades of time with thousands of different employees, how many occurrences have there been? It would be very difficult, if not impossible, to find any records of such an event, but it can happen. But that is not what HACCP is about. HACCP is not about being perfect; HACCP is about due diligence. It is the proactive identification of hazards *far in advance* of incidents of injury or illness occurring.

Hazard evaluation is probability versus possibility. Yes, it is possible for anything to happen. But is it probable? It is possible to get struck by a meteor and lightning at the same time, but it is not very probable. Structuring daily activities as if this event were highly probable would lead to never leaving a shelter or seeing the light of day. This is not a very practical action to a highly unlikely event. So, pose the question: Is this hazard *reasonably likely to occur* under these given conditions? If it is unreasonable to expect the hazard to occur, then it is a mere possibility.

The issue of probability and HACCP is still a highly debated topic, with no clear methods for determining with absolute certainty all of the hazards that should be managed in the HACCP plan and those that should not. The process of analyzing hazards is constantly being challenged as new processes and products are developed, and as new information is obtained and new hazards become known. The key is doing the best job possible each and every time a HACCP plan is developed or verified using the best resources available.

DOCUMENTATION AND ONGOING EFFORTS

Documentation of the hazard analysis must be complete, clear, and made readily available to the organization. The complete hazard analysis, with all supporting documents—including, but not limited to, references, audit reports, and scientific evidence—should be kept on file in one central location. It is not uncommon for the same information to be used for multiple HACCP plans throughout the company.

On a local basis, the hazard analysis documentation for each material and processing step evaluation should be available and be part of the final HACCP plan. The HACCP plan should also list all of the supporting documentation and identify the official file location.

The only proper way to do a hazard analysis is by using the three actuals: the analysis must be done on the *actual product*, at the *actual production location*, with the *actual people* who know the product and the potential hazards the best. The hazard analysis is based on facts, not assumptions and conclusions like "we've never had a problem." The hazard analysis requires research and a variety of technical knowledge about many different topics. The proper HACCP team with the right support and information is critical to the accurate identification of the potential hazards for a product. The identification is the foundation for an effective HACCP plan and the protection of the consumers.

REFERENCE

1. Association of Food and Drug Officials, *Medical Device HACCP Training Curriculum*, Draft Edition (York, PA: AFDO, 1999).

4

Principle #2—Determine Critical Control Points

DISTINGUISHING BETWEEN CRITICAL CONTROL POINTS AND CONTROL POINTS

A critical control point (CCP) is defined as "a step at which control can be applied and which is essential to prevent or eliminate a food safety hazard or reduce it to an acceptable level."[1] The medical device industry uses the term *essential control point* (ECP) instead of CCP. An ECP is "a point, step, or procedures at which control can be applied and which is essential to prevent, eliminate, or reduce a hazard to an acceptable level."[2] Controlling factors or variables at CCPs is described as implementing control measures. Control measures, then, describe actions and activities taken at the CCP to prevent, eliminate, or reduce the identified hazard. Every significant hazard must have a control measure to reduce the likelihood for the hazard to occur. The control measures are dependent on the reliability of the food safety control system.

As "a point, step, or procedure" in the production process, a CCP does not focus on the supporting manufacturing infrastructure, such as sanitation, equipment maintenance, pest control, personnel programs, transportation and storage requirements, premise maintenance, and recall and traceability requirements. As will be discussed in chapter 12, product safety issues pertaining to these and similar areas must be controlled through prerequisite programs. A detailed set of prerequisite programs outlines how product safety will be assured and simplifies identification of CCPs by focusing on process steps rather than plant infrastructure.

A CCP differs from a *control point* (CP). A control point is "any step at which biological, physical, or chemical factors can be controlled."[3] As such, a control point usually is related to quality or production issues. A control point normally is not associated with product safety, unless the control point supports a CCP. For instance, a dry ingredient mix facility may place screens, magnets, and a metal detector in the production line to prevent metal contamination of the finished product. The screens and magnets are control points; only the final point of control, the metal detector, is a CCP.

To differentiate between a control point and a CCP ask two questions. First: If I lose control of this step, is there a succeeding step (for example, a kill step, a chemical wash, a freezing step) that could effectively control the hazard? If the answer to this question is "yes," then the step is probably a control point. If the answer is "no," ask another question: If I lose control of this step, could the product cause serious illness or injury?[4] If the answer is "yes," the step is probably a CCP.

COMMON SOURCES OF CRITICAL CONTROL POINTS

CCPs often are found in the areas of raw materials, ingredient handling and receiving, processing, packaging, and distribution.

Raw Materials

Product contamination by microbiological, chemical, and physical hazards—such as pathogens, pesticides, herbicides, antibiotics, naturally occurring toxins, and metal fragments—are in raw materials. When a processor has control measures in place to prevent contaminated raw materials from entering the plant, these materials and the act of their receipt can be CCPs. This is especially true if no step exists in the process to eliminate or reduce the hazard, for example, a thermal processing step to eliminate a microbiological hazard. If a significant hazard may be associated with a raw material, then a supplier quality assurance program should be in place to control the hazard to the best of the supplier's ability.

A raw material decision tree can be used to determine if an incoming raw material might be considered a CCP.[5] A raw material decision tree can be used to answer the following questions.

Question #1: Is a significant hazard associated with this raw material? This first question can be answered by the hazard analysis. If identified hazards are sufficiently severe and likely enough to occur that they could harm someone, then the answer to this question is "yes." Proceed to question two. If the answer is "no," then ask question one of the next raw material.

Question # 2: Will this hazard be processed out of the product? If no way exists to reduce a hazard to an acceptable level or eliminate it during processing, then this hazard probably occurs in the finished product. Options to control the hazard include adding a process step—such as heat treatment—to reduce or eliminate the hazard, or designating the relevant raw material as a CCP. In the latter case, it may be possible to identify control programs for the raw material before it reaches the production plant.

Other less accurate methods of control are "hold and test" programs that require acceptable test results before a raw material can be used. Usually, Certificates of Analysis or "hold and test" methods are not considered acceptable means of preventing or eliminating hazards at the raw material level because it is unlikely that these methods will detect minute levels of contamination. In cases where they are the only possible methods of control, sampling and testing methods must be stable and capable of ensuring the accuracy and reliability of the results.

Question # 3: Is there a cross-contamination risk to the facility or to other products which will not be controlled? If the answer to this question is "no," proceed to the next raw material. If the answer is "yes" then process steps or prerequisite programs may be put in place to eliminate or reduce this risk.

Ingredient Receiving and Handling

If an incoming raw material contains biological, chemical, or physical hazards, the manner in which it is received, handled, or stored might be a CCP. For instance, the improper storage of some dry ingredients can result in aflatoxin production or insect infestation. If control measures are not in place under the prerequisite programs to reduce or eliminate these hazards, then these steps can be considered CCPs. Control measures for this type of CCP include sifters, magnets, temperature and humidity control, and regular chemical treatment to avoid infestation.

Processing

Process steps are commonly identified as CCPs. Examples of these steps include rework, cooking, chilling, and formulation control.

Rework. Rework and salvage processes may be CCPs, particularly if any of the products contain allergenic ingredients and a risk of cross-contamination with other products is possible. Control measures include production scheduling, product handling, sanitation, and mixing rework into identical products only.

Cooking. Because heat inactivates pathogens and eliminates or greatly reduces biological hazards, heat processing steps can be CCPs. Several variables are responsible for the effectiveness of any heat processing step. These variables can include time, temperature, pressure, container fill, container agitation, size of solid ingredients, and chemical and physical properties of liquids and solids. All relevant CCP variables must be in compliance with the determined critical limits for the step to be considered under control and validated by a scientific study.

Chilling. Cooling or chilling may be a CCP. Bacteria spores could germinate or grow during the cooling or chilling process and become a serious health hazard. Therefore, both time and temperature variables can be CCPs if bacterial spores have not been destroyed with a cooking step, or prevent the growth of *S. aureus* to prevent toxin formation.

Formulation Control. Formulation of the product may be a CCP. During formulation, ingredients can affect the product's ability to support microbial growth, cause allergic reactions, and adversely affect consumer health if maximum allowable limits are exceeded. Variables include: ingredient proportions such as weights and volumes, pH, A_w, ingredient concentrations, ingredient inventory monitoring before and after the batch is mixed to ensure that the correct amounts of sensitive ingredients are used, adequate agitation or mixing times to ensure a homogeneous mix, and verification testing of the finished mix to ensure the correct usage of certain key ingredients. Thus, mixing of the product may be a CCP.

Packaging

Packaging is a step in the production process that should be considered during CCP determination. During the packaging step a number of factors can be considered CCPs. For instance, the integrity of the package seal may be considered a CCP. Other activities at the packaging level that might be considered a CCP include detection of metal and other foreign material or the presence of a proper vacuum or proper gas mixture in modified atmosphere packaged products.

Ensuring that package ingredient declarations are correct can be a CCP in cases where ingredients may cause allergic reactions or have controlled regulatory health limits. Issues such as correct coding for traceability are usually considered part of a recall and traceability prerequisite program.

Distribution

Time, temperature, and humidity might need to be controlled during the storage and transportation of a product. A comprehensive prerequisite program for transportation and storage might be adequate to control the safety of the product. However, in some cases these variables are critical to the safety of the product. In those instances a CCP might be identified at the storage and/or transportation steps. When in doubt, ask the question: If I lose control of this step, could the product cause serious illness or injury? If the answer is "yes" then the step may be a CCP.

Remember that CCPs are "points, steps or procedures" under the *manufacturer's* control. If customers are responsible for transportation and storage, the CCP will be part of the customer's HACCP plan. Many factors that control hazards related to certain products are beyond the control of the manufacturing facility (these may occur at the retail level, in the food service arena, and within homes, for example). A medical device intended for hospital use is tested under certain fairly controlled environmental conditions. That same device used in a home environment may be taken outdoors where the temperature is colder or warmer or used in the bathroom where the humidity is high. Those extremes may adversely affect the medical device. During the hazard analysis the HACCP team should attempt to identify and document key health hazards, even ones that may occur beyond the manufacturer's control. While it may be impossible to eliminate these hazards, steps may be taken to lessen their impact. For instance, temperature-indicating sensors may be incorporated into packaging to ensure that temperature abuse is evident, or label instructions added to identify key storage or handling requirements.

IDENTIFYING CRITICAL CONTROL POINTS

Critical control point decision trees are tools recommended for use during the CCP determination step. These trees provide the HACCP team with a systematic and logical approach to determining CCPs. Decision trees also provide a basis for documenting the reasons for selecting or rejecting a step as a CCP.

Considerations When Selecting a Decision Tree

The most widely used decision trees include those developed by Codex Alimentarius (1997 version), the U. S. National Advisory Committee on Microbiological Criteria for Foods (NACMCF, 1998 version), and the Canadian Food Inspection Agency (1995 version). These decision trees, as well as one commonly used in the medical device industry, are shown in Figures 4.1 through 4.5. Regardless of the decision tree used, the results obtained should be tested against the experience and knowledge of HACCP team members.

Important considerations when using any decision tree include:

- Each process step identified in the flow diagram must be considered in sequence.

- At each step, the decision tree must be applied to all identified hazards.

- Use a decision tree to determine CCPs only after the hazard analysis has been completed and the significance of each hazard has been evaluated.

- A CCP may have more than one control parameter within its control measure. For instance, a pasteurization CCP could include both time and temperature variables.

- More than one hazard may be controlled by a specific control measure.[6]

- The number of CCPs that may be identified is unlimited.

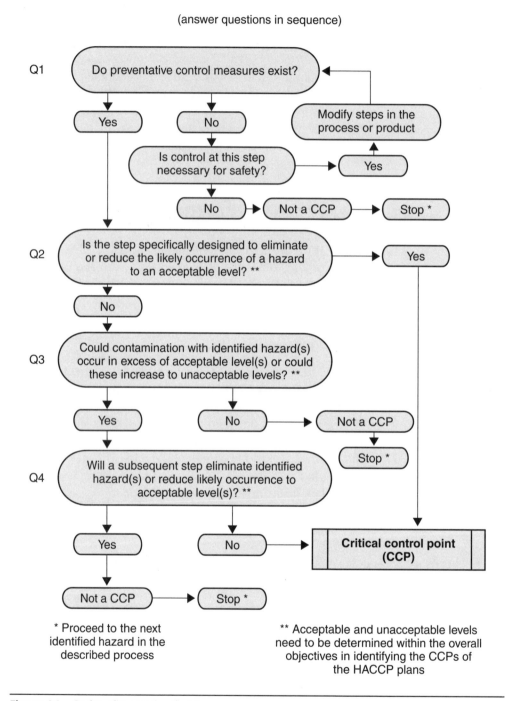

(answer questions in sequence)

Q1 — Do preventative control measures exist?

Yes — No — Modify steps in the process or product

Is control at this step necessary for safety? — Yes

No — Not a CCP — Stop *

Q2 — Is the step specifically designed to eliminate or reduce the likely occurrence of a hazard to an acceptable level? ** — Yes

No

Q3 — Could contamination with identified hazard(s) occur in excess of acceptable level(s) or could these increase to unacceptable levels? **

Yes — No — Not a CCP — Stop *

Q4 — Will a subsequent step eliminate identified hazard(s) or reduce likely occurrence to acceptable level(s)? **

Yes — No — **Critical control point (CCP)**

Not a CCP — Stop *

* Proceed to the next identified hazard in the described process

** Acceptable and unacceptable levels need to be determined within the overall objectives in identifying the CCPs of the HACCP plans

Figure 4.1 Codex Alimentarius decision tree.

Q1. Does this step involve a hazard of sufficient likelihood of occurrence and severity to warrant its control?

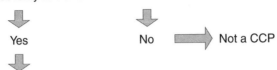

Q2. Does a control measure for the hazard exist at this step?

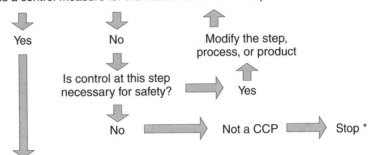

Q3. Is control at this step necessary to prevent, eliminate, or reduce the risk of the hazard to consumers?

Yes   No ➡ Not a CCP ➡ Stop *

CCP

* Proceed to next step in the process

Figure 4.2 NACMCF decision tree 1.

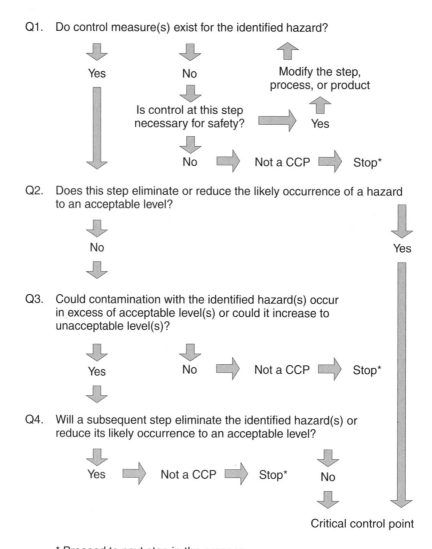

Q1.   Do control measure(s) exist for the identified hazard?

Q2.   Does this step eliminate or reduce the likely occurrence of a hazard to an acceptable level?

Q3.   Could contamination with the identified hazard(s) occur in excess of acceptable level(s) or could it increase to unacceptable level(s)?

Q4.   Will a subsequent step eliminate the identified hazard(s) or reduce its likely occurrence to an acceptable level?

* Proceed to next step in the process

Figure 4.3   NACMCF decision tree 2.

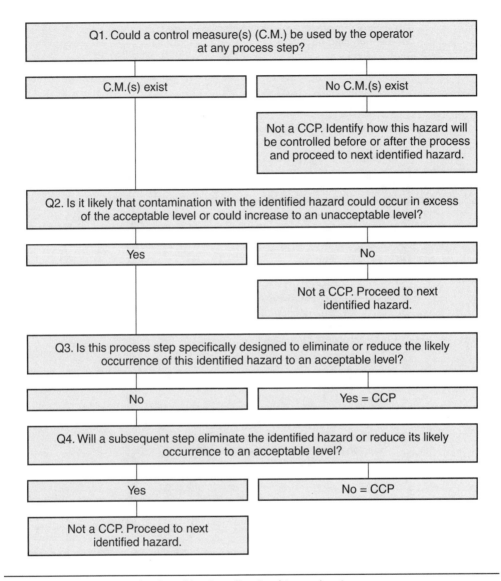

Figure 4.4 Decision tree developed by Canadian Food Inspection Agency.

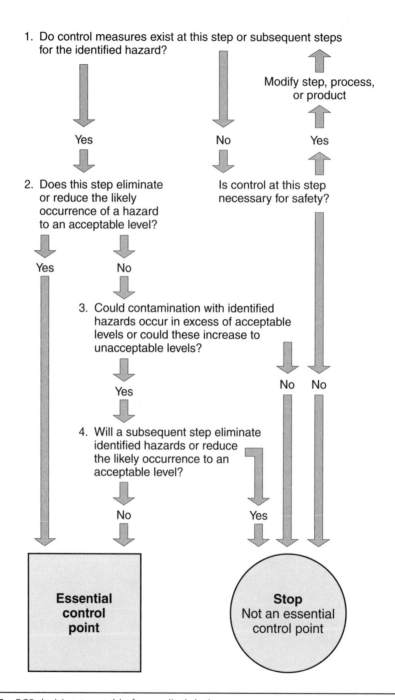

Figure 4.5   ECP decision tree table for medical devices.

As shown in Figure 4.6, two questions should be answered before a decision tree is used to determine CCPs:

A. Does this step in the process involve a hazard of sufficient likelihood of occurrence and severity to warrant its control? This question is asked as part of the hazard analysis. If the answer is "yes," proceed to the next question. If the answer is "no," then this step is not a CCP. Ask this question of the next process step.

B. Is this hazard fully controlled by a prerequisite program? Specific process steps, such as cooking or sifting, are never completely controlled by a prerequisite program. Equipment prerequisite areas may include the calibration and preventive maintenance of an oven but not the actual cook time and temperature. On the other hand, training and education programs on employee hand washing may be sufficient to ensure that the hazard of "microbial contamination during employee handling" is controlled. Another example may be the ability of sanitation programs to fully control microbial or chemical hazards on equipment. If the answer to this question is "yes," then this is not a CCP. Proceed to the next process step and ask the question again. If the answer is "no," proceed to the next question.

Using a Decision Tree

If the answers to both of the previous questions indicate that a process may be a CCP, then a decision tree may be used as a tool to determine CCPs and document the reason for their selection as such. The following questions are commonly asked on a decision tree such as the one shown in Figure 4.7 to determine CCPs.

Question 1: Do control measures exist for the identified hazard? Question 1 asks whether the operator could use any control measure at this step or elsewhere in the process to control the identified hazard.

If the response to this question is "yes," clearly describe what measure(s) the operator could take to control the hazard, for example, "Yes—metal detector" or "Yes—cooking," then proceed to Question 2.

If the answer is "no," ask if control at this step is necessary for the safety of the product. If the answer to this question is "yes," then determine how the identified hazard could be controlled before, during, or after the manufacturing process. Often a step, process, or product can be modified to add a control measure. If control at this step is not necessary for safety, the step is not a CCP. Proceed to the next step in the process.

Question 2: Is this process step specifically designed to eliminate or reduce the likely occurrence of this identified hazard to an acceptable level? "Specifically designed" means that the procedure or step is intended to specifically address the identified hazard. For example, a metal detector has been "specifically designed" to detect and reject products containing certain steel and stainless steel fragments. Other examples include pasteurization (a heat process designed to kill harmful organisms), retort (the process of canning products in a vessel—resembling an oversized pressure

Process Step	Is this hazard of sufficient likelihood of occurrence and severity to warrant its control? Yes—Proceed to next question. No—Not a CCP	Is this hazard fully controlled by a prerequisite program? Yes—Not a CCP No—Proceed to next question.	Q1: Do control measures exist for the identified hazard? Yes—Proceed to next question. No—Either not a CCP or need to modify step, process, or product.	Q2. Is this process step specifically designed to eliminate or reduce the likely occurrence of this identified hazard to an acceptable level? Yes—CCP No—Proceed to next question	Q3. Could contamination with the identifed hazard(s) occur in excess of acceptable level(s) or increase to unacceptable level(s)? Yes—Proceed to next question. No—Not a CCP	Q4. Will a subsequent step eliminate the identified hazard(s) or reduce its likely occurrence to an acceptable level? Yes—Not a CCP. Identify subsequent step. No—CCP	CCP Number

Figure 4.6   CCP determination form.

A. Is this hazard of sufficient likelihood of occurrence and severity
    to warrant its control?

B. Is this hazard fully controlled by a prerequisite program?

Q1. Do control measures exist for the identified hazard?

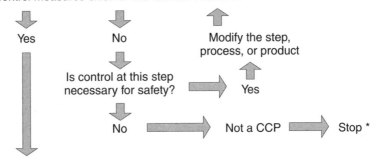

Q2. Is this process step specifically designed to eliminate or reduce the likely
    occurrence of this identified hazard to an acceptable level?

Q3. Could contamination with the identified hazard(s) occur in excess of
    acceptable level(s) or increase to unacceptable level(s)?

Q4. Will a subsequent step eliminate the identified hazard(s) or reduce its likely
    occurrence to an acceptable level?

    * Proceed to next step in the process

Figure 4.7 A CCP decision tree.

cooker—at a high temperature to kill pathogens), and acidification (adding acid to lower the pH of foods to make conditions unfavorable to bacterial growth).

If the process step is specifically designed to eliminate or reduce the likely occurrence of the hazard to an acceptable level, the answer is "yes" and this step automatically becomes a CCP. Caution should be taken when more than one step in the process has been "specifically designed" to eliminate or reduce the hazard. In that case, only the final control measure is the CCP. For instance, in a process with several magnets or metal detectors in the same line, only the final metal detector is the CCP. The other control measures are control points.

If the step is not specifically designed to eliminate or reduce the likely occurrence of an identified hazard, the answer is "no." Proceed to Question 3.

Question 3: Could contamination with the identified hazard(s) occur in excess of acceptable level(s) or increase to unacceptable level(s)? This question is included in all decision trees. If the significance of the hazard has been carefully evaluated as part of a hazard analysis, the question has already been answered. Basically, this question assists the HACCP team in determining whether the hazard has a significant impact on product safety.

It is important to note that this question also asks if the hazard could increase to an unacceptable level. The growth of microorganisms during processing, storage, or distribution could result in microbial numbers increasing to an unacceptable level even though these numbers were acceptable at an earlier point in the process.

If the answer to this question is "yes," then proceed to Question 4. A "yes" response should be accompanied by a documented description of the scientific literature or data on which the decision was based, particularly if this was not done during the evaluation stage of the hazard analysis.

If your answer is "no," then the hazard is not known to have an impact on product safety and the step is not a CCP. Proceed to the next step in the process.

Question 4: Will a subsequent step eliminate the identified hazard(s) or reduce its likely occurrence to an acceptable level? This question assists in the identification of multiple points at which control measures may be used to control a hazard in a single process. In this case, only the final point is considered a CCP; the others are considered control points. For example, in the making of marinara sauce, the washing of tomatoes is a control point. Thermal processing is a subsequent step that will "eliminate the identified hazard." Therefore the time and temperature parameters for the thermal processing are the critical control points that must be controlled. During the production of an electronic circuit for a medical device each of the components can be tested individually prior to placing them on the circuit board. Testing of each of those components is a control point. The final electronic circuit board is functionally tested after the assembly operation. That test would be considered a critical control point.

If no subsequent step(s) is (are) scheduled in the process to control this hazard, answer "no" and this particular process step becomes a CCP. If there is (are) subsequent step(s) later in the process that will eliminate the identified hazard or reduce it to an acceptable level, answer "yes" and this step is not a CCP. As part of its CCP documentation, the HACCP team will need to identify the subsequent step(s) that control the hazard before proceeding.

Factors Leading to CCP Misidentification

A number of factors can lead to the misidentification of CCPs. The following are common mistakes that can lead to the misidentification of CCPs:

- Using a decision tree without first determining the hazard's significance and whether it is controlled by a prerequisite program

- Missing a process step in the process flow diagram and in the hazard analysis

- Failing to identify all possible hazards

- Assigning the wrong level of significance to a hazard

- Inadequate development or implementation of the prerequisite programs

- Misapplication of the decision tree

- Lack of scientific evidence in support of hazard identification

DOCUMENTING CRITICAL CONTROL POINTS

CCP determination should be clearly documented. Figure 4.6 provides an example of the type of form that can be used. Also, CCPs can be sequentially numbered on the process flow diagram, CCP determination form, and HACCP plan for convenience. Many organizations identify CCPs numerically with a category qualifier for biological ("B"), physical ("P"), and chemical ("C"). For example, if the first CCP identified controls a biological hazard, it is recorded as CCP-1B. If the second CCP identified controls a chemical hazard, it is recorded as CCP-2C. If a biological and a chemical hazard are controlled at the same processing step, and this is the fifth CCP, then the CCP number used is CCP-5BC. This identification protocol sequentially identifies CCPs independent from process step numbering and informs the user of the HACCP plan which type of hazards need to be controlled at a particular process step.[7]

REFERENCES

1. U.S. National Advisory Committee on Microbiological Criteria for Foods (NACMCF), *Hazards Analysis and Critical Control Point Principles and Application Guidelines* (Washington, DC: U.S. Food and Drug Administration, 1997).
2. Association of Food and Drug Officials, *Medical Device Training Curriculum*, Draft ed. (York, PA: AFDO, 1999).
3. NACMCF, *Hazards Analysis.*

4. Sara Mortimore and Carol Wallace, *HACCP: A Practical Approach,* Second ed. (New York: Chapman and Hall, 1995): 51.

5. Ibid., 61.

6. Kenneth E. Stevenson and Dane T. Bernard, *HACCP—A Systematic Approach to Food Safety*, Third ed. (Washington, D.C.: The National Food Processors Institute, 1999): 82.

7. Canadian Food Inspection Agency, *Food Safety Enhancement Program Implementation Manual* II (Ottowa, Canada: Government of Canada, 1995): 57–58.

5

Principle #3—Establish Critical Limits

WHAT ARE CRITICAL LIMITS?

The third HACCP principle of setting critical limits (CLs) follows two very important stages in the development of a HACCP plan. Once a thorough hazard analysis has been conducted and the correct critical control points (CCPs) have been determined, the next crucial step is the determination of critical limits. The National Advisory Committee on Microbiological Criteria for Foods (NACMCF) defines a *critical limit* as "a maximum and/or minimum value to which a biological, chemical, or physical parameter must be controlled at a CCP to prevent, eliminate, or reduce to an acceptable level the occurrences of a food safety hazard."[1] Codex Alimentarius defines a critical limit simply as "a criteria which separates acceptability from unacceptability."[2] In other words, critical limits are defined processing boundaries that cannot be exceeded. If a critical limit is exceeded, then corrective action must be taken.

Parameters commonly utilized in establishing critical limits and controlling biological hazards include time, temperature, weight/size, humidity, water activity, pH, preservatives, salt level, chlorine level, and viscosity.

An example of setting critical limits occurs in the cooking of meatballs. A critical limit would be cooking the meatballs to an internal temperature of 160°F (71°C) or greater.[3] This critical limit is set to ensure that all pathogens or disease-causing microorganisms are killed. This critical limit may be achieved several ways. For example, the actual temperature of the meatballs may be measured after cooking. Or, the meatballs may be cooked using a validated process. If this latter system is used factors such as the size of the meatballs, cooking time, cooking temperature, and cooking conditions must be controlled to ensure that the cooked product is safe.

Yet another example of the setting of a critical limit occurs with the cooling of a cooked meat product. The maximum internal temperature of a cooked product should not remain between 80°F (27°C) and 130°F (54°C) for more than 1.5 hours nor between 40°F (4°C) and 80°F (27°C) for more than 5 hours.[4] This ensures that recontamination of the cooked product and exponential growth of bacteria do not occur.

ESTABLISHING CRITICAL LIMITS

A scientific basis needs to be used to set critical limits. To do this, companies may utilize external sources of information to augment internal sources of knowledge. Sources of information to use in the setting of critical limits for biological, chemical, and physical hazards may include literature searches, government regulations, industry standards, trade association technical committees, in-house research or studies, generic food safety models, equipment manufacturers, and trained industry consultants. Once the critical limits are established for a CCP, processing limits can be developed to more tightly control the process or simply to keep it within normal boundaries. Critical limits should define unacceptable processing conditions from a safety perspective. If the critical limit is exceeded, corrective actions must be initiated. Critical limits differ from operational limits. Operational limits define normal processing conditions and should be set more tightly than critical limits.

Microbiological

Microbiological finished product testing or performance standards are rarely used as critical or operational limits simply because of the delay factor between the time of sampling and the receipt of testing results. An example is the USDA/FSIS performance standard of 6.5 $\log_{10}$ reduction of *Salmonella* for cooked poultry products. This is to ensure that the cooked chicken will no longer cause a food borne illness due to *Salmonella*.

Sampling of the product for microbiological issues can be rather ineffective, especially if the pathogen is present at a low level or is not randomly distributed throughout the production lot. A better method to ensure microbiological safety is to define the processing conditions needed to achieve specific time/temperature parameters, thus ensuring that the microbiological performance standards are met. Controlling the process allows immediate corrective actions to be made if a process's critical limits are exceeded so that risks resulting from the production of a product are minimized or averted.

Chemical

Chemical limits take a number of different forms. Chemicals can be both naturally occurring and added. Examples of naturally occurring chemical hazards include shellfish toxins, aflatoxins, and vomitoxins. Critical limits for shellfish toxins can relate to the time of year and the harvest water location. For vomitoxin, which occurs in wheat, corn, and other grains, entire regions can be affected or problems can be localized, based on weather. In this case, whether a flour mill or feed mill, regular testing of the supply source must take place.

Other naturally occurring chemical hazards, such as lead, mercury, or even dioxins, can come from a contaminated environment. This can be controlled, for example, by a critical limit that specifies "no lead as provided by a supplier source guarantee." Potential chemical hazards such as pesticides, hormones, antibiotics, preservatives, colors, vitamins, and nitrites are most effectively controlled through good manufacturing practices (GMPs), good agricultural practices (GAPs), and prerequisite programs.

Physical

Defining critical limits on physical hazards is straightforward. Equipment such as magnets, metal detectors, sifters, and screens remove many physical hazards. For a magnet, the critical limit could be described as "no hazardous metal" whereas for a metal detector the critical limit can be based only on the metal detector's capability to find ferrous, non-ferrous, and stainless steel material. The proper functioning of the kick-out device should be defined and monitored. All kick-outs should be carefully checked to investigate the source of the metal.

ESTABLISHING OPERATIONAL LIMITS

Once the critical limits are established, operational limits can be established. Operational limits are designed to prevent routine deviations of the critical limits. Operational limits are set tighter than the critical limits to provide a safety factor for the processor. These limits need to take into account various factors such as accuracy and precision of the measurement process, process and product variation, and limits needed to achieve quality requirements. If the potential exists for occurrence of a process deviation, operational limits provide the processor with the opportunity to adjust the process and bring it back into control prior to the production of a product that violates the critical limit.

REFERENCES

1. U. S. National Advisory Committee on Microbiological Criteria for Foods, *Hazard Analysis and Critical Control Point Principles and Application Guidelines* (Washington, DC: U. S. Food and Drug Administration, 1998): 762.
2. Codex, 1997.
3. USDA/FSIS, Appendix A: "Compliance Guidelines for Meeting the Lethality Conformance Standards for Certain Meat and Poultry Products." 1999. http://www.fsis.usda.gov.\oa\fr\95033f-b.htm
4. USDA/FSIS, Appendix B: "Compliance Guidelines for Cooling Heat-Treated Meat and Poultry Products (Stabilization)." 1999. http://www.fsis.usda.gov.\oa\fr\95033f-b.htm

6

Principle #4—Establishing Monitoring Procedures

WHAT IS MONITORING?

The activity of monitoring critical control points (CCPs) is essential to the success of a HACCP-based system. Appropriate monitoring procedures must be established and used to ensure that critical limits are not exceeded. To establish and effectively conduct monitoring procedures, the questions of who, what, where, when, why, and how must be answered. Such procedures should primarily be observations or physical measurements that can be readily carried out without imposing unrealistic time delays or extreme costs in production processes.

Within a HACCP-based system, monitoring is the act of scheduled testing and/or observation, recorded by the company, to report the findings at each CCP. Monitoring is an action that is normally carried out on the line by production personnel. Monitoring may be performed continuously by an instrument such as a temperature recorder or pH recorder. Since monitoring consists of continuing observation, it also requires management attention and action to sustain the HACCP process and to ensure that appropriate actions are taken when critical limits are exceeded. It is not something that can be set up, turned on, and ignored.

Examples of monitoring procedures include:

- sampling and inspecting of raw materials

- checking and documenting product temperatures

- checking temperature and humidity in dry storage rooms

- checking inventory control

- checking amounts of additives used for each batch/lot
- product sampling for bacterial analysis
- scheduled checking of net weights
- scheduled checking of labels used
- periodic checking of process control specifications
- visually inspecting product and equipment
- checking equipment maintenance.

The monitoring procedures used for each CCP must be specific and should be designed to monitor the control of each hazard identified.

Obviously, monitoring is done to collect data and to subsequently have information upon which to base decisions and take appropriate actions. Monitoring also provides an early warning that a process is either losing control or is in fact out of control. When done properly, monitoring can help to prevent or minimize loss of product when a process or handling deviation occurs. It can also help to pinpoint the cause of the problem when control is lost. Without effective monitoring and recording of data or information, there is no HACCP-based system.

COLLECTING DATA

Monitoring is a data collection activity. Thus, it is important to understand how to properly collect data. In general, there are ten steps to follow in designing a data collection or monitoring activity:

1. *Ask the right questions.* The questions must relate to the specific information needed. Otherwise it is easy to collect data that are incomplete or that answer the wrong questions.

2. *Conduct appropriate data analysis.* What analysis must be done to get from raw data collection to a comparison with the critical limit(s)?

3. *Define where to collect.* Where are the specific locations for data collection?

4. *Ensure unbiased data collection.* If the data are biased, the data do not describe the manufacturing conditions and the data subsequently cannot be compared to the critical limits. Therefore it will not be possible to determine if the products being manufactured are safe.

5. *Understand the needs of the person collecting the data.* This may include special environment requirements, training, and experience.

6. *Design simple but effective data collection forms.* Forms used to collect and record data should be self-explanatory, must permit the recording of all appropriate data, and should be designed to reduce the opportunity for error.

7. *Prepare instructions.* Operating instructions are powerful tools to help employees conduct the monitoring process in a consistent manner.

8. *Test the forms and instructions and revise as necessary.* The person or employee who developed a form may think it is easy to use. However, a form may not be easy to use by the operator under production conditions.

9. *Train the person(s) collecting the data.* Operators need to know how, where, and when to collect the data, and how, where, and when to properly record their observations.

10. *Audit the collection process and validate the results.* Audits provide a tool to ensure that a HACCP system is (1) operating as planned and (2) operating in an effective and efficient manner.

Monitoring can be done by either observation or measurement at CCPs. In general, an observation gives a *qualitative* index of control; a measurement results in a *quantitative* index. Thus, the choice of whether the monitoring will be an observation or a measurement, or both, depends upon the established critical limit and available methods. Potential time delays and costs should also be considered.

Monitoring by Observation

Observation is the most basic means of data collection. While monitoring by measurement often is recommended because it gives "unbiased" numbers, the importance of observations cannot be overlooked. Of course, the observations must be compared to the CCP's critical limit(s). This requires a manual analysis by the observer and, in many cases, a subjective interpretation. Extreme care must be taken when selecting, training, and standardizing observers.

Monitoring by Measurement

Monitoring by measurement can include physical, chemical, or microbiological indices. The most common process measurements taken are time, temperature, and pH. However, for raw materials, chemical tests for toxins, food additives, contaminants; and microbiological tests for coliforms, *E. coli*, *Salmonella*, and other microorganisms are often used.

As expected, measurement monitoring requires some extra care. Equipment must be calibrated and quality control procedures for data collection must exist. Monitoring with an uncalibrated thermometer or one that does not read to the desired decimal point can do more harm than good.

RECORDING DATA

Measurement data can be recorded in a number of ways. The easiest way is with a data sheet. Data sheets should record information in a simple format. However, as in observation monitoring, the person recording and collecting the data must be instructed sufficiently to perform the data analyses relative to the critical limit. In the example shown in Figure 6.1, the person collecting the data must know that any internal temperature below 180°F (82°C) is cause for a corrective action.

The trend for measurement monitoring is toward full automation. Micro-processing systems can have visual and/or sound alarms when critical limits are exceeded. Automation can produce data sheets as well as control charts and check sheets. If calibrated and maintained correctly, automated systems can help to reduce the risk of human error.

Processing line 1 critical limit: Temperature not less than 180°F		
Time	**Temperature**	**Notes:**
0800	181°F	
0830	181°F	
0900	180°F	
0930	180°F	
1000	179°F	1005—Increased steam flow
1030	180°F	
1100	180°F	
Operator: <u>Joe Smiley</u> Date: <u>mm/dd/yy</u>		

Figure 6.1   Temperature data sheet.

CONTINUOUS VERSUS INTERMITTENT MONITORING

If monitoring is not continuous, the question of when to monitor becomes extremely important. It is no less important for in-process monitoring than for monitoring on an individual lot basis. Intermittent or noncontinuous monitoring must reliably indicate that a hazard is under control.

Intermittent monitoring quickly leads to a discussion on statistics. If monitoring is on a per-lot basis (for example, raw material), the question becomes "How much do I sample?" If a production line is to be intermittently monitored, an additional question to ask is "How often do I sample?" These questions are best answered through statistical analysis. Management must decide on the amount of risk it is willing to accept by consulting literature or competent statistical authorities. These sources can help answer the "when" question so that appropriate intervals can be incorporated into the development or modification of a firm's sampling plans.

DETERMINING MONITORING POINTS

Monitoring in a HACCP-based system is performed at CCPs. It must be done at a location where a CCP accurately reflects the state of a critical limit. For example, if the critical limit of a cooking CCP is an internal temperature of 180°F (82°C), then monitoring should be performed during or immediately after cooking when the maximum temperature has been reached. However, the ideal is to monitor where there is minimal interruption in the production flow.

With regard to other monitoring location options, the key to establishing "where" is to learn to ask the right questions. Only then can effective data collection occur. The following questions should be asked; sample answers using the internal temperature example above are provided.

Q: What questions need to be answered?

A: What is the internal temperature of the cooked product at the completion of cooking (or after a certain amount of time)?

Q: What means will be used to get the answer?

A: Measuring the internal temperature.

Q: What data analysis must be done, and how will the results be communicated?

A: The internal temperature must be at least 180°F. Results can be communicated by an electronic alarm, by continuous monitoring of a temperature recorder, or by periodic examination of a temperature control chart.

Q: What type of data is needed?

A: Internal temperature data recorded to the nearest 0.1°F is needed.

Q: Where in the process can data be obtained?

A: Data can be obtained from the cooked product as it exits the cooker.

Some of these questions and answers are self-evident, and it might appear foolish to follow this process for every critical limit. However, the important concept is that, in deciding where to collect data, the process works backwards. Before asking what data it needs, a firm should determine what questions need to be answered. This better defines data needs and subsequently suggests where the data should be collected.

QUALIFICATIONS OF THE PERSON COLLECTING THE DATA

The qualifications of the person collecting the data must be based upon the how and where of monitoring. Certainly, the designated employee must have easy access to the CCP, as well as the skills and knowledge to understand not only the production process but also the purpose, importance, and process of the monitoring activity. In cases such as organoleptic determination of decomposition or chemical or microbiological analyses, the person must have a high level of training and experience. Of course, the person should also be unbiased. All things considered, the "who" should be someone in whom the company can place its trust.

7

Principle #5—Establish Corrective Action Procedures

WHAT IS CORRECTIVE ACTION?

No matter how well the HACCP system has been designed and implemented, deviations from the processes established as part of the HACCP plan may occur. Once hazards have been identified, corresponding critical limits determined, and monitoring procedures set up, it is necessary to establish corrective action procedures. Corrective action is defined as "action to be taken when the results of monitoring at the CCP indicate a loss of control."[1]

It is a general sign that a process is out of control when the critical limits at a CCP are exceeded. When this occurs, corrective actions must be taken to bring the process, and the affected product, back into control. The HACCP plan must be designed so that deviations from the critical limits can be discovered quickly. The early detection and subsequent elimination or reduction of deviations enables corrective actions to be taken as early as possible. This minimizes the production of nonconforming product. Specific corrective action plans should be developed for each CCP since variations result from many causes. Actions that would be considered corrective action include: isolating and holding product for safety evaluation, diverting the affected product or ingredients to another line where deviation would not be considered critical, reprocessing, rejecting raw material, and destroying product.

Personnel responsible for implementing corrective actions must be properly trained; possess a thorough understanding of the HACCP plan, the process, and the product produced; and have the authority to see that the corrective action is properly taken. Additionally, the corrective action should be documented.

GOALS OF CORRECTIVE ACTION

Corrective action has two goals. The first is to identify, correct, and eliminate the cause of the deviation. The second is to determine the scope of the problem so that nonconforming product can be properly identified and disposed. These two elements apply when the deviation is associated with exceeding critical limits and should lead to restoring control of the process.

There are four general steps to any corrective action. They are to (1) identify the cause of the deviation, (2) determine product disposition, (3) record the corrective action, and (4) reevaluate the HACCP plan.

Identifying Causes of Deviations

Identifying the cause of a deviation usually involves some form of root cause analysis. A root cause is "a fundamental deficiency that results in a nonconformance and must be corrected to prevent recurrence of the same or similar nonconformance."[2] The misidentification of the root cause could lead to an improper corrective action.

Determining Product Disposition

Determining the appropriate method for disposing of nonconforming product is important, as it is undesirable for nonconforming or unsafe product to enter commerce. Product destruction should be witnessed and documented. Disposal, however, is a short-term correction designed to contain a problem. Long-term corrections address the underlying cause and are expected to solve a problem permanently without resulting in the occurrence of a new problem. To address the problem correctly, the manufacturer needs to identify the hazards and their causes. The company must improve the manufacturing processes, revise company procedures, and train employees to follow the new procedures. The processes used to determine the short- and long-term solutions should be included in the corrective action plan.

Recording the Corrective Action

All corrective actions taken must be documented. Corrective action records assist the company in the identification of recurring problems, and may be used to determine whether the HACCP plan requires modification. The documentation should identify the product, describe the deviation, detail the action to be taken (including the method to be used for final disposition of the affected product), and state the name and job title of the person responsible for making the correction. Any reevaluation of the HACCP plan should be noted in the minutes of the verification meetings.

All corrective action records should be filed separately. Additionally, corrective action records may be filed with the records that illustrate the deviation. This method of double filing permits fast and efficient evaluation of the deviations noted, and their subsequent corrections, by company personnel and outside auditing bodies.

One additional record, called a Notice of Unusual Occurrence and Corrective Action (NUOCA), may be used for corrective actions. It is designed for use in those situations where an applicable predetermined corrective action is not available for a given scenario. This record is completed using the formal steps described above, and filed with the other corrective action reports. The acronym "NUOCA" often is used to mean any corrective action report, and, in fact, many companies title their corrective action reports as NUOCAs. This supports the position that corrective actions should be unusual occurrences.

Reevaluating the HACCP Plan

Many firms miss the final but extremely important step involved in corrective action: reevaluating the HACCP plan. This step can be used to (1) identify gaps in the HACCP plan, (2) identify hazards that may have been overlooked initially, (3) determine whether corrective actions taken are sufficient to correct deviations, (4) establish whether critical limits are properly set, (5) determine if monitoring activities are adequate, (6) determine if new technologies are available which could reduce the likelihood of the occurrence of a hazard, and (7) determine if new hazards must be addressed in the HACCP plan.

CORRECTIVE ACTION PLANS

Corrective action plans are usually written in an "if–then" format. Corrective action plans should be as specific as possible, but it is not necessary for them to be extremely long. A description of what actions will be taken when a specific deviation occurs is sufficient. Following are several examples of corrective action statements.

> *"If temperature of milk at pasteurizer drops below the critical limit, then milk flow is diverted until temperature recovers. Diverted milk is repasteurized. Check the operation of the heating/cooling units to determine the reason for the temperature deviation that caused the flow diversion. Repair if necessary, reestablish control and resume production."* (AFDO-Seafood HACCP Alliance)

> *"If product does not reach required internal temperature for the required time, then recook or destroy the product."* (AFDO-Seafood HACCP Alliance)

> *"If the internal dimensions of components do not meet specifications, then reject the lot of components."* (AFDO-Medical Devices)

> *"If sterilization parameters are not met, then quarantine product, review records and determine through sampling and testing if product is releasable, can be resterilized, or if it must be discarded."* (AFDO-Medical Devices)

REFERENCES

1. Codex, 1997, page 1, Annex to Appendix II.
2. ASQC CQA Brochure

8

Principle #6—Establish Verification Procedures

OBJECTIVES OF THE VERIFICATION PROCESS

The complexity of the verification process makes it the least well-defined of the seven HACCP principles, because it attempts to address several principles under the concept of one principle. Many believe that the verification process is simply calibration and record review. While these are integral elements of verification, the principle embodies much more.

The verification principle is designed to assist a firm in the accomplishment of three HACCP objectives. First, the verification process is used to ensure that the HACCP plan is working. In other words, it confirms that the written plan is implemented, and that the implemented plan is identical to the written plan. Second, verification ensures that the HACCP plan is valid. When used in this manner it is a science-based review of the rationale behind each part of the HACCP plan, such as the hazards analysis, CCP determination and verification strategies, and the establishment of critical limits. Finally, verification ensures that the HACCP plan is relevant. Since the HACCP plan is not intended to be static once developed and implemented, it must be reviewed periodically to ensure that it remains current and effective.

At a minimum, verification of the entire HACCP system should take place annually. This ensures that all plan elements are reviewed to validate the adequacy of the plan in the identification and control of significant hazards. In addition, the annual review assesses whether the HACCP plan is functioning as designed, and ensures that it continues to accurately reflect the firm's product and operational requirements.

TYPES OF VERIFICATION

Verification should occur at several points throughout the HACCP plan development and implementation, as well as on an ongoing basis. Several types of verification activities will be explored in this chapter. Selecting the appropriate approach to use in a specific instance is an integral part of an effective HACCP system.

Verification can be defined as methods, procedures, and tests used to determine if the HACCP system is in compliance with the HACCP plan. The HACCP team needs to decide which methods, procedures, and tests the company should perform to verify that the HACCP system is working effectively. The HACCP plan should specify these actions, state the frequency at which these actions will be performed, and identify the person(s) responsible for performing the actions. Verification uses methods, procedures, or tests separate from and in addition to those used in monitoring (chapter 6) to determine whether the HACCP system is in compliance with the HACCP plan or whether the HACCP plan needs modification.

Verification reports should include information about the HACCP plan and the person(s) responsible for administering and updating the plan, the status of records associated with CCP monitoring, and direct monitoring data of the CCP gathered while observing the operation. Certification that monitoring equipment is properly calibrated and in working order, and results of records review and any samples analyzed to verify that CCPs are under control should be included in the report. Training records of the individuals responsible for monitoring CCPs and the HACCP team members should be reviewed and documented as well.

Several categories of verification are discussed following.

Validation

The primary type of verification is the validation that the critical limits at the CCPs are sufficient for their intended purpose. Validation is the initial step in which the HACCP plan is tested and reviewed prior to implementation. This may require the assistance of external resources to identify the biological, chemical, or physical hazards that are intrinsic to the raw materials, ingredients, or processes. A scientific or technical review of the critical limits is necessary to verify that the specifications that are set are adequate to control the hazards that are likely to occur, and in some cases that the specifications comply with regulatory requirements. The CCPs, critical limits, and monitoring activities must be repeatedly challenged and statistically demonstrated to prevent or control identified hazards in the company's normal operations. Microbiological or analytical testing can be used effectively to verify that the process is in control and that acceptable product is being produced. The results of the validation process provide clear evidence that the HACCP plan elements adopted by the company are effective and sustainable.

Ongoing Assessment

The second type of verification is an ongoing review that ensures that the company's HACCP plan is functioning effectively. A functioning HACCP system minimizes the need for extensive product sampling and testing since the appropriate preventive measures are built into the production controls. Firms rely on verification of their HACCP plan to ensure that the plan is being followed correctly, for review of CCP records, and to determine that appropriate risk management and product disposition decisions are made when deviations occur.

A schedule of verification activities is developed as part of the HACCP plan. This includes the procedures or methods to be utilized, frequency, and person(s) responsible for performing the activity. Examples of HACCP plan verification activities that should be considered as part of a HACCP program include:

- Reviewing the HACCP plan for completeness

- Confirming the accuracy of the flow diagram

- Reviewing CCP monitoring records

- Reviewing deviations and their resolution or corrective action, including the disposition of finished product

- Calibrating temperature or other critical measuring equipment

- Visually inspecting operations to observe if CCPs are under control

- Analytically testing or auditing monitoring procedures

- Randomly collecting and analyzing samples of in-process or finished product

- Sampling for environmental and other concerns

- Reviewing consumer or customer complaints to determine whether they relate to the performance of the CCPs or reveal the existence of unidentified CCPs

- Reviewing personnel records to determine employees' amount of training in HACCP system responsibilities

- Reviewing written records of verification inspections that certify compliance with the HACCP plan or specify deviations from the plan and corrective actions taken

- Checking for the presence of prerequisite programs

- Reviewing modifications to the HACCP plan.[1]

Designated personnel must periodically review records to ensure that specific record keeping requirements are being met. They are then responsible for documenting that this task was in fact performed, and for recording the findings of the records review. Records should be complete: at a minimum they should include the company's name and location, date and time of activity, initials of the operator, and identity of product and product code. The HACCP plan should stress the responsibility for accurate documentation and address the seriousness of falsification. Regulatory agencies may copy records to document deficiencies, provide information for agency review, document record falsification, and facilitate the next inspection.

Review of Monitoring Records. Continuous monitoring with measuring and recording devices such as automatic time–temperature equipment is optimal as it provides a permanent record that can be reviewed and evaluated. Noncontinuous monitoring is used when a continuous approach is not feasible, such as for visual examinations; monitoring ingredient specifications; measuring pH, water activity (A_w), and product temperatures; or for attribute sampling. When dealing with noncontinuous monitoring, the frequency of review is critical to ensure that the hazard is under control. Random testing at a CCP or statistically based sampling may be utilized to verify effectiveness of the CCP, critical limit, and monitoring activities. Review of these records includes the determination that monitoring has been performed as specified, critical limits have been met, and corrective action has been taken when necessary. Review should ensure that actual values, rather than conclusions, are recorded, as well as the date and time of monitoring, initials of operator, identity of product, and the company's name and location. The signature of the person performing the review and the date reviewed should be recorded, with follow-up, being performed on a timely basis, generally within one week.

Review of Corrective Action Records. The review of corrective action records determines that all critical limit deviations have been properly addressed following the predetermined corrective action plan. Additionally, the date of corrective action, initials of operator, identity of the product, and the company's name and location is confirmed. The signature of the person performing the review and date reviewed should be recorded, with follow-up being performed on a timely basis, generally within one week.

Review of Verification Records. The review of verification records includes confirmation that calibration and product testing is being conducted consistent with the HACCP plan, that the process flow diagram is current, that audits are performed with the appropriate corrective action taken as identified, and that record review is being completed on a timely basis.

Calibration. Instrumentation that is used to measure, monitor, and control the parameters identified as critical limits must be calibrated to ensure the accuracy of the results. The calibration schedule should be identified for all classes of equipment, for instance, thermometers, thermocouples and temperature/humidity recorders, and feedback loops. The method of calibration, frequency at which calibration should occur, and standards to be utilized should be specified in the plan. Primary standards that are used to calibrate routinely used equipment, such as certified thermometers calibrated and traceable to national or international standards, should be identified and maintained in a controlled manner with limited access.

Testing and Analysis. As mentioned, testing and analysis may be performed during initial validation to support the selection of CCPs, critical limits, and monitoring activities. Once the plan is implemented, random samples should be collected and analyzed independently to confirm the effectiveness of each CCP in the system. The HACCP plan should specify what tests will be performed and the appropriate corrective action to be taken, including disposition of affected products, in the event of a failure.

Observation and Audit. Verification audits range in scope from observation of a company's operations or monitoring activities to an in-depth audit performed by internal or third-party resources. Verification audits should be performed periodically and may include unannounced audits. Such audits ensure that selected CCPs are continuously under control. Additional rationale for performing audits may include the determination that intensive coverage of a specific hazard is needed because of new information concerning the hazard and associated risk; when a company's products have been implicated as a vehicle of injury, illness, or associated health complaint; and to verify that changes have been implemented correctly after a HACCP plan has been modified.

Revalidation

The third type of verification consists of documented periodic revalidation, or reassessment, independent of audits or other verification procedures that are performed to ensure the accuracy of the HACCP plan. Revalidation is performed on a regular basis, for instance annually, and/or whenever significant product, preparation, or packaging changes require modification of the HACCP plan. The revalidation process includes a documented on-site review, and verification of all flow diagrams and CCPs in the HACCP plan. Revalidation is similar to validation in that it considers whether the plan is adequate in general rather than focusing on the plan's daily operations. It is also similar to validation in that it must be done by someone thoroughly trained and knowledgeable in HACCP principles. However, validation occurs when the HACCP plan is initially tested and reviewed prior to implementation.

Revalidation of the HACCP plan is required when there is an unexpected system failure; a significant product, process, or packaging change; or when new hazards are recognized. Changes in raw materials or ingredients, finished product distribution systems, or even in the intended use or consumers of the finished product should initiate the revalidation process.

The significance of revalidation cannot be overestimated. It is the element of verification that prevents the HACCP plan from becoming obsolete and therefore ineffective. In the event of a system failure or the recognition of a new hazard, revalidation of a HACCP system should be undertaken immediately. When considering changes in product formulations, packaging, and so on, the impact of these changes must be assessed prior to the change so that any modifications to the HACCP plan can be made concurrent with the change.

EXTERNAL REVIEW

In specific regulated industries, the relevant governmental agencies have the regulatory responsibility to review and approve the company's HACCP plan to ensure that the system is functioning satisfactorily. This constitutes an external form of verification. It may include document review, direct observation or measurement, and/or product sampling and analysis. A HACCP system may be found to be inadequate if the plan, in operation, does not meet regulatory requirements, personnel are not performing required tasks, HACCP records are not being maintained, or adulterated product is being produced or shipped.[2]

Verification activities should be realistic within the scope of the company's operations, and defined for each CCP in the HACCP plan. Over time, verification can assist the HACCP team in identifying and improving plan or operational weaknesses, eliminating unnecessary controls, and assuring continuous effectiveness of the system.

REFERENCES

1. U. S. Public Health Service, U. S. Department of Health and Human Services, "Annex 5: HACCP Guidelines," in *1999 Food Code* (Washington, D.C.: U. S. Food and Drug Administration, 1999).
2. Ibid.

9

Principle #7—Establish Record Keeping and Documentation Procedures

IMPORTANCE OF RECORD KEEPING

The seventh principle of HACCP is the establishment and implementation of a comprehensive record keeping system. Documentation provides factual evidence that a particular activity has been adequately performed to predetermined specifications. Under a HACCP system, the documentation generated must be in the form of a formal, written record that demonstrates that the activity has been performed in a timely manner and conducted in accordance with established procedures. Once a record has been created, a formal record keeping system must be implemented. This system must establish procedures for the identification, storage, retrieval, maintenance, protection, and disposition of documents.

Some firms view HACCP record keeping as a nuisance since these records require time to record and maintain. As a result, their reason for developing and maintaining records often is solely to meet regulatory requirements. Other firms embrace HACCP records as the appropriate way of doing business and have incorporated them as an essential part of their quality management system. In this instance, records are viewed as tools for simplifying business life, for streamlining operations, and for offering other long-term benefits to the company.

Internal Benefits

Firms that have embraced HACCP as a way of life, or as part of their quality management system, recognize four internal benefits to having a comprehensive record keeping system. First, these records provide a reasonable certainty that a firm took responsible actions when product was manufactured; for example, that safety parameters were met. Second, they offer reassurance that appropriate corrective actions have been taken to reformulate the products or redesign the process when critical limits were exceeded. Third, products whose safety has been compromised are identified and contained, thereby preventing subsequent transfer of risk to the marketplace. Fourth, to any party reviewing or auditing the manufacturing system, a record keeping system shows that the manufacturing process is under control. Records present a comprehensive picture that can be used to show that hazards have been detected, minimized, or controlled. This in turn suggests that these potential hazards no longer pose a significant risk to a consumer's health or general well-being.

Regulatory Compliance

Regulatory agencies, on the other hand, use HACCP records to evaluate the state of control and/or compliance of a manufacturing firm. Inspectors routinely make professional judgments and reach conclusions as to whether responsible manufacturing practices were conducted. A company's failure to take corrective actions when critical limits are exceeded raises substantial regulatory concerns about the product safety controls employed by them. A company that takes immediate corrective actions after critical limits are exceeded, including further preventive steps to ensure that the problem(s) do not occur again, is viewed more positively by the regulatory agency and regarded as responsible.

Indirect Benefits

The design and implementation of a comprehensive record keeping system is a significant aspect of a successful HACCP system. In addition to the benefits listed above, several indirect benefits result from a firm's adherence to record keeping procedures. First, records provide management with a mechanism for appraising the effectiveness of processing controls and procedures, and suggest trends toward noncompliance during production. Second, records can be used to evaluate personnel and to provide a foundation for an effective training program. Finally, records that are routinely shared with employees can be used to motivate them to sustain their manufacturing practices, particularly if the monitoring results show that all critical limits have been met.

TYPES OF RECORDS

Under a HACCP system, the records of primary importance are CCP monitoring records, corrective action records, and verification records. CCP monitoring records confirm that the critical limits have been achieved at each CCP. Corrective action records document that appropriate actions have been taken when critical limits have not been met. Verification records confirm that the HACCP plan is being followed and that the HACCP system is valid and effective.

Commonly maintained HACCP system records include observations of measurements obtained during production (time, temperature, tolerances, and so on), corrective action records in response to critical limit deviations, and verification records (calibration records, laboratory analyses, annual HACCP plan review, and so on). These records are specifically required for certain regulated products, but numerous other records should be maintained and controlled under the HACCP system. Examples of these records include:

- Documents supporting the HACCP plan and hazard analysis
- Written Standard Sanitation Operating Procedures (SSOPs)
- Process flowcharts
- List of HACCP team members and their qualifications
- Data supporting critical limits, including laboratory analyses
- Outline of prerequisite programs and preliminary steps
- Employee training records
- Supplier guarantees/Certificates of Compliance/importer verification
- Shelf life studies
- Consultant reports
- Records of laboratory analyses (for example, pyrogen testing, water phase salt, pH, microbial challenge studies, and so forth)
- Packaging design and validation records

Monitoring Records

Monitoring records are the records that confirm that the critical limits at a CCP have been met. The minimum information to be included on all HACCP monitoring records include form title, company name and location, time and date, product identity (by type/model, lot number, and so on), actual observations or measurements, critical limits, operator's signature or initials, reviewer's signature or initials, and the date of review. Examples of monitoring records are shown in Figures 9.1 through 9.6.

Corrective Action Records

Corrective actions are taken in response to critical limit deviations. Information contained in corrective action records provides an evaluation of the actions taken, including a description of the deviation and any corrective action taken, in addition to a notation as to final disposition of the affected product. The name of the individual responsible for taking the corrective action should be included. A sample corrective action report is shown in Figure 9.7.

Raw Material Evaluation Sheet

Name of company
Address of company

Date _____ Time of evaluation _____

Product _____ P.O. number _____

Lot number_____ Supplier _____

Sample method and size _____

Sample no.	1	2	3	4	5
Wt.	_____	_____	_____	_____	_____
Size	_____	_____	_____	_____	_____
CCP item	_____	_____	_____	_____	_____
Color	_____	_____	_____	_____	_____
Shape	_____	_____	_____	_____	_____

Certificate for CCP item (Yes/No): _____

Operator/QC/Receiver: _____

Reviewed by: _____ **Date:** _____

Figure 9.1 Raw material evaluation sheet.

Note: In Figure 9.1 the items in bold are the HACCP record. In some instances it may be desirable to separate the CCP items from the control record for the non-safety items. The critical limit for this particular record is the certificate for the CCP item.

Supplier Certificate of Conformance

Name of company
Address of company

Date
Name of your company
Address of your company

Dear Mr. John Doe:

This certifies that in accordance with your purchasing specification, this shipment of (product) meets specifications for these hazards—*Supplier name, Lot number 12345.*

Yours truly,

I. B. Honest
QC director,
Name of supplier

Reviewed by: _____   Date: _____

Note: Make sure that the supplier meets all the specifications for the product you want on the certificate of analysis or supplier guarantee. A blanket statement does not always ensure that the product will meet your specifications.

Figure 9.2   Supplier certificate of conformance.

Processing Log

Name of company
Address of company

Date: _____   Product: _____

Critical limits: _____   Line: _____

Operator: _____

Line number	Lot number	Time of day	Temp MIG	Temp recorder	Comments

Reviewer: _____   Date: _____

If critical limits are exceeded, notify shift supervisor, and separate and identify the batch involved.

Figure 9.3   Processing log.

Label Room Inspection Log

Name of company
Address of company

Date: _____

Product: _____

Critical limits: _____

Line: _____

Label room supervisor: _____

Lot number	Time of day	Labeling requirement Yes/No	Presence of CCP item	Comments

Reviewer: _____   Date: _____

Figure 9.4 Label room inspection log.

Temperature Measurement

Instrument/Equipment

Name of company
Address of company

Instrument/equipment: _____

Location in plant: _____

Serial number: _____

Model number: _____

Schedule of calibration date: _____

Date calibrated	Calibration results	Method of calibration	Performed by	Reviewed by

Figure 9.5   Equipment calibration log.

Finished Product Report

Name of company
Address of company

Date: _____   Sample no. _____

Vendor: _____   Analyst: _____

The results of the analyses of sample XXXX consisting of xx amount of samples identified as batch 1 to 4 are as follows:

Batch	APC/G	Coliforms/ 10g	E. coli/10g	S. aureus/G	Salmonella/ sample

Remarks:
The above sample was analyzed using methods found in the *FDA Bacteriological Analytic Manual*, Eighth Edition.

I. M. Wright
Laboratory Director
AAA Laboratories
Address of lab

Reviewed by: _____   Date: _____

Figure 9.6   Finished product report.

Corrective Action Report

Name of company
Address of company

Date: _____   Lot ID:_____

Description of problem:

_____

_____

_____

_____

Action taken:

_____

_____

_____

_____

Date problem solved:_____

Current status:

_____

_____

Supervisor: _____

Reviewer: _____   Date: _____

Figure 9.7 Corrective action report.

Verification Records

Verification records document that the HACCP system is valid and is being consistently implemented. Unlike daily CCP monitoring records, verification records are typically conducted periodically and on a predetermined schedule. Verification records include:

- the HACCP plan and modifications to the HACCP plan (for example, changes in ingredients, formulations, processing, packaging, and distribution)

- processor records verifying supplier compliance with guarantees or certificates

- calibration records to verify the accuracy and calibration of all monitoring equipment

- analytical records, microbiological challenge tests, environmental tests, periodic in-line tests, and finished-product testing

- audit records of in-house, on-site inspections

- validation records of equipment-evaluation tests

Figures 9.8 through 9.11 are samples of potential HACCP verification records. For the meat and poultry industry, USDA/FSIS has specific format, review, and signature requirements.

DESIGNING A RECORD KEEPING/ DOCUMENTATION SYSTEM

The design of HACCP system records is not specified by formal regulation. Many approaches have been successfully used to design monitoring records. Some companies prefer to use one form for each production step. Others incorporate multiple items on one comprehensive form. Regardless of the method used to design the HACCP records system, the company should review the documentation in place and determine how to incorporate these HACCP activities throughout the entire system. These forms must be consistent with the HACCP plan, and should specify all steps required by HACCP including analyzing hazards; identifying CCPs; determining, controlling, and monitoring critical limits; taking corrective actions; and verifying results.

The successful design of a record system requires the involvement of a variety of personnel from production, quality control/assurance, and management. The resulting diversity of perspectives representing multiple disciplines creates a comprehensive picture of the entire HACCP system. Such a design also empowers employees and facilitates the communication, training, and acceptance of the record system by all personnel.

Another objective in designing a record keeping/documentation system is to provide for contemporaneous recording of events as they happen, with verification done independently by one or more persons unrelated in functions or units. Human errors can be significantly reduced by requiring dual signoffs, one from a person in production and another by someone in the quality department, as a verification step.

Laboratory Report

Name of company
Address of company

Date: _____   Sample number: _____

Vendor: _____   Critical limit: _____

Examined by: _____

Remarks:
The above sample was analyzed for the presence of the CCP item using official AOAC recognized methods.

I. M. Wright
Laboratory Director
AAA Laboratories
Address of lab

Figure 9.8   AAA laboratory report.

Processing Research Laboratory and/or University Extension Unit

Address of unit

Date of letter
Name of your company
Address of your company

Dear Mr. John Doe:

Various published studies document that a process that provides the parameters set for your process is adequate for that process. This supports our studies revealing that the process will meet the parameters you have set.

Sincerely,

I. M. Helpful
Processing Research Laboratory
Address of lab

Figure 9.9   Process validation letter.

Processing Research Laboratory and/or University Extension Unit

Address of unit

Date of letter
Name of your company
Address of your company

Dear Mr. John Doe:

On date of evaluation, during a visit to your company, your equipment was tested to meet the parameters for your process by setting our testing equipment to the equipment. Test results from three production runs indicate the parameters continue to operate as designed.

On this date, different sample sizes were also run in the equipment at your process time. These tests met your HACCP plan's critical limits.

Sincerely,

I. M. Helpful
Processing Research Laboratory
Address of lab

Figure 9.10 Equipment validation letter.

Employee Training Record

Name of company
Address of company

Employee: _____

Training course	Date of course

Figure 9.11 Employee training record.

Modify Existing Forms versus Create New Forms

CCP monitoring records may be integrated into established records systems. Purchase orders, invoices, inventory control records, and so on, can be modified for this purpose. An obvious advantage to doing this is that employees are already familiar with how to fill out these records and very little transitional training has to be done. Some firms are hesitant, though, to modify current purchase orders, invoices, or inventory control records because these forms release a substantial amount of information to regulatory agencies that is unrelated to HACCP or other regulatory requirements.

Some firms elect to revamp their entire record keeping system. This requires a substantial investment in time needed to retrain some employees, and redirect others to perform administrative work and technical training necessary for making the system work. The advantage to this approach is that it allows employees to understand the entire system, rather than just a small step of the system or the process in which they work.

Balanced Approach versus Overkill Approach

A balanced approach in record keeping is important. Records should be designed to be simple and easy to follow, with all monitoring steps clearly indicated. Essential information to include should describe who, what, where, when, and how.

It is neither practical nor desirable to develop a record for every activity within the processing environment. An overkill method frequently results in companies generating too many records. This becomes burdensome to employees, limits controls to the critical aspects of the process, and increases storage space needed for files.

Simplified versus Complex Records

An example of a simple record is shown in Figure 9.12. A more complex variation of the same record is illustrated in Figure 9.13. Figure 9.12 contains all of the information needed to check the CCP; Figure 9.13 includes the purchase order (P.O.) number to review for information needed to check the CCP at the receiving step, if any problems occur. Both are adequate from the regulatory standpoint, but the second one requires more traceback review and its accuracy cannot be determined until two records are reviewed.

There are many advantages to developing a HACCP record keeping system that is simple and concise. Well-designed, simplified records provide assurances that records generated during monitoring will be focused and timely. They also reduce the time required for management review and can reduce documentation errors. While most CCP monitoring records and some Standard Sanitation Operating Procedures (SSOP) records require the entry of an actual observed value (for example, 45°F, 150 ppm, 35 sec.), many records can be simplified by the use of "yes/no" or "pass/fail" entries.

Date	Product	Vendor	Amount/ Quantity	Specifications	Meets specifications Yes/No	Inspected by	Comments

Reviewed by: _____   Date: _____

Figure 9.12 CCP receiving record.

Date	Product	P.O. number	Specifications	Inspected by	Pass/Fail	Comments

Reviewed by: _____   Date: _____

Figure 9.13 CCP receiving record.

Computerized versus Manual Records

Some firms use computerized records to document their HACCP activities. Certain processing activities lend themselves to computerized formats. Using computerized records to monitor CCPs, however, can be problematic. The absence of key personnel, or complex systems that require multiple documentation files, can make it difficult or impossible to retrieve needed records. Further, computerized records can become impractical since monitoring needs to be conducted as the activity is observed. Finally, unless the manufacturing activity itself is computerized, monitoring using computerized records becomes susceptible to the repetitive recording of values, or "dry labbing," in the absence of actual observations.

While these problems certainly can be addressed by operational improvements, computerization of HACCP records must be carefully designed to ensure contemporaneous documentation of events, adequate security for records maintained within the system, adequate storage capacity of records, and verification of authorized electronic signatures *prior* to product releases. After computerizing the HACCP activities, whether in full or in part, an active review of the process—from beginning to end—is advisable to ascertain whether adequate controls have been put in place for the automated HACCP.

PREVENTING DOCUMENTATION ERRORS

All quality and HACCP systems require human involvement. It is common to find errors across the entire spectrum of documents required within a processing operation. Common documentation errors include the lack of a specific monitoring record at a CCP, such as the temperature of a cooler at a storage CCP, or the safety of water under an SSOP record. These types of errors usually are a result of monitoring activities that may have little variation in actual value. As practices become routine in cases like this, very little analysis or thinking goes into jotting down observations on records, and errors are easier to make.

Significant errors can also be found simply because the specifics of the HACCP plan are not being followed. These errors include improper monitoring frequencies for both monitoring activities, untimely review of records, lack of corrective action records, and the repetitive recording of values known as "dry labbing."

An effective means for minimizing errors in documentation is the implementation of a comprehensive training program and the timely review of records. Training should encompass the specifics of monitoring (what, when, why, how) and the significance of the monitoring value. This not only ensures accurate records, but provides for timely corrective action when critical limits are exceeded. A regularly scheduled training program should be a continuing activity within each processing firm. However, this must be coupled with timely review of records and audits from quality department personnel or management.

In reality, HACCP is record keeping.

Part III

Implementing HACCP

10

HACCP Plan Implementation and Maintenance

SUPPORTING STRUCTURES FOR HACCP IMPLEMENTATION

The implementation and maintenance of a HACCP system requires effort and commitment comparable to that exerted for any major organizational change or continuous improvement initiative. While the drivers of the HACCP initiative may reside primarily in the company's technical community, HACCP plan implementation and maintenance is ultimately multidisciplinary in nature. It requires careful planning, deployment of resources, ongoing monitoring, and constant adjustment. Quality practitioners will recognize the opportunity for application of W. E. Deming's "Plan-Do-Check-Act" principle in HACCP plan implementation. Modern project management methodologies are well-suited for coordination of the various resources and tasks required for successful implementation.

Auditors of HACCP plans should seek evidence that the extensive planning and organizing that precedes successful implementation has been conducted. An appropriate HACCP plan is effectively sustained as new knowledge is brought to light, as the environment dictates, or as organizational change demands.

Management Commitment

Ethical and environmental factors make product safety the highest business priority, but senior management may feel secure that existing quality systems alone can meet this objective. However, the hazard analysis and critical control points approach to product safety outlined by HACCP can be justified as a means to effectively strengthen or supplant less comprehensive or effective product safety conventions. As discussed in chapter 2, upper management's understanding and commitment are essential for ensuring companywide support and commitment for HACCP plan implementation.

The core team may first identify the need for or the relative merit of implementing a HACCP plan. These reasons may include:

- HACCP is required by regulation in some sectors of the food industry, for example, meat and seafood operations, where U.S. Department of Agriculture (USDA)/Food Safety Inspection Service (FSIS) regulations require HACCP systems. Additional segments of the industry are expected to eventually have HACCP mandated by regulation.

- Customers often require formal HACCP plans regardless of regulatory imperative. The HACCP "convention" has been increasingly defined, refined, and promoted by various technical bodies and advisory committees and is gaining widespread recognition as a superior means of assuring product safety. An example is the National Advisory Committee on Microbiological Criteria for Foods (NACMCF), who published the first HACCP criteria in 1992 and revised them in 1997. The committee's "seven principles" approach has developed a common language. This and other organized "bodies of knowledge" create the need for producers to adopt the convention to demonstrate appropriate technical sophistication in their approach to product safety. The adoption of HACCP may simplify and ease communication with discriminating customers.

- Internal experts identify the need to adopt HACCP. This may be driven by a realization that existing product safety measures are inadequate or inconsistently applied. An industry or company may, for example, be faced with mounting technical evidence that its products pose a unique or previously unidentified or elevated safety risk. Inspection-oriented systems may not adequately reduce risk. Finally, inspection-oriented systems to assure product safety may result in a high incidence of internal failure—high costs associated with detecting failures after they have occurred. The "problem prevention" nature of HACCP can be demonstrated to be more cost-effective than inspection-and-testing oriented schemes for controlling product safety.

HACCP entails extensive planning, commitment of resources, and new transaction disciplines (monitoring, record keeping, audit/verification procedures, and trend analysis techniques). Senior management must agree with the need for HACCP and fully endorse the initiative so that sufficient time and money are allocated (to assure equity with competing demands). Upper management support also ensures that middle level and operational managers place proper emphasis on the transactions necessary for implementation. When the need for HACCP is demonstrated, then accepted, visible upper management commitment indicates to the company that the benefits realized justify the outlay of resources.

Product Safety Policies and Objectives

An effective means of demonstrating companywide commitment to product safety is the development of a formal product safety policy. Such a policy is developed by upper management and draws cross-functionally upon the company's technical, regulatory compliance, and legal experts to ensure accuracy and precision. HACCP is a tactical component of a comprehensive product safety policy.

An effective HACCP-based product safety policy will include statements of objectives that:

- Designate product safety as a top business priority and make the distinction that product safety is not negotiable (unlike product quality level).

- Endorse the implementation of prerequisite programs to support product safety.

- Specifically support the development of appropriate HACCP plans.

- Endorse and name a cross-functional steering team of technical resources and subject matter experts to train and educate others throughout the company and to coordinate the resources necessary to implement HACCP and the supporting prerequisite programs. This steering team should, in turn, appoint a leader or overall HACCP coordinator.

- Establish timelines for program implementation.

The steering team responsible for the implementation of HACCP will develop the specific objectives and ultimately establish companywide responsibilities for all aspects of the HACCP program's design, development, and implementation. A typical summary of responsibilities for implementation of a HACCP system is shown in Figure 10.1.

The specific responsibilities assigned will vary from company to company, but cross-functional involvement is essential. Many organizations recognize the value of involving the sales/marketing and business development functions in the early stages of HACCP plan development. These functions are especially useful in providing insight into the intended use of the finished product, an important factor to consider when performing an effective hazard analysis.

Prerequisite Programs

A solid foundation of prerequisite programs is necessary to the support of a HACCP system. Prerequisite programs are "the basic environmental and operating conditions that are necessary for the production of safe and wholesome foods."[1] Since many prerequisites are broader in scope than product safety, some are directly linked to HACCP while others are managed outside of the HACCP system.

Controls for many serious hazards, but not CCPs, should reside in prerequisite programs. While the relatively few CCPs in a process should be addressed in the core HACCP program, the importance of the broader prerequisite controls must not be

---

Policy and Objectives Development

Primary responsibility: Management. Support: R&D, Quality Assurance, and Marketing/Sales.

HACCP Plan Procedure Development

Primary responsibility: Quality Assurance. Support: R&D, Operations.

Approval of Procedures

Primary responsibility: Management. Support: R&D, Marketing.

HACCP Training and Education

Primary responsibility: Quality Assurance (identifies subject matter experts). Support: R&D, Management.

HACCP Plan Implementation

Primary responsibility: Operations (HACCP Team). Support: R&D, Quality Assurance.

HACCP Plan Verification (including initial scientific validation)

Primary responsibility: Quality Assurance. Support: R&D.

HACCP Plan Improvement and Revision

Primary responsibility: R&D, Quality Assurance. Support: Operations (HACCP Team).

Verification of a Fully Functioning HACCP System

Second and/or third party verifications will need to be scheduled. Primary responsibility: Quality Assurance.

Figure 10.1 HACCP system implementation responsibilities.

---

overlooked. An early step in preparing to implement HACCP is to monitor mandated prerequisites in the organization's regulatory environment. Prerequisite programs must be systematically identified and examined as part of the overall HACCP system implementation.

In preparing to develop or audit a HACCP plan, it is necessary to assemble a list of all pertinent prerequisite programs (including any mandated by regulation) to locate and review related procedures, work instructions, and records. Many, if not all, of these will reside in the company's current quality and operating manuals. Likewise, in auditing it is essential for audit teams to reference and familiarize themselves with regulations where pertinent. These regulations pose an appropriate standard upon which to judge compliance and effectiveness.

Each industry segment under consideration must implement prerequisite programs necessary to assure a safe operating environment. Prerequisite programs create the environment for the safe production of a food or a biomedical device. In some industry segments, pertinent regulations prescribe certain prerequisite programs, thus effectively linking them with HACCP.

Chapter 12 discusses prerequisite programs in detail and can be used as a guide for the areas that may be controlled by prerequisite programs. The discussion in chapter 12 focuses on prerequisites that apply to various food processing industry segments. A company may elect to utilize existing system or process auditing teams to evaluate prerequisite programs in conjunction with HACCP implementation. Common prerequisite programs are often listed along with generally stated "standards" for the audit team to use as a reference in compiling audit checklists. These may include:

- *Plant and grounds construction.* Flow and traffic control should be implemented to reduce potential for cross-contamination.

- *Processing equipment design.* The equipment should be constructed according to sanitary design principles and should be properly maintained to prevent deterioration and product contamination.

- *Pre-start-up inspection.* Cleaning, sanitizing, and housekeeping efficacy should be verified prior to start of production.

- *Specification system.* The company will maintain written specifications for all ingredients, package materials, and finished products.

- *Vendor/Material control.* Vendors' quality systems will be verified to be effective.

- *Master sanitation schedule and cleaning procedures.* Cleaning and sanitizing activities related to product safety are scheduled and monitored.

- *Storage, shipping, and handling.* Supplies/materials/finished products must be stored, shipped, and handled properly. This includes ensuring that temperature is controlled as appropriate and that cross-contamination is prevented throughout distribution.

- *Chemical control.* Potential toxic, caustic, or injurious substances whose use is unavoidable in and around product manufacturing must be effectively segregated.

- *Recall and material traceability.* The ability to identify or recover stock at any stage of production and distribution must be ensured through appropriate coding and records of use.

- *Pest control.* An appropriately qualified and licensed pest control operator will conduct an effective program in concert with applicable regulations.

- *Operator/Employee training.* Operators must be appropriately trained to properly conduct their assigned tasks.

- *Calibration and standardization.* Calibration schedules shall be established for all CCPs in the manufacturing process, as well as for laboratory and analytical equipment used in monitoring.

- *Environmental monitoring.* Microbiological evaluation of the processing and production "environment" (drains, air handling systems, and so on) will be conducted as appropriate to control pathogens.

- *Allergen controls.* In food and related industries, cross-contamination of products with undeclared allergens (substances known to induce an adverse immunological response in susceptible individuals) will be exercised through labeling control, and prevention of physical cross-contamination.

- *Foreign material control.* In various industry sectors, metal detectors and other foreign material exclusion devices will be employed.

HACCP implementation involves a close examination of prerequisite programs, rather than a cursory review. The implementation of a HACCP system will probably result in the need to upgrade certain prerequisite programs. The act of doing a thorough hazard analysis (HACCP Principle #1) often brings new knowledge or different perspectives about hazards to the company. This analysis often appropriately concludes that control of some hazards must revert to prerequisite programs. These programs, which may have been previously installed in the absence of a HACCP perspective, will need to be revised. Auditors must take into account the company's understanding of both new and familiar elements.

HACCP TEAM FORMATION AND TRAINING

Effective companywide implementation of HACCP is a multidisciplinary task that requires an effort equal to that supporting any major organizational change or improvement initiative. Team formation and training are important aspects of HACCP implementation.

Team Formation

A combination of cross-functional and natural work teams is the best formation to thoroughly implement HACCP. For larger companies, a hierarchy of at least two tiers of teams is recommended in HACCP implementation.

Steering Team. The first tier is the steering team comprised of staff level management and technical/subject matter experts. A technical leader, or HACCP coordinator—usually selected from the company's quality, research and development, or compliance group—assumes a leadership role and assembles the core team.

Organized to initiate full-scale HACCP implementation, this team is responsible for identifying the need for implementation and for garnering visible upper management commitment to the initiative. This steering team should assist in the development and communication of an overall product safety policy with HACCP as an essential component. After initial implementation, the steering team monitors the regulatory and competitive environment for new knowledge related to product safety and incorporates that knowledge into control plans.

This steering team also is responsible for organizing others for the actual implementation. These responsibilities may include forming or appointing operations teams (product teams, plant teams, or site teams) to be trained and to ultimately take responsibility for on-site HACCP implementation; and identifying internal and external experts to assist in the development of HACCP-related bodies of knowledge and to deliver training.

Operations Teams. The second tier may consist of the site-specific operations teams (product teams, plant teams) assembled, trained, and empowered to implement HACCP at the establishment level. The steering, or core team, and senior management should work together to select an operations team that includes personnel from cross-functional and natural work team elements. The selection of these individuals is among the most important considerations in implementing HACCP. Cross-functional representatives will include site quality assurance, engineering/maintenance, and production management personnel. As with the companywide core team, the cross-functional perspective is important in assuring technical integrity of the initiative, but at the establishment level. A site coordinator, often a quality assurance professional, should be appointed to lead the site team.

The "natural work team" element refers to the inclusion of appropriate "process owners" on the operations team. These process owners are often line supervisors and/or operators, and their inclusion helps ensure that operational details are addressed in the development of plans. Organizations that have developed ISO 9001–based quality systems and subscribers to total quality management (TQM) recognize the value of including trained operating-level personnel in the development of work instructions. Likewise, the inclusion of these employees in planning for HACCP system implementation benefits the entire organization. Operating team membership criteria may differ by organization or industry segment, but ultimately team makeup must ensure that members are able to understand and apply the significant, scientifically based body of knowledge upon which successful HACCP implementation builds.

Team Training

Upon auditing a HACCP plan or companywide implementation, an auditor should seek evidence that training plans are complete, and that training objectives are indeed realized and documented. Training must be well-conceived and appropriate to the company's HACCP implementation plans. A company implementing HACCP will need to demonstrate that appropriate expertise has been assured in the design and execution of training.

Extensive team training is essential to support HACCP implementation. When planning for training, the organization should first seek to understand specific external requirements. Certain regulated industry segments specify training requirements. For example, both seafood and meat and poultry HACCP regulations require training in HACCP for a designated individual in a food company. Logically, this person would be the HACCP leader or coordinator for the company.[2] Increasingly, customer requirements include specific training requirements. Obviously these and any other requirements must be met. Records must be kept of any training provided to assure customers and to provide evidence to auditors that appropriate training has indeed occurred.

Significant consideration must be given to the "depth" of training that is appropriate to the organization's HACCP implementation. While external requirements (regulations, customers) often require the training of coordinators, or single initiative leaders, effective implementations are assured through appropriate training of a "critical mass" of individuals responsible for overall implementation, execution, and maintenance of the HACCP plan. Line supervisors, quality control staff, line operators, as well as individuals involved in the purchasing and distribution of goods, should be trained to the appropriate degree since these individuals are essential to effective site teams. Each organization will address the question of training "depth" differently and must consider the costs/benefits of extensive training. Training should be considered a prudent preventive quality cost.

Training must be formal, and may require the use of external expertise, at least in the development of initiative leaders. Many companies mistakenly interpret the considerable body of knowledge related to HACCP and rely solely on internal agents to draft HACCP plans without any outside training and influence. To successfully implement HACCP, an organization should carefully consider all available resources when designing an appropriate training intervention to support HACCP implementation. Industry trade groups and associations (composed of both primary producers and suppliers), regulators, academia, and private sector consultants—used individually or collectively— provide potential resources upon which to draw for training. The use of these external experts ensures that potential microbiological, physical, and chemical hazards of public health significance are fully considered in the development of the company's HACCP plan. External experts also provide perspectives on the dynamic regulatory and consumer environment. However, an external agent's efforts must be integrated with company-specific activities to assure local buy-in and relevance.

Many organizations define the qualifications required to become an external HACCP consultant prior to awarding a contract for training. Desired qualifications include: a demonstrated understanding and subscription to the seven principles of HACCP as outlined by NACMCF (or Codex Alimentarius Commission); a demonstrated ability to prepare HACCP plans; industry experience and product category knowledge specific to the industry under consideration; and prerequisite knowledge of good manufacturing practices (GMPs), product safety, and sanitation/environmental standard operating procedures (SOPs). Additionally, actual business references and access to a contemporary client base may be required, as is appropriate professional liability insurance. Finally, consultants must demonstrate an understanding of recognized auditing techniques.

Ultimately, the selection of external experts/consultants to assist in the training of the HACCP implementation team resides with the organization's overall HACCP coordinator. Specific details on training delivery and expectations should be developed. Additionally, the need and policies for periodic training refresher courses—or retraining—should be identified.

Training interventions must be carefully designed to ensure that participants receive the most for funds expended. In-house training, delivered by a qualified training consultant (as outlined above) is often an excellent approach. Training should include initiative leaders, as well as line level participants. The focus of the training should be on company-specific applications (products, unit operations, and so on). A two to three day in-house course is often used by organizations implementing HACCP. The expenses and logistics associated with in-house training must be weighed versus the relative merit and convenience of attending off-site professional training courses.

Off-site training is often appropriate, provided participants are exposed to material specific to their company's area of operation. Off-site training, such as public course offerings, is often cost-effective and allows participants the opportunity of interchange and infusion of ideas that comes with exposure to other organizations. When off-site training is chosen, the training organization should be selected according to the criteria outlined above. Off-site seminars of two to three days in length should provide participants with the opportunity to select exercises and applications to the industry segment under consideration. Ideally, off-site or public courses provide participants with useful reference materials and "after session" opportunities to clarify any questions or considerations that may follow training.

Off-site training courses can be used to train internal trainers, who should, in turn, bring acquired knowledge in-house for delivery. Off-site courses may be regarded as "train the trainer" opportunities, provided participants in off-site courses are competent to bring acquired knowledge "in-house" and, in turn, train participants accordingly. HACCP training plans must ultimately ensure that a critical mass of individuals is appropriately prepared to implement and maintain the HACCP initiative. Finally, regardless of the training method used, training and reference materials should be assembled and made available for future reference and consultation as necessary.

In some cases, expert training in specialized subject matter may be needed. For example, advanced, specialized training in scientific validation and verification of HACCP plans may be necessary in certain circumstances. Trade and regulatory affiliated organizations increasingly offer such courses. This type of training is advised in situations where called for by close regulation or customer requirements, and should be targeted for HACCP initiative leaders.

Many companies embrace the use of commercially available software products to aid in the implementation of HACCP plans. While software may be useful in assuring adherence to certain conventions in flowcharting, analyzing hazards, and so on, software is no substitute for training in the underlying principles and concepts essential to the effective implementation of HACCP. Software programs that adhere to the seven underlying HACCP principles are a useful aid in deploying HACCP, but cannot replace extensive training of personnel.

Many small companies face practical problems associated with the costs of training to support HACCP implementation. State or local initiatives that provide training and development funds for organizations in need may be consulted for assistance, especially in cases where the implementation of HACCP is essential to company competitiveness and employee retention. Small companies should consider identifying such sources of funding and applying to secure them.

PILOT PROJECTS/OPERATIONAL QUALIFICATION OF HACCP PLANS

Failure to link the training of operations/site teams with a relevant and immediate application is a common mistake. Training should be immediately followed by the opportunity to apply principles learned at the establishment level. Ideally, a manageable "pilot project"—also called a demonstration project or trial—will be identified, and integrated into the training that precedes HACCP implementation. The execution of a pilot project integrates training and preparation into the actual HACCP implementation. Training should conclude with the development of detailed work instructions that are relevant to actual on-site application. This enables training participants to "take home" relevant operational plans that apply to actual on-site applications and immediately design a HACCP plan, at least on a trial basis.

Pilot projects provide an organization with the opportunity to apply HACCP plans on a limited basis while studying all aspects of implementation. Results must be carefully examined so that necessary adjustments can be made to ensure success when HACCP is deployed companywide. Implementation plans should list specific projects (as identified by the guiding coalition and site teams) along with timetables for their implementation. Here, trained site teams assume primary responsibility for the implementation. In multi-site organizations, at least one pilot project should be conducted per site.

Pilot project selection may be limited to a specific unit operation, or a limited family of products or processes at a specific operating site. A pilot project should be regarded as a trial to ensure that the organization can execute all aspects of implementation. A pilot plan is used to confirm that procedures have been learned and can be applied, that CCPs can be monitored and scientifically validated as planned, that corrective action plans can be executed, that all forms and records are usefully employed and understood, and that deviations are appropriately recognized and the reasons for them understood. While a viable trial or demonstration project may be limited to a specific aspect of manufacture, it needs to be designed in such a way as to demonstrate the organization's ability to successfully execute the seven principles in extended areas.

During the pilot project, special attention must be paid to the scientific validation of HACCP plans (this validation will be repeated as HACCP is extended company-wide). Specifically, validation consists of making sure that each CCP is identified and that the critical limits associated with them are based upon sound technical information. Monitoring of CCPs should ensure that identified hazards have been prevented, eliminated, or reduced to an acceptable level. At this juncture, the company must prove that scientific validation is based on supporting scientific information from appropriate authoritative sources. Such sources will differ by industry segment; specific regulation or convention may prescribe scientific validation. Evidence of scientific validation should be recorded and made part of the permanent implementation plan.

Some companies will elect to keep external experts/consultants on hand throughout the entire pilot phase. If this is not possible, organizations are encouraged to maintain access to external experts for assistance in evaluating results and making adjustments to the plan.

Pilot projects and their examination are essential to successful HACCP plan implementation. They provide the opportunity for all involved to learn and apply every aspect of the system, and to make adjustments as necessary, prior to companywide deployment of HACCP. Many operational nuances are identified through pilot projects. Many companies widely publicize or otherwise call attention to HACCP pilot projects. For example, to call attention to the impending program and changes in operational methodology, HACCP demonstration teams may identify the location of CCPs on the production plant floor by posting HACCP-related instructions at or near the location of each CCP. The posting will identify the CCP by location and number, and will include a description of the critical limits and SOPs for monitoring, response, and corrective action.

Trial length needs to be carefully considered and will differ by organization, depending on the relative complexity of the operation. Organizations often conduct HACCP pilot projects/trials as they do new product development efforts: a relatively short initial trial (with evaluation, critique, and adjustment), followed by "scaled-up" or longer experimental runs of the plan. A key to maximizing learning from pilot projects is running them for a significant length of time, over representative conditions, so as to allow the usual sources of variation in materials, machinery, and manpower to become factors.

HACCP pilot projects/trials results should be summarily evaluated after a predetermined period of time or after a certain defined number of production repetitions. Site team members should verify that all activities planned were in fact executed. The site HACCP coordinator should assemble team members and operators for a rigorous critique of all aspects of the pilot project/trial. If third-party/external expert or corporate team oversight of the trial has taken place, that input will need to be assembled as well.

The formal evaluation of the HACCP pilot projects/trials should:

- Be conducted in a manner that is rigorous and systematic. It is advised that specifically designed checklists or schedules, rather than participants' notes and observations, be used to sequentially evaluate each progressive step (the seven principles) in designing and implementing HACCP. NACMCF and other sources cited provide reference material to help design the checklists.

- Result in a judgment that trials determined the plan to be either (1) sound, and the team may move forward with companywide deployment without making any or only minor adjustments to the plan, or (2) in need of significant improvements (procedures, retraining, and so on) to the degree that a retrial may be required.

- (Where improvements are required) provide that all indicated actions are captured, with assignment of responsibilities and completion dates for distribution to appropriate parties. If repeat trials are necessary, the evaluation should state any expected changes in timing for companywide deployment of HACCP.

Since communication and organizationwide learning are critical, provisions should be made for a thorough review of HACCP pilot projects, at least among individuals responsible for further deployment of the HACCP initiative. Some recommend going so far as to provide a one-hour presentation to all company personnel to acquaint them with the new HACCP system and their role in producing safe products for consumers.[3]

COMPANYWIDE HACCP DEPLOYMENT

The same cycle of preparation, execution, review, and adjustment used in pilot projects applies to companywide deployment of HACCP. Site teams remain responsible for actual implementation of HACCP plans, but the leadership and technical resources are significantly diluted as the initiative is expanded among, and more comprehensively within, operational sites. For this reason, all significant adjustments, retraining, and so on, should be identified at the pilot project level.

One problem faced by implementation teams is maintaining an appropriate uniformity in the content, execution, and appearance of HACCP plans when the system is deployed throughout the company. Some uniformity and standardization is assured through appropriate team training. Undesirable differences can be further worked out during the analysis of pilot projects. Successful multi-unit organizations often organize regular, formal networks of HACCP coordinators to meet regularly or exchange information. Uniformity in appearance of the program (often important from a customer's point of view) can be achieved through the use of centrally administered, version-controlled documents and forms. Paper or electronic forms may be adapted to a company's specific needs. The various appendices to the sources cited throughout this work also provide excellent guidelines with respect to document and record content.

HACCP PLAN MAINTENANCE

NACMCF and others similarly define verification as those activities, *other than monitoring,* that determine the validity of the HACCP plan and that the system is operating according to plan. An important aspect of verification is the initial validation of the HACCP plan to determine that the plan is scientifically and technically sound.[4]

In excluding monitoring from the definition and designating initial validation as *an aspect* of verification, the 1997 NACMCF *Guidelines for Application of HACCP Principles* helps eliminate a common source of confusion among the terms. Verification is a more comprehensive set of activities and usually conducted by someone other than operators of the HACCP plan.

In implementing a HACCP plan, then, leaders and teams must provide for a comprehensive set of activities that go beyond routine monitoring and initial validation. Verification procedures are detailed comprehensively in chapter 7 and are not difficult to understand. Yet organizations often fail to provide for appropriate, periodic, systematic execution of verification procedures. These should be conducted by qualified individuals, then analyzed and interpreted to make a determination (supported by evidence) as to whether the plan is operating as intended. A good system of HACCP plan verification provides precisely that, and does so formally and with scheduled regularity.

Auditors will recognize that overall HACCP plan verification has similarities to planning, conducting, and reporting a quality systems audit of the overall quality system, but with a narrower focus on systems directly supporting product safety. As is the case with all audits, extensive checklists are necessary and useful to compare what is actually occurring with the plan. Numerous suggested guidelines, such as the 1997 NACMCF *Guidelines,* and proposed schedules are available for consultation when developing verification plans. Organizations are cautioned, however, to regard this specific plan as somewhat simplified, and perhaps not comprehensive enough for certain environments.

In arranging a verification plan, organizations must first look to the regulatory requirements that may prescribe specific verification activities in a certain industry or segment. FDA and USDA/FSIS, for example, detail certain aspects of verification requirements in those regulations that apply to their respective industry segments. USDA/FSIS issues an excellent *HACCP Plan Review Checklist* that is readily adaptable to a broad segment of industries.

In industries where the HACCP convention is being adopted, increasingly, discriminating customers are elevating the level of scrutiny around HACCP plans. As most recognize the critical nature of verification, many now extend those verification activities to suppliers. These specifics also need to be taken into account when designing verification procedures.

A very general outline of the steps taken in planning and conducting a verification audit follows:

- Schedule formal verification activities and allocate resources.

- Examine all HACCP documentation (SOPs, work instructions) and sample all pertinent records, including exceptions and deviation reports. This may be done prior to the audit through a formal request for information.

- Review initial validation, and verify revalidation for any significant process change, ingredient change, system failure, and so on.

- Plan site visit and prepare detailed checklist. Focus on the actual observation of work (is CCP monitoring understood, done consistent with plan, and so on?).

- Monitor prerequisite programs that support HACCP. This is especially critical where a significant hazard is identified during hazard analysis, and control reverts to a specific prerequisite program. Instrument or testing equipment calibration procedures that directly enable CCP monitoring should be examined as well.

- As the verification cycle progresses, review previous verification reports and determine that corrective actions were implemented and plan adjustments made.

- Review all written directions issued by qualified internal experts and endorsed by the organization's HACCP steering team that call for the incorporation of new knowledge into the HACCP system. Verify that actions have been taken.

- Prepare a written report. Orally review the report upon exit from the site and distribute corrective action requests.

- Follow up on corrective action as indicated.

It is recommended that formal verification activities take place at regular intervals. In general, independent records reviews should be conducted at least monthly, especially within the first year of HACCP implementation. Comprehensive verification audits (including site visits and work observations) should be scheduled, and results documented at least yearly. Most importantly, verification should be conducted immediately subsequent to any major change in process, ingredient, CCP selection, or critical limit designation. Verification should include revalidation of CCPs as necessary. These guidelines are recommendations only; any schedule can be set—adherence to it is the primary goal.

Formal verification entails a comprehensive audit, and is not to be confused with day-to-day monitoring activities. Parties performing formal verification procedures should be independent of the operating site reporting structure. For example, many companies assign internal verification duties to independent staff groups, such as quality assurance, to ensure independence, adequate technical orientation, and auditing acumen.

Second-party (or customer) verification is required by some companies and allows HACCP plans to be calibrated to customer expectations. Third-party (contractors independent of the company, customer, or supply chain) verifications are advantageous to ensure adequate independence from the site being audited, and can provide infusion of new knowledge and expertise. Internal second- or third-party auditors must be adequately qualified. In addition to general auditing skills and subject matter expertise, auditors should possess qualifications similar to those outlined in the section of this chapter pertaining to selection of trainers.

EXTENDING THE HACCP SYSTEM
TO THE SUPPLY CHAIN

A comprehensive HACCP system optimally extends to the company's sources of supply and into the system of product distribution. In the food industry, for example, it has become common to refer to HACCP as a program of food safety assurance that extends from "field/farm to table." Increasingly, as part of HACCP implementation, organizations have realized that the HACCP/prerequisite convention must be extended to ensure cooperation with suppliers and distributors of goods. "Each specific process (growing/harvesting, distribution, product processing, final preparation) must have its own HACCP program to ensure a final product that meets the safety and regulatory standards of today."[5] Other types of operations, both upstream (suppliers) and downstream (distributors) may pose opportunities for the introduction of potential hazards of public health significance. Operations related to temperature control of microbiologically sensitive goods, or even simple storage conditions, are examples of such factors.

Again, in applying the underlying premise of HACCP, hazards manifested as a result of conditions at the manufacturers will rarely be reliably identified through examination of goods or products at the point of customer (intermediate or final) receipt. Where appropriate then, control needs to be exercised at those critical steps in the process. Any company whose finished product integrity depends on events in the supply chain beyond its immediate control should consider requiring HACCP plans of key suppliers and distributors. That activity brings about the practical and problematic challenge of managing these plans. Seldom will a company be intimately involved with designing and implementing HACCP in a supplier's location. As a result they will be essentially limited to conducting verification audits to judge the efficacy of the plans.

As the HACCP "convention" based on the NACMCF (or Codex Alimentarius Commission) seven principles gains wider acceptance, this common language and consistency in approach will aid in providing a basis for inter-organizational coordination of product safety activities. Organizations should designate a technically competent individual to monitor the supply chain and apply HACCP principles. Supply partnerships, manufacturing/distribution alliances, and the like, have blurred modern organizational distinctions considerably. ISO 9001–oriented organizations accumulate considerable documentation related to purchased goods and services, including requirements for approved testing methods, certificates of analysis, and material qualification protocols. Typically, statements requiring the manufacture of materials and goods under a HACCP plan are contained in this type of supplier-related documentation. As part of the due diligence and pre-qualification of suppliers, HACCP plans and hazard analysis documents should be obtained and reviewed. Ideally, firsthand observations of supplier and distributor activities and site inspections of suppliers should include examination of HACCP plans, and especially observation of work related to the monitoring of CCPs. HACCP-related audits should be performed against standards outlined in NACMCF.

REFERENCES

1. U.S. National Advisory Committee on Microbiological Criteria for Foods (NACMCF), *Hazard Analysis and Critical Control Point Principles and Application Guidelines* (Washington, DC: U.S. Food and Drug Administration, 14 August 1997): 9.
2. Donald A. Corlett, Jr., *HACCP User's Manual* (Gaithersburg, MD: Aspen, 1998): 23.
3. Ibid., 125.
4. NACMCF, *Hazard Analysis,* 19.
5. William L. Bennet and Leonard L. Steed, "An Integrated Approach to Food Safety," *Quality Progress* (February 1999): 40.

Part IV

Applying HACCP to the Food Processing Industry

11

Food Industry in General

FOOD COMPONENTS

Food is a complex biological system. The principle components of food products are cellular tissues from plants or animals, or other products of animal origin such as milk and eggs. These commodities are combined with chemicals to form food. Chemicals are added to a food product for a number of reasons: to fortify it with nutrients, to improve flavors, and to enhance other sensory aspects. Chemicals also can inhibit spoilage, including microbial spoilage.

Plant tissue used in food products can come from roots, stems, leaves, nuts, or fruits. This means that plant tissue can come in contact with a wide variety of potentially hazardous agents, including pollutants and intentionally applied toxic chemicals (pesticides). However, the primary hazards on plant material are microorganisms originating in the soil.

Muscle, the primary source of animal tissue, is traditionally classified in the following manner:

- Meat—sourced primarily from domesticated cattle, swine, lambs, and goats

- Poultry—sourced primarily from chicken, turkey, and squab

- Fish—includes fin fish (both fresh and salt water), shrimp, crab, and molluscan shellfish

Animal tissue and products of animal origin can present special food borne disease hazards because animals can be infected with zoonotic microorganisms. Even animals that are disease-free can harbor or carry microorganisms that cause food borne disease in humans.

SOURCES AND TYPES OF FOOD HAZARDS

Food products are in a constant state of change. These changes can be caused by natural mechanisms or by humans during food processing operations. These changes start on the farm and continue through food processing operations. In addition, a finished food product is not immune to changes.

Changes to food can be beneficial or detrimental. Once a plant is harvested or an animal is slaughtered, the natural defense mechanism of the plant or animal is compromised, and the tissue starts to decompose. This decomposition can be caused by internal or external sources. Internal decomposition is autocatalytic and enzymatic in origin. External decomposition is caused by some external living system such as microorganisms, other animals, chemical reactions, or physical actions.

On the farm, beneficial changes include the maturing of vegetables, fruits, or animals. Another example of a beneficial change is the hydro-cooling and packaging of fresh-cut vegetables for the fresh produce market. Detrimental changes observed in animals include diseases or tumors. Detrimental changes to plant tissue include bruises, tumors or gauls, or infections.

A number of microorganisms play an essential role in the production of fermented foods such as cheese, yogurt, pickles, sauerkraut, some types of sausage, and alcoholic beverages. Other microorganisms are detrimental to human health. For example, *Aspergillus flavus,* a mold that produces mycotoxins that can cause tumors in mammals, can infect plant material and cause a human health hazard.

Chemical changes may be enzymatic or non-enzymatic chemical reactions that may cause beneficial or non-beneficial changes to food. Beneficial chemical changes include the development of a brown crust during the baking of bread. The bread crust turns brown as a result of the Maillard reaction—a reaction between reducing sugars and the amino groups of amino acids, peptides, and proteins. A classical undesirable chemical reaction is the formation of nitrosamines, a carcinogen, during the improper curing of fermented meats or sausage.

Physical changes include size reduction. Size reduction can add value to food products by cutting plant or animal tissue into useable sizes and by separating edible portions of animal or plant tissue from inedible portions. However, if the size reduction process is not controlled properly it can increase the rate of autolysis of the tissue by disrupting an excess number of cells.

Commercial food processors expect that ingredients entering the processing plant, including farm-based commodities, will meet proper specifications. This minimizes the need for incoming inspection and sorting. Many food processors require farmers to apply the principles of HACCP to the production of agricultural products. Chapter 13 describes the application of HACCP to the meat and poultry industry, while chapter 14 discusses the application of HACCP to the seafood industry. The dairy industry is discussed in chapter 15. Chapter 16 describes how farmers and food processors can reduce hazards in some food components by applying HACCP principles to fresh fruit and vegetable production. Finally, chapter 17 details the relationship of HACCP to the retail and food service industries. In all of these instances, the primary changes in food products typically start with the changes that occur with harvesting or slaughter and continue through food processing, packaging, storage, and delivery.

Food processing is designed to enhance beneficial changes and to reduce the rate of detrimental changes. Converting raw ingredients into a tasty food product that can be served as a meal is an example of a beneficial change. Processed food can undergo two types of detrimental changes:

- Spoilage that makes the food inedible. The following four factors affect the spoilage rates in food: time, temperature, oxygen, and water. The spoilage of food can be catalyzed by biological, chemical (enzymatic or non-enzymatic), or physical mechanisms.

- Contamination of the food with a biological, chemical, or physical hazard. Biological hazards are the primary cause of food safety hazards. HACCP provides a mechanism to ensure that all hazards are properly addressed and controlled.

Food processing cannot prevent the deterioration of food, but it can retard the spoilage rate. Even if the product is commercially sterilized and packaged in a hermetically sealed package, non-enzymatic chemical changes can occur during the shelf life of the product and render it esthetically unpleasing.

The following food processing steps are used to retard the deterioration of food: drying, heating, cooling (which includes both refrigeration and freezing), fermenting, irradiating, and packaging. Packaging is used to control the amount of oxygen that contacts the food product or to prevent contact from occurring. In addition, packaging can protect the product from physical abuse, contamination by microorganisms or vermin, or human tampering.

Biological Hazards

Microorganisms, the primary cause of biological hazards in food, are present throughout the environment. Microbial actions can be beneficial, innocuous, or detrimental to human health. Most types of microorganisms are innocuous to humans. However, those that are harmful to human health can cause death. HACCP auditors are encouraged to study a standard food microbiology text or to access the U.S. Food and Drug Administration's *FDA Bad Bug* Web site for details on the growth of pathogens and the incidence of implicated foods. Table A.1 (Appendix A) lists some of the microorganisms that can cause biological hazards in foods.

To sustain their growth, microorganisms require environmental conditions similar to those required by humans. Key elements for growth include: time, optimum temperature, nutrients, and water. Some microorganisms require oxygen for growth while others occur only in anaerobic conditions. For example, *Clostridium botulinum* is a strict anaerobe that produces the deadly toxin that causes botulism. In contrast, *Listeria monocytogenes*, which has caused food borne disease outbreaks in prepared meats, cheeses, and fresh vegetables, is an aerobic organism.

Since food is a natural source of nutrients and water for microorganisms, food processors use the following processes to control the growth and level of microorganisms.

Heat. Depending on the actual temperature of the product, heat has several affects on microorganisms. At temperatures just above the optimal for the species, heat will inhibit microbial growth. Pathogens normally will not grow in food that is held above 140°F (60°C). Organisms are killed as the temperature is increased further. The lethality depends on two physical factors: the temperature of the product and the length of time the product is held at that temperature. Increasing a product's temperature reduces the amount of time necessary to kill pathogenic cells. Vegetative microorganisms can be killed when a product is heated to temperatures of less than 212°F (100°C). If a low-acid food product is hermetically packaged, the product must be commercially sterilized to kill spores of *Cl. botulinum*. Temperatures used to kill bacterial spores are usually in excess of 250°F (121°C). A process authority must develop the specific time–temperature relation for commercial sterilization processes. For example, the FDA and USDA recognize organizations such as the National Food Processors Association as well as competent personnel in the Cooperative Extension Service as having expertise to develop these processes.

Pasteurization can be defined as the time–temperature relation that provides sufficient lethality to kill all vegetative pathogenic microorganisms and reduce the non-pathogenic microorganisms to an appropriate level in a specific food product. Commercial sterilization can be defined as the time-temperature relation that provides sufficient lethality to kill all pathogen microorganisms (both vegetative cells and spores) in a specific food product. Commercial sterilization is not designed to totally sterilize a food. Commercially sterilized foods may contain thermophilic microbial spores that are not pathogenic.

Cold. A decrease in temperature below the optimal growth temperature for the species will reduce the growth rate of organisms. Most microorganisms that can affect food safety will not grow at temperatures below 40°F (4°C). However, food must be frozen to completely stop the growth of microorganisms. Most foods start to freeze at temperatures of 28°F (-2°C). Frozen food is held at temperatures of less than 0°F (-18°C) to inhibit undesirable chemical reactions. Freezing of food may reduce the level of viable microorganisms in a food product. However, refrigeration or freezing rarely can be used as a control strategy to eliminate a food borne disease problem.

Chemicals Used in Food Products. Food processors can control microorganisms by controlling the physical properties of food through chemical or physical methods.

Microorganisms require water for growth. Water can be present in two forms in food: free water and bound water. Water that is bound in various degrees to food constituents is available to microorganisms for growth. Food technologists use water activity (A_w) as an estimate of the amount of water available for microbial growth. A_w is the ratio of the vapor pressure of the food to the vapor pressure of pure water. As A_w

decreases, the amount of water available for microbial growth declines. *Cl. botulinum* does not grow in food with an A_w content of less than 0.91. In general, bacterial pathogens do not grow in food products that have an A_w of less than 0.85. The lower limit for yeast growth is 0.7 to 0.75 and for mold growth is 0.6. A_w can be lowered in foods by adding ingredients such as salt or sugar. In addition, the water content of foods can be reduced by evaporation or drying.

The hydrogen ion concentration, or pH, also affects the growth of microorganisms. *Cl. botulinum* can grow in foods when the pH is greater than 4.8. Therefore, foods with a pH of less than 4.5 are classified as high-acid foods, and foods that have a pH of greater than 4.5 are classified as low-acid foods. Low-acid canned foods must undergo a thermal process to destroy *Cl. botulinum* spores. If the food product has a pH of less than 4.5, the thermal process is less severe because it needs to kill only the vegetative pathogens.

Various chemicals can be used to either retard the growth of or kill microorganisms. These chemicals can be divided into two major types: chemicals that can be added to food products or packages and chemicals that cannot be added to food products or packages. In addition to food grade acids, which are used to reduce the food's pH, other antimicrobial agents include benzoic acid, sorbic acid, propionic acid, nisin, natamycin, nitrate, nitrite, sulfite, and sulfur dioxide. Compounds such as hydrogen peroxide are used as a chemical sterilant in aseptic packaging systems.

Chemicals Used in the Food Processing Plant. Food processors use other chemicals at the processing plant to aid in the control of biological hazards.

The cleaning of food processing equipment can be classified as both a physical and chemical method that is used to control the growth of microorganisms. Cleaning physically removes residual foods that can be a source of nutrients and water for microorganisms. In addition, cleaning agents can physically kill microorganisms by disrupting their cells. If cleaning is not done periodically, the food processing equipment will serve as a source of contamination for future lots of food. Equipment must be cleaned prior to sanitizing.

Sanitization is a chemical process used to kill viable microorganisms that may be left on equipment after the cleaning process. A number of sanitizing compounds have been approved for use in food processing plants including chlorine, iodophores, and quaternary ammonium compounds. Sanitization must take place to reduce the chance of cross-contamination. It is not a substitute for proper cleaning of equipment or facilities.

Pesticides are used in processing plants as part of an insect and rodent control program. Insects and rodents harbor microorganisms, add filth to food, and can cross-contaminate food. To ensure the safe production of food, these chemicals must be stored and used in a manner that complies with federal regulations. The proper use of these chemicals is necessary to ensure that the HACCP prerequisite pest control program is effective.

Physical and Mechanical Control. In addition to controlling temperature and water activity, food processors can use other mechanical means to control microbial growth.

Packaging material provides a physical barrier that can be used to reduce microbial spoilage. Packaging material protects food products from microbial contamination during storage, transportation, distribution, and retail sales. Sources of contamination include handling by humans, environmental contamination, or cross-contamination by pests. Packaging systems have been developed to control the atmosphere of fresh-packed foods. The oxygen and carbon dioxide levels are controlled at levels that inhibit microbial growth in products, such as ready-to-eat vegetable salads, that use this type of packaging.

Radiation. Ionizing radiation is used to cold-pasteurize foods without changing the character of the raw food product. Ionizing radiation disrupts the genetic material of living cells, and kills parasites, insects, and pathogenic bacteria. In addition, radiation reduces the level of non-pathogenic bacteria in food. Food irradiation will *not* make the food radioactive. In recent years, the FDA has approved the irradiation of a number of foods including spices, vegetables, poultry, and red meat.

Chemical Hazards

Food can become contaminated with chemical hazards during any stage of the manufacturing process. There are a number of different types of chemical hazards that can occur from natural or human origin.

Some food components cause allergic responses in sensitive individuals. The primary causal agents in allergic reactions are proteins. Food proteins implicated in food allergy reactions come from a wide variety of sources including peanuts, tree nuts, eggs, milk, shellfish, wheat, and soy. Other chemicals implicated as allergens include some artificial colors and sulfites. The primary control measure for allergens is proper labeling of food and the proper cleaning of food processing equipment after a product that contains a known allergen has been produced.

Plant or animal tissue can be contaminated with chemical hazards by environmental contaminants or the improper use of agricultural chemicals such as pesticides, antibiotics, or hormones. One primary source of environmental contamination is contaminated water. For this reason, some HACCP prerequisite programs include a water testing requirement.

Food may also be contaminated in the manufacturing plant. Most of these problems can be attributed to contamination with industrial chemicals, such as cleaning agents, sanitizers, pesticides, and/or lubricants. Control measures include ensuring the proper use and storage of these chemicals. Food additives should not cause a chemical hazard in foods when added to foods at the proper levels and used within limits established by regulatory agencies.

Physical Hazards

Physical hazards can enter a food product during any stage of the production (farming), manufacturing, or distribution process. Mortimore and Wallace classify physical hazards as:

- items that are sharp and could penetrate the skin or gastrointestinal tract

- items that are hard and could cause damage to teeth

- items that are capable of blocking the respiratory tract and could cause choking[1]

Many sources exist for physical hazards. These sources include inadvertent contamination on the farm (such as stones, insects, wood, dirt, and so on), inadvertent contamination during processing (bone fragments, wood, glass, plastic, metal fragments, and so forth), and contamination during distribution because of packaging failure. In the United States, the Food and Drug Administration states that the presence of poisonous or deleterious substances in food makes the food adulterated. However, the FDA also recognizes that some substances may be unavoidable contaminants in food since they may be necessary for food production or may be an inherent component of the food. Therefore, tolerances have been set at levels that pose no inherent hazard to human health. Regulatory action can be taken only if the defect level is exceeded. However, it is illegal for a food processor to knowingly blend out a contaminant to reduce its level in a food product so that it is below the regulatory limit.

Control measures for physical hazards include using inspection and sorting procedures to remove contaminants and maintaining the proper preventative maintenance systems to ensure that food is not contaminated during production, packaging, storage, and delivery.

NEW FOOD BORNE DISEASES AND NEW TECHNOLOGIES

Food safety and the control of pathogenic microorganisms is not a static science. In recent years, food microbiologists have identified a number of pathogenic microorganisms including *Campylobacter jejuni, Yersinia enterococlitica*, and *E. coli* O157:H7. In addition, food technologists currently are developing a number of processing strategies to control microbial contamination in food. Strategies under development include ohmic and inductive heating, micro- and radio frequency waves, high voltage arc discharge, pulsed electric fields, oscillating magnetic fields, pulsed light technology, ultrasound, high pressure processing, and pulsed x-rays.

To effectively audit HACCP programs, professionals must be aware of new developments in food safety and control mechanisms.

REFERENCE

1. S. Mortimore and C. Wallace, *HACCP: A Practical Approach* (Gaithersburg, MD: Aspen, 1998): 87.

12

Prerequisite Areas for Food Safety

EVOLUTION OF PREREQUISITE PROGRAMS

Many government regulations and food industry guidelines respecting food safety have been established around prerequisite programs, or procedures that address operational conditions and provide the foundation for a HACCP system. Chapter 2 distinguishes between prerequisite controls and critical control points (CCPs). This chapter discusses the evolution of and identifies common categories for prerequisite food safety programs.

Prerequisite programs originally came from food regulations and voluntary food industry programs. The most familiar progenitor of these programs is the current good manufacturing practices, or GMPs, codified in Code of Federal Regulations, Title 21, Part 110.[1] GMPs were established to help define for the food industry the minimal sanitary conditions for processing safe food products. They include such areas as personal hygiene, operational practices, cleaning and sanitation, water safety, foreign material control, and sanitary design. The GMP programs in most quality-oriented firms exceed the federal regulatory requirements.

The Seafood HACCP Regulation,[2] CFR Title 21 Part 123, requires GMPs and sanitation standard operating procedures (SSOPs) as prerequisite requirements for the HACCP program. These address eight areas: pest control; employee hygiene; water safety; protection from adulterants; prevention of cross-contamination; condition of hand washing, hand sanitizing, and toilet facilities; condition and cleanliness of food contact surfaces; and labeling, storage, and use of toxic compounds. The USDA/FSIS has also established its version of SSOPs for the meat and poultry industries.[3] These prerequisites are divided into two categories: preoperational procedures and operational sanitation. The preoperational procedures include the cleaning of food contact surfaces, cleaning of equipment, and cleaning of utensils, while the operational SSOPs include equipment cleaning, employee hygiene, and proper product handling. In 1998, the FDA published the *Guide to Minimize Microbial Food Safety Hazards for Fresh Fruits and Vegetables*.[4] This publication addresses prerequisites or "good agricultural practices" used to minimize biological hazards common to the growing, harvesting, washing, sorting, packing, and transporting of fresh fruits and vegetables sold in an unprocessed or minimally processed state.

Numerous industry guidelines that specify higher standards than those imposed by regulatory GMPs have evolved over time. Originally developed for the purpose of self-inspection and continual improvement, these standards are now also used by many companies for the purpose of supplier certification. A sample guideline is AIB International's "AIB Consolidated Standards for Food Safety."[5] This document has been further developed to address numerous sectors of the food industry, such as dairy products, fresh-cut produce, raw (unprocessed) fruits and vegetables, and food distribution centers. Using a sector-specific approach, these guidelines develop and emphasize quality issues for the specific food industry and the prerequisite programs most applicable to food safety.

As previously noted, prerequisite food safety programs can be described and categorized in many ways, depending on the regulatory perspective and industry sector. CCPs—not prerequisite programs—are normally used to address significant food hazards, but even this varies from one industry sector to another. In one industry segment a certain prerequisite may be of minor importance, while in another the same prerequisite may be essential to ensuring product safety.

If the prerequisite program is used to create an environment where a hazard is not likely to occur, it can be essential to ensure product safety. When this occurs, the prerequisite program must be properly designed and implemented. In addition, the company should take actions to check, inspect, and document its continued effectiveness.

TYPES OF PREREQUISITE PROGRAMS

Because of the various perspectives described above, many different categories have been developed for prerequisite food safety programs. From a regulatory HACCP perspective six key prerequisites should be implemented: *good manufacturing practices, trace and recall, cleaning and sanitation, pest control, chemical control,* and *customer complaints—food safety*.[6] Sperber et al. describe eight prerequisite program categories: *facilities, raw material controls, sanitation, training, production equipment, production controls, storage and distribution,* and *product controls*.[7] The NACMCF 1997 HACCP Guideline lists 11 prerequisite programs in its Appendix A: *facilities; supplier control; specifications; production equipment; cleaning and sanitation; personal hygiene; training; chemical control; receiving, storage, and shipping; traceability and recall;* and *pest control*.[8]

In an effort to consolidate these different programs while still addressing the diverse needs of the food industry, this book will describe prerequisite programs according to the following categories: *good manufacturing practices; chemical control; cleaning and sanitation; microbiological control; sanitary design and engineering; preventive maintenance; trace and recall; pest control; receiving, storage, and shipping controls; supplier control; water safety; air safety; food safety training; equipment calibration; customer complaints—food safety;* and *audits and inspection programs.* This list is comprehensive, but not exhaustive, and many of the categories overlap in the web of quality systems used to manage food safety.

Good Manufacturing Practices

For the purpose of this discussion, GMPs will be divided into three subcategories: *personal hygiene, good operational practices,* and *foreign material and glass control.* Personal hygiene involves procedures used by employees, contractors, visitors, and other on-site personnel to protect food products from such contaminants as hair, jewelry, clothing, pathogens, and other human-transmitted hazards. Good operational practices denote methods and techniques that protect food from contamination during manufacturing and storage process steps. These steps include receipt and storage of raw materials, transfer and handling of ingredients, operational appearance, and shipping. Foreign material and glass control involves the use and management of protective devices for prevention of foreign material contamination.

Personal Hygiene. Personal hygiene programs focus on preventing product contamination due to the interface of employees and food process zones. Companies typically establish GMP rules and train employees in compliance. Clothing and garment rules cover the use of clean, appropriate outer garments (limitations on buttons, fuzzy sweaters, and so on) or uniforms, the use of hair and beard restraints, restrictions on hair ties and pins, limitations on the wearing of exposed jewelry, the use of proper foot wear, the control of items in top pockets (or elimination of pockets), and the use of strong perfumes, false eyelashes, false fingernails, and fingernail polish. A more recent trend that could result in potential food hazards and should be addressed through these policies is exposed body piercing jewelry.

Personal hygiene also addresses disease control. Without proper safeguards, biological hazards such as *Shigella* and hepatitis A may be transmitted from personnel to food products. Employees must wash and, in most cases, sanitize their hands before reporting to their workstations and after use of restrooms or after breaks and lunch. For sensitive product areas, some companies require the use of protective devices such as gloves, sleeve guards, and facemasks. No person with boils, sores, open and infected wounds, or a food-transmittable disease should be allowed to work in food process areas; illness should be reported to supervisory personnel. Supervisory personnel should be trained to recognize signs of biological hazards, such as a jaundiced appearance in individuals with hepatitis A. It is also important to distinguish between contagious illnesses that could be hazardous to coworkers, and infectious agents that are a threat to food products.

GMPs also address eating, drinking, gum and tobacco chewing, smoking, and using toothpicks near food processing areas or "product zones." Food operations typically permit drinking water only from fountains/coolers or plastic water bottles in these sensitive areas, while providing break areas, smoking areas, and lunchrooms for other activities.

Good Operational Practices. Procedures that prevent contamination of food during handling and transfer of products fall into the good operational practices category. This includes keeping all ingredients and finished products off the floor, eliminating and/or cleaning spills and leaks, cleaning ingredient containers before use, handling rubbish and food waste properly, discarding any food that falls on the floor, and using good housekeeping in process areas.

Good housekeeping includes the proper storage of parts, equipment, and utensils after use; storing personal effects and clothing in lockers or other designated areas; hanging air and water hoses back on designated racks and reels after use; and other activities that prevent intrusion of potential contaminants into process areas. The work area should be maintained in a reasonably sanitary condition, with a minimum of operational debris. Dedicated scoops and other utensils should be used for specific raw materials and ingredients. Ingredients and process aids should be properly labeled and stored after use to prevent cross-contamination.

Foreign Material Control and Glass Control. Procedures and equipment should be utilized to prevent the inclusion of objectionable or harmful foreign objects into food products. Objectionable items include burned product, hair, insects, and paper, while harmful contaminants include metal, glass, Plexiglas, and wood splinters. Harmful contaminants may cause traumatic injury such as laceration of the mouth, tongue, throat, stomach, or intestine, as well as injury to the gums and teeth. GMPs require that measures must be taken to prevent the inclusion of metal or other extraneous material in foods. According to FDA policy, food is considered adulterated if it is ready-to-eat and contaminated with hard or sharp objects that measure 7 to 25 mm in length.[9] Customer and market-driven requirements in this area are more demanding, and usually require preventing inclusion of metal contaminants bigger than a 1 to 3 mm diameter sphere.

Foreign materials may originate from raw materials and ingredients, from food processing equipment, from the food plant environment (walls, ceiling, and so on), from employees, from food service product preparation, and from retail tampering. Since most food processing equipment is fabricated from metal materials, metal is a universal physical hazard in most segments of the food industry.

Equipment utilized to control metal hazards includes magnets, filters, traps, and electronic metal detectors. Non-metallic foreign objects such as stones, bones, wood, glass, and insects can be controlled through the use of sifters, product grading screens, rock traps, destoners, wash tanks, aspirators, and x-ray detection equipment. In cases where equipment may not be sensitive or sophisticated enough to remove foreign objects, inspection conveyors may be required so that employees can manually remove contaminants. Regardless of the equipment or procedure used to detect and remove foreign materials, findings should be logged on an ongoing basis and sources of contamination investigated.

Standard operating procedures should also be utilized to prevent physical hazards. Food plants should adopt a glass policy that outlines requirements for shielding fluorescent tubes and light bulbs in process areas; for protection or removal of glass gauges, emergency lights, thermometers, and wall clocks; for control of glass containers in process areas; for the safe use of laboratory glassware; and for handling breakage of glass packaging materials.

Self-inspection is also used to identify and control physical hazards. Regardless of whether equipment or procedures are used, there must always be a method to evaluate physical contaminants. A process should be in place to determine if contaminants are incidental or continuous in nature, and if further corrective actions should be taken.

Best practices and new technologies in good manufacturing practices include infrared activated toilets and sinks, automated hand sanitizers, automated floor foamer (a spray sanitizer replaces boot dips and forklift wheel dip), posted hand wash signs in restrooms, computerized defect removal equipment, metal detectable ear plugs and bandages, computerized networked metal detector management equipment, shielded mercury vapor bulbs, employee health screening, glass breakage programs for glass pack lines, electronic inspection equipment for glass bottles and jars (100 percent glass breakage inspection), washing of incoming glass jars and bottles, and management of employee practices through behavioral management theory.

Chemical Control

Chemical hazards include such items as sulfites, yellow #5 (tartrazine), sanitation chemicals, allergens, mycotoxins, pesticides, refrigerants, solvents, acid, caustics, and sanitizers. They may originate from raw materials, such as histamines in scromboid fish; from allergenic ingredients, such as peanuts; from food additives, such as sulfites; and from chemicals used in food plants, such as ammonia (a refrigerant) and sodium hypochlorite. In general, chemical control relates to procedures used for the receipt, storage, use, disposal, and record keeping of chemicals needed for processing, sanitation, pest control, and maintenance. Due to the broad array of potential hazards, preventive prerequisite programs have been identified here as sanitation chemical handling, process aid chemical control, plant pesticide control, maintenance chemical control, agricultural chemical control, and allergen control.

Sanitation Chemical Handling. The first step in any food plant chemical control program must be an inventory of all approved chemicals. This master list should include sanitation chemicals, maintenance chemicals, process aids, chemical ingredients, and pesticides used at the plant. Food plants typically maintain this master list as part of an OSHA-required hazard communication program.

Cleaning chemicals and sanitizers should be appropriate for use in food processing areas. In the past many companies relied on the U.S. Department of Agriculture (USDA) screening and rating system for chemical products approved for use in meat and poultry facilities, but this program has been discontinued. Chemicals not previously rated by USDA as safe for food plants will require supplier or third-party certification as proof that they are food grade or safe for a food plant.

Primary containers of chemicals should be stored in a segregated, locked, and identified area, rather than near food process zones. Some chemicals, such as acids and chlorine compounds, may require physical segregation. Storage areas should have spill containment equipment, such as containment walls or spill pallets, in the event of container breakage. All containers should be closed and secured after dispensing. Secondary containers in regular use near food zones should be stored a safe distance from the food zone and closed after each use to guard against spillage.

In facilities that utilize clean-in-place equipment, piping used for chemicals should be identified with signage or labels. These pipes should not run directly above exposed product zones. Chemical make-up tanks must also be appropriately identified.

The contents of all primary and secondary chemical containers and application equipment must be properly identified. Identification includes the name of the chemical and hazard rating (from the material safety data sheet). Before use, cleaning chemicals and sanitizers generally require dilution to proper concentrations. Dilution rates are usually specified on product labels. Test kits are available to test concentrations of many of these chemicals, such as chlorine, caustics, and quaternary ammonium compounds. Where equipment is used to automatically dilute chemicals, calibration of the equipment should be a regular practice. Biocides are categorized as pesticides by the U.S. Environmental Protection Agency (EPA), are regulated by Federal pesticide law, and carry an EPA registration number. Use of these materials should be regularly logged to ensure compliance with the labeled application rate. Finally, the application of these chemicals must be carefully controlled. Applications must not be made to food products or to process zones during production. Written procedures should be developed to identify proper dilution, testing, and application for all sanitation chemicals.

Best practices and new technologies in sanitation chemical handling include the use of color-coded buckets and other containers for use of different types of chemical solutions, automatic chemical dilution and dispensing units, waterproof labels on containers in wet areas, spill control kits, spill control pallets, chemical storage areas with spill containment barriers, and employee safety programs (hazard communication, Hazwopper, lock-out/tag-out, process safety management, and so on).

Process Aid Chemical Control. During the processing of foods, process aids such as fungicides, microbiocides, disinfectants, defoamers, and chelating agents are used. These include items such as hypochlorites, chlorine gas, ozone, mineral oil, peracetic acid, sprout inhibitors, sulfites, and chlorine. All of these chemicals should be food grade. Any non–food grade chemicals used would face regulatory scrutiny and sampling. If contaminants were found, regulatory actions might follow. Labels and material safety data sheets should be on file for each chemical. As with sanitation chemicals, storage should be controlled and all materials properly labeled.

Application of processing chemicals should be closely monitored. Those chemicals that carry an EPA registration label must be applied only at the rate listed on the label, and application should be logged to indicate amount used, where used, rate of application, concentration, date, name of applicator, and EPA registration number. Proper application should be validated periodically through end product testing for chemical residue levels. Microbial testing may also be necessary for treated process water.

Plant Pesticide Control. When rodenticides, avicides, and insecticides are applied at processing facilities, strict controls are needed to prevent product contamination. These materials should be stored in a locked, well-ventilated storage area with the proper signage. The materials should be FDA/USDA approved for food plants, and sample labels and material safety data sheets should be on file. Rodenticides should be applied only to exterior areas of the facility in locked, tamper-proof bait stations. All containers of pesticides should be properly labeled. Special keyed bait stations, bait-securing devices for bait stations, and employee safety programs are a few of the best practices and new technologies in the area of plant pesticide control.

Maintenance Chemical Control. All lubricants used in process zones should be certified as food grade. Application of lubricants should be carefully controlled to prevent product contamination. Lubricants should be applied only during line downtime, and there should be a written standard operating procedure for proper application techniques. Bearings, hydraulic drives and lines, and conveyor drives should be located outboard to process lines, and catch pans should be installed under bearings located directly above process areas. Lubricants should be labeled and stored in the same manner as pesticides and sanitation chemicals.

A spill control procedure should be developed for lubricants and other maintenance-related chemicals (such as solvents, anhydrous ammonia). Forklift battery charging areas should not be located near process zones, and should be designed with spill containment barriers. Best practices and new technologies in the area of maintenance chemical control include spill "pigs" (containment devices), greaseless bearings, and employee safety programs (hazard communication, Hazwopper, and so on).

Agricultural Chemical Control. Control of crop chemicals requires appropriate documentation of agricultural chemical applications to raw materials during growing, and a pesticide-screening program of incoming raw materials and finished products. Grower application cards are typically supplied to processors to document proper application levels. Samples of finished food products should be periodically screened for pesticide residues.

Allergen Control. Allergen control concerns chemical hazards attributed to raw materials and ingredients. An allergen control program should be established when manufactured food products have allergenic ingredients. Such a program evaluates and controls the risks from allergen cross-contamination and mislabeling by addressing product design, manufacturing, and packaging processes. Key components of an allergen control program include screening and control strategies.

The screening process involves assessing all ingredients, raw materials, process aids, and packaging to determine if any of these items will induce allergic or chemical sensitivity reactions. These materials include, but are not limited to, peanuts, tree nuts, milk, eggs, soy, wheat, fish, shellfish, celery, sesame, yellow #5, sulfites, monosodium glutamate, and lactose. A documented inventory of these items will demonstrate the need for or exemption from implementing an allergen control program. If allergen or allergen-like materials are processed in the facility, the inventory should identify which process lines these materials are run on, and if the lines are "stand-alone," or are shared by non-allergen-containing products. A finished product inventory that lists all finished food products containing allergens and identifies which allergen(s) each product contains should also be developed. Such an inventory is an important tool in planning the sequence of production runs to avoid allergen cross-contamination.

Numerous control strategies can be used to manage allergens, depending on the type of allergenic ingredients/raw materials, and type of finished food product. The starting point is a hazard analysis, which should be used to identify all allergen food hazards in raw materials, ingredients, the processing system, and packaging. The hazard analysis will assess the likelihood and severity of each potential allergen hazard, and will distinguish those significant hazards that should be controlled through a HACCP system from hazards that can be controlled through prerequisite programs. In some cases a typical prerequisite program, such as cleaning and sanitation, may be elevated to a CCP for allergen control. This occurs when the hazard analysis has determined that failure to properly clean equipment or surfaces could lead to a life- or health-threatening condition.

Where non-allergen-containing products are run on the same process lines as allergen-containing products, the hazard analysis should evaluate the effectiveness of cleaning after allergen-containing product runs, and also should include testing of the non-allergen-containing products for cross-contamination from allergens.

Receiving controls should be in place to address allergens. These include certification of incoming materials as allergen-free, labeling incoming pallets of allergenic ingredients, segregated storage of allergen-containing materials, and review of incoming packaging materials to ensure that ingredient listings include allergenic ingredients where required.

There are many control steps for allergens during processing and packaging. Where possible, allergen-containing products sharing the same process line as non-allergen-containing products should be scheduled to be run last, followed by a full cleanup. Dedicated utensils, containers, tools, uniforms, and scaling equipment should be used for allergen-containing product runs. It is critical that all allergenic raw materials and ingredients be listed properly in the ingredient declaration on packaging material. This can be monitored through manual operator checks and by automated optical scanning of UPC codes on packaging material that automatically rejects product or shuts down the manufacturing line if allergen-containing product is detected.

Cleaning is one of the most important controls for allergens. Procedures for allergen cleanups should be thorough and documented. Post-cleaning visual inspection is critical to ensure that all allergenic residue is removed from process lines; inspection may be augmented by ATP bioluminescence swabbing.

Lines must be properly engineered to control allergen cross-contamination. Allergenic ingredients should be added at the furthest point in the process flow towards packaging. Lockout of three-way valves and allergen applicators should be used on shared product lines. A dust removal system should be installed to filter finely divided allergenic materials (such as peanut flour). Traffic flows from allergen scaling areas into process areas should be carefully evaluated.

Training is key for all of the above controls. Employees need to be aware of allergen control procedures, and training should be conducted for new hires and on an annual refresher basis. As always, results of training should be documented.

Where the same process line is used to run allergen-containing and non-allergen-containing product, the allergen control program must be validated by end product testing. "First-off" product from non-allergen-containing food product process lines should be tested for presence of cross-contaminating allergens on a routine basis.

Best practices and new technologies in the area of allergen control include the labeling of incoming allergenic ingredients, allergen warnings on product labels, UPC code scanning during packaging to ensure correct packaging material is used for allergen-containing products, chemical labels and material safety data sheets, dust removal systems for areas handling powdered allergens, lockout for allergen application equipment, allergen mapping, and rapid ELISHA test kits for egg, dairy, and peanut allergens.

Cleaning and Sanitation

Cleaning and sanitation is an important prerequisite that deals with housekeeping, cleaning, and sanitizing procedures used to control possible contamination in the manufacturing facility. Cleaning generally refers to the removal of soils, debris, and chemicals from food processing equipment and environmental surfaces. Sanitizing, on the other hand, is the application of microbiocides to cleaned surfaces for the purpose of killing microorganisms. The sanitation process follows the cleaning process.

Key components of a cleaning and sanitation program include a master cleaning schedule (MCS), a daily housekeeping schedule, written cleaning procedures, and housekeeping practices. A master cleaning schedule is a tool used to ensure that other-than-daily cleaning tasks are completed on a timely basis. It identifies all key cleaning tasks for equipment, outside grounds, building areas, and food utensils; the required frequency of cleaning; the responsible position or person; and provides a means to track completion dates and employee sign-off. A daily housekeeping schedule is used to inventory tasks that must be completed routinely in plant areas to ensure that they are clean, safe, and orderly. This also includes "on-the-run" cleaning. The overall goal of using cleaning schedules is to (1) provide a method to manage a large number of important tasks that cannot be practically assigned to memory, and (2) to schedule cleaning activities with a frequency that will disrupt the lifecycles of insects and microorganisms.

Written cleaning procedures are used to document the sanitation program. These are work instructions which detail how to clean plant equipment, what types of chemicals are necessary, procedures for using application equipment and other cleaning devices (high-pressure guns, low-pressure hoses, clean-in-place [CIP] tanks, clean-out-of-place [COP] tanks, foaming vessels, line cleaning air-actuated bullets ["pigs"], and so on), and safety procedures that need to be practiced when handling chemicals and equipment (such as personal protective equipment, lock-out/tag-out). A cleaning procedure should be developed for each key piece of food processing equipment, as well as for the food processing environment (floors, walls, ceiling). Procedures should be written in simple language, preferably by the personnel who will be performing the actual cleaning and sanitation.

Best practices and new technologies in the area of cleaning and sanitation include the use of color-coded brushes, utensils, and other cleaning equipment to prevent cross-contamination between raw and finished product work areas; peracetic acids for equipment sanitation; use of digital cameras to document cleaning procedures; training programs for sanitation crews; automated titration and tracking of chemicals during CIP and COP cleaning; automated belt washers; a high-pressure cleaning attachment ("mouse") for pipe washing; rapid results ATP bioluminescence swabbing equipment for monitoring cleaning effectiveness; and chemical spill pallets.

Microbiological Control

Microbiological control involves a program to monitor, assess, and control the risk of microbial contamination. Typically cleaning and sanitation address control of microbiological hazards, but this additional prerequisite is needed for facilities where control of such hazards as *Listeria* and *Salmonella* is critical.

Key methods of microbial control include equipment swabbing, environmental monitoring, line profiling, and product testing for microbiological contamination. Swabbing is used to evaluate the effectiveness of cleaning and sanitizing on process equipment and to problem-solve product contamination issues. Line profiling involves product sampling at different locations along the process flow to determine sources of microbial loading in food products. Samples of raw materials, intermediate product from various process steps, and finished product are tested for total plate count, yeast and mold, coliforms, and specific pathogens to build a microbial profile of the process system. Environmental monitoring is the central component of a *Listeria monocytogenes* control strategy, and involves sampling surfaces in areas where cooked, refrigerated, or perishable products are processed and packaged. These surfaces include floors, walls, ceilings, drains, trash cans, trolleys, conveyor frameworks, storage hoppers, sinks, HVAC equipment, and other potential environmental sources of pathogens. Where food products are cooked or there is a pathogen kill step, it is especially critical to monitor areas between the kill step and packaging. *Salmonella* monitoring may be conducted in areas where products with a history associated with Salmonella are used such as dried dairy products, eggs, and meat-processing areas.

Other important components of microbial control include self-inspections and audits, hand washing, hand dipping, foot baths, control of plant traffic, sanitary design of process lines, and clean gloves and uniforms. Vigorous hand washing must be done for a minimum of 20 seconds with hot, soapy water to remove most microorganisms. Many of these items are part of other prerequisite programs. Finally, microbial testing and timely corrective action to issues identified during audits ensure that pathogens are controlled or eliminated.

Best practices and new technologies in microbiological control include rapid swabbing test kits; sponge sampling kits for *Listeria;* floor foams; color-coded cleaning equipment and maintenance tools; Microban-impregnated paints, conveyor belts, toilet and door handles; and drain sanitizers.

Sanitary Design and Engineering

Production facilities and process lines should be designed to prevent contamination of food products. Proper design impacts on many areas: the building, equipment, electrical systems, construction, maintenance, cleaning, solid waste handling systems, pest control systems, and foreign material control.[10] Sanitary design criteria depend on the specific industry segment and inherent food hazards (such as dairy processing versus flour milling), although certain engineering requirements pertain to all food plants.

Each facility or food company should develop a set of sanitary design standards to serve as a guide for constructing new process lines and production facilities. These industry-specific guidelines are also an important training and compliance tool for company maintenance personnel and outside contractors. For example, guidelines provide directives for the use of sanitary welds during equipment installation and line construction. Ground and polished sanitary welds ensure that equipment and surrounding surfaces can be fully cleaned and sanitized, thus augmenting microbial control.

These universal requirements relate to basic building design and location. Plants should be located away from feedlots and landfills. Adequate drainage and dust control must be incorporated into outside grounds through drains and paved lots. Landscaping should not attract birds, insects, rodents, and other pests; low shrubs and grass are preferred over trees, but shrubs should not be planted next to buildings. Lighting should not be mounted on the building, but rather on poles or other fixtures that illuminate the building from a distance and draw insects away from the facility. Design features incorporated into the facility to prevent rodent entry include outside drainpipe screens, metal flashing installed below loading docks, door seals, and a graveled perimeter.

The interior of the plant should be designed to facilitate cleaning. Equipment should not rest directly on the floor. Services such as pipes and electrical conduits should be mounted away from walls. Where applicable, an equipment loft should be incorporated into the plant design so that utilities such as steam, air, power, and water can be supplied to process equipment from directly overhead.

Air handling systems must be designed to prevent contamination. Generally positive pressure is desired in process areas, and air should flow from finished product areas to raw material areas, not vice versa. Ductwork may need to be insulated to prevent condensation buildup over process zones.

Restrooms and hand washing areas are a regulatory requirement. Hot and cold water must be supplied to hand wash stations, and valves should be foot or electronically activated to prevent recontamination of hands. Restrooms must not open directly into production areas.

Raw material preparation areas should be segregated from intermediate and finished product processing areas. Design should take employee and forklift traffic flows into account to minimize the potential for cross-contamination.

Best practices and new technologies in sanitary design and engineering include 3-A Standards, National Sanitary Foundation (NSF) design standards, Baking Industry Sanitation Standards Committee (BISSC) design standards,[11] European Union design standards,[12] antimicrobial additives for paints and plastic materials, utility lofts, and a sign-off process for new equipment and process lines.

Preventive Maintenance

Preventive maintenance involves the use of a predetermined schedule to service the physical building, equipment, and processing utensils with the goal of preventing food product contamination. This prerequisite ensures that structural beams, supports, walls, ceiling, and floors are maintained on a regular basis to eliminate contamination from paint chips, insulation, metal, plastic, or wood. Overhead light fixtures must be properly maintained to ensure that they are adequately shielded against glass breakage. Equipment such as conveyor belts, bearings, drive motors, chain guards, augers, and pumps must be serviced on a regular basis to prevent contamination from leaking lubricants, conveyor clips, belt threads, rubber gaskets, and metal shavings from metal-on-metal wear.

The core to a good preventive maintenance program is a schedule and a work order system. The schedule is a management tool that ensures that equipment and structures are routinely serviced before they become a source of contamination. The work order is used to track scheduling and completion of both preventive maintenance and non-scheduled repairs. Work orders should include a priority system that gives an urgent status to food safety–related repairs. A good preventive maintenance program should also address the removal of project debris after completion of work by maintenance personnel or contractors.

Best practices and new technologies in the area of preventive maintenance include predictive maintenance, computerized preventive maintenance systems, contractors' food safety requirements, and total productive maintenance systems.

Trace and Recall

Trace and recall is a program used to track and control the movement of food products, from receipt of ingredients and raw materials to end point distribution of finished goods. This level of control is established to enable a food company to retrieve product from the distribution system and marketplace in the event a product is defective or becomes contaminated during manufacturing or retailing. The elements of a good recall program include a written product withdrawal and recall policy, including a defined recall process; a recall action team; proper lot coding of all retail and food service packaged units; product complaint handling procedures; a system of notification for company personnel, customers, and regulatory agencies; and a means to recover and dispose of recovered food products.

Facilities should maintain accurate records of lot or batch numbers assigned to food products. Lot or batch numbers should be incorporated into distribution documents such as shipping manifests or bills of lading to facilitate product tracking, and copies of these records should be held for at least the shelf life of the product. Food companies should periodically test the effectiveness of their trace and recall program through mock recall exercises. The results of these exercises should be summarized, documented, and maintained on file.

Best practices and new technologies in the area of trace and recall include tracking lot numbers of raw materials in production records, semiannual mock recall exercises, computerized warehousing and recall tracking, company spokespersons, crisis management plans, pre-planned press releases, disposal certification, monitoring of coding equipment, and printed lot codes.

Pest Control

Pest control involves a program to limit pest activity through documented programs and practices. Key target pests include birds, rodents, and insects.

A written pest control program should be on file, describing practices used to control birds, rodents, and insects. The program should include the following documents: overview of program, current applicator license and liability insurance for the pest control operator (PCO) or in-house applicator, written procedures for chemical application, sample labels and MSDS for all pesticides, a schematic showing the location of all pest control devices, service reports for the PCO, and a pesticide application log. If restricted-use pesticides are used, the applicator must be properly licensed, whereas application of general use pesticides requires a trained applicator (requirements may vary, depending on local and state laws).

Controls to limit rodent activity may include exterior bait stations, interior mechanical traps, glue boards, hardware cloth, door seals, and graveled or paved zones around the plant. Rodent activity should be limited by proper sanitation to remove food debris and to eliminate harborage areas.

Insect controls may include insect light traps, door and window screens, pheromone traps, glue boards, fumigation, fogging, and spot spraying with insecticides. Sanitation is also an important preventive measure in controlling insects, and efforts must be made to remove sources of food, water, and harborage.

Bird control is typically addressed through a combination of strategies. The first approach should be removal of all sources of food and sites for roosting and nesting.

Tools used to facilitate bird control include gang spikes, plastic owls, predator balloons, hardware cloth and bird nets for exclusion, pellet guns, screened windows and doors, and avicides.

Best practices and new technologies in pest control include pest findings trend analysis, use of personal digital assistants to scan pest control devices (electronic logging), monitoring with non-toxic bait blocks, pheromone monitoring, CO_2 fumigation, tin cat mechanical traps, 18–24 inch (0.5–0.67 m) inspection aisles, 30–36 inch (0.75–1 m) gravel perimeter, exterior bait stations every 50–100 feet (15–30 m), interior mechanical traps every 20–25 feet (6–8 m) and flanking doors, non-electrocuting insect light traps (glue boards), 30-foot (9-meter) buffer zones between electric grid insect light traps and exposed process zones, annual changeout of insect light trap tubes at peak insect season, solar fly traps, and parasitic wasps for outdoor fly control.

Receiving, Storage, and Shipping Controls

Food products must be handled in a safe and sanitary manner during the receipt and storage of raw materials, and the storage and distribution of finished food products. Receiving, storage, and shipping controls utilize numerous practices to prevent product contamination at the beginning and end of the food manufacturing process.

Receiving controls include inspection of all incoming carriers for sanitary condition, inspection of all incoming ingredients for potential contamination, proper documentation of all incoming raw materials and ingredients, temperature evaluation of all incoming perishable raw materials, and proper documentation of incoming product safety, such as certificates of analysis. Results of incoming material inspections should be properly documented, rather than reported by exception. Tracking should include date, supplier, lot number, temperature (if applicable), condition of carrier, evidence of tamper seal on carrier, carrier identification, and condition of product and pallets. Certificates of analysis should arrive prior to or with incoming shipments and must be examined to ensure compliance with company written specifications.

Company written specifications are typically developed for all raw materials, packaging, ingredients, process aids, and finished food products. Included in a specification are a product description, transportation and storage requirements, and required analytical test results for quality attributes and known biological, physical, and chemical hazards. In addition, some operations pull samples of incoming materials for acceptance testing of microbiological, visual, physical, and other product attributes.

Once received, all raw materials should be dated directly on their containers rather than on shrink-wrap to ensure first-in first-out (FIFO) utilization. It has also become common to specially identify pallets containing allergenic ingredients. Raw materials and ingredients should be stored in areas segregated from processing and packaging areas, and often allergen-containing ingredients are further segregated. Holes and tears in ingredient containers created in the unloading or storage process should be inspected for contamination, and the product should either be discarded or the damage repaired by taping and labeling tears. Perishable and frozen ingredients must be placed in storage at the appropriate temperature, and temperatures should be monitored and recorded on at least a daily basis.

Storage areas must be maintained in sanitary condition. This requires appropriate cleaning and pest control measures. Palletized ingredients and raw materials should be stored at least 18 inches (0.5 m) off the floor, preferably in racks, and should be at least 18 inches (0.5 m) away from walls and ceilings to allow for maintenance aisles. Where it is necessary to store goods on the floor, slip sheets should be used as a sanitary barrier.

Programs for finished goods are parallel to those for incoming ingredients. Food products should be stored in a safe manner, in clean areas with appropriate pest controls. A segregated sanitary storage area is typically established for damaged goods; these areas need daily scrutiny to manage spillage and potential food sources for pests. The temperature of refrigerated and frozen goods must be routinely monitored and logged to prevent quality and food safety issues. As in receiving areas, storage of finished food products must be separated from storage of chemicals, including food grade chemicals used as ingredients or process aids. Outgoing carriers must also be inspected to ensure they are free from odors, toxic chemicals, debris, foreign materials, rodents, and other hazards. Company-owned distribution vehicles should be cleaned on a regular basis to ensure sanitary condition.

Best practices and new technologies in receiving, storage, and shipping controls include the examination of shipping records for the prior three cargoes transported by outgoing carriers, color-coded FIFO pallet tags, and allergen labeling.

Supplier Control

Supplier control refers to a program of company criteria for the evaluation and approval of suppliers, raw materials, ingredients, and services in order to minimize food product contamination. Without effective supplier control, even the best prerequisite and HACCP systems cannot fully ensure product safety.

The starting point is clearly-defined expectations for suppliers, usually in the form of specifications and a supplier approval checklist. Ingredient specifications should outline requirements for control of food hazards in supplied materials. Compliance to these specifications is usually demonstrated in COAs accompanying each shipment (see previous section).

It has become standard practice to establish a supplier approval program to further protect the customer from contaminated raw materials. Typical expectations for suppliers include an implemented HACCP program, participation in a third-party sanitation audit program with a favorable audit rating, a product liability insurance policy for $3 million, a documented trace and recall program, a continuing pure food guarantee of product safety, and an on-site qualifying food safety and quality audit conducted by a customer representative.

The formation of partnerships and alliances, the identification of select supplier programs, Internet accessibility to supplier specifications, and supplier performance review meetings are a few best practices in the area of supplier control.

Water Safety

Although water safety is addressed in the GMPs, numerous recent issues with potability and contamination of drinking water with pathogens such as *E. coli* O157:H7 is justification for putting more emphasis on this important prerequisite. A water safety program mandates a process to manage the safety and quality of water used as a food ingredient, water used in processing, water used in cleaning operations, ice and steam used for food contact, and drinking water consumed by employees.

Only potable water can be used by food processing operations for the purposes listed above. An annual potability certification that verifies compliance with State and/or EPA drinking water regulations should be maintained on file for water used in the facility. For water supplied by a municipality, documentation of compliance typically is supplied by a water department or company upon request. When well, lake, or river water is used by a food company the water must be tested on a routine basis by the company to certify compliance to EPA potability requirements. In addition to EPA requirements, non-city water should be microbiologically tested on a weekly basis to document effectiveness of water treatment systems and freedom from coliforms and pathogenic bacteria (and in some cases, protozoa). Where water is a predominant food product ingredient (such as in beverages), further written specifications should be developed to outline other important criteria, such as hardness, off odor and flavor, chlorine levels, and particulate levels.

Water treatment must be carefully monitored and logged by the processing facility. Daily testing of chlorine gas, calcium or sodium hypochlorite, or ozone levels is necessary to monitor correct chemical application levels and desired microbial kill. Non-chemical treatments such as ultraviolet or heat pasteurization systems also need to be carefully monitored and logged to ensure correct operation. Where food grade steam is utilized, careful management of boiler treatment chemicals is necessary to prevent product contamination. Personnel should ensure chemicals are FDA approved, that they are added at the appropriate concentrations, and that chemical labels and MSDS are maintained on file.

Food plants must be properly engineered to prevent backflow or siphonage of wastewater, wash water, septic lines, or other non-potable water into potable water lines. Backflow devices should be installed on potable water lines used for drinking water, cleaning water, ice production, and processing water supply. Plumbing must be done to eliminate dead legs (or back legs), removing areas where microorganisms can grow. Installations must comply with federal, state, and/or local regulations. These devices should be inspected periodically by maintenance personnel or third-party agencies.

Best practices and new technologies in water safety include filtration of all ingredient water with a 10 micron filter, backflow blueprints, and annual backflow certification.

Air Safety

Air safety describes a program to manage the safety and quality of air and gases used in a facility HVAC system, used as a food ingredient, used in processing, used in cleaning operations, and used in packaging operations. Failures related to this program can result in such hazards as airborne microorganisms, airborne peanut protein, hydrocarbon contamination from air used in packaging machines, and chemical contamination of carbon dioxide used in carbonated beverages.

Air used in either the HVAC system or supplied to equipment such as dryers and classifiers should be filtered to remove dust, insects, and other small contaminants. For microbiologically sensitive food products, HEPA filtration may be necessary. Filters should be cleaned or replaced on a regular basis, managed through the preventive maintenance or master cleaning schedule. Evaporative coolers also need regular cleaning and maintenance to prevent microbial growth in the water spray system and on evaporation media units.

Gases and air used to process and package food products must be food grade to prevent contamination. Toxic lubricants, dirt, water, and other materials must be removed from compressed air that contacts food products. Compressed air should be filtered to remove particles at least 50 microns in size. Traps and filters require maintenance on a regular basis and results should be logged.

Gases such as nitrogen and carbon dioxide that are used as ingredients or process aids must be food grade. Specifications from suppliers should stipulate this status, along with certificates of analysis received with each incoming shipment.

Best practices and new technologies in air safety include microbiological air sampling, the use of charcoal and HEPA filters, and the use of food grade gases.

Food Safety Training

Many prerequisite programs have a training component. This includes training in good manufacturing practices, cleaning and sanitation, personal hygiene, allergen control, and preventive maintenance. Due to the extensive amount of training required to effectively manage prerequisite programs and HACCP, it is key that a system be established to provide for the scheduling, presentation, and tracking of employee training.

Training venues can be group presentations or individualized learning from interactive programs. An important part of this program is identifying appropriate educational materials from the wide variety of videos, interactive CD-ROMs, manuals, and other commercially available material.

Upon completion of all training sessions, employee learning should be evaluated and results documented. Documented training must include the date, subject matter, name of student, title of subject matter, and results of written or oral subject matter testing, along with a roster of all employees attending the training session. Training records should be retained in the employees' personnel files or other appropriate locations.

A calendar or master schedule is a useful tool for ensuring timely completion of required training. Typically food safety training is required for all new employees, with annual refresher courses given in such areas as cleaning practices and GMPs.

Best practices and new technologies in food safety training include computerized tracking programs for completed training, interactive Internet and CD-ROM training programs, and the establishment of learning centers for individualized training.

Equipment Calibration

Equipment calibration involves the standardization and calibration of analytical and processing equipment utilized to control food safety hazards. Thermometers used to track microbial kill temperature in food products must be calibrated on a regular basis to ensure reliability. Scales used to weigh out food additives that have regulatory tolerances should be standardized with certified weights on a frequent schedule. Examples of other equipment that may require calibration include pH meters, moisture analyzers, vacuum gauges, and micrometers.

Where possible, a certificate should be obtained through a national or international standards organization for calibration devices such as standardized thermometers and metal detector test balls. Calibration should be performed on a scheduled basis and results documented. Standard operating procedures are typically developed to outline the approved process for performing equipment calibration. The use of calibration management software and calibration labels is a highly recommended practice.

Customer Complaints—Food Safety

This prerequisite program involves review of marketplace risk associated with customer complaints, and investigation and corrective measures needed to prevent recurrence. The program focuses only on *product safety–related* complaints, and must have a mechanism to identify complaints, trends, and frequencies that may deem product withdrawal or recall necessary.

A written program should be developed to describe procedures for handling food safety complaints, including forms for tracking the complaint from receipt through resolution. Most companies share complaint information with employees to aid in rapid troubleshooting and corrective action to eliminate the root cause of product contamination.

In many cases, investigation of complaints may require analytical capabilities to properly identify the product contaminant. Examples of testing include analysis for microbial pathogens, glass flame and chemical tests, foreign material analysis, insect analysis, hair identification, and chemical testing.

The following are excellent methods of tracking complaints: computerized complaint tracking programs, complaint trend analysis, complaint log books, complaint measurement, and normalization of data by units produced/sold/distributed.

Audits and Inspection Programs

Prerequisite programs require ongoing management and evaluation. Audits and inspections are used to evaluate effectiveness of these programs and must be utilized to ensure constant improvement and control of food safety hazards. Audits identify program defects, verify that systems are in place, and are a starting place for corrective actions. Audits and inspections include monthly food safety self-inspections, pest control inspections, post-cleaning inspections, GMP inspections, third-party food safety and sanitation audits, and supplier approval audits.

The starting point for an inspection or audit should be a standard, guideline, or standard operating procedure that defines expectations for the area, system, or equipment under review. For example, company GMP and personal hygiene rules for employees outline requirements that will be evaluated during the plant floor GMP inspection.

Results of audits and inspections should always be documented. Upon completion of the review, results should be recapped with the appropriate personnel or workgroup. Opportunities and defects should be prioritized for corrective actions.

In some cases, a score or measure may be developed from an audit. This measure of program effectiveness should be communicated to all personnel, from line workers to executive management, to facilitate corrective actions, to acquire needed resources, and to identify progress made in food safety and sanitation programs.

Best practices and new technologies in auditing and inspection include the use of personal digital assistants and handheld computers for plant inspections, and the use of food safety teams for management of self-inspections and corrective actions.

REFERENCES

1. U.S. Food and Drug Administration, *Current Good Manufacturing Practice in Manufacturing, Packing, or Holding Human Food* (Title 21 Code of Federal Regulations Part 110, 1986).
2. U.S. Food and Drug Administration, *Procedures for the Safe and Sanitary Processing and Importing of Fish and Fishery Products* (Seafood HACCP Regulation) (Title 21 Code of Federal Regulations Part 123, 1995).
3. U.S. Department of Agriculture, *Hazard Analysis and Critical Control Point (HACCP) Systems* (Meat and Poultry HACCP Regulation) (Title 9 Code of Federal Regulations Parts 416 and 417, 1996).
4. U.S. Food and Drug Administration, *Guidance for Industry: Guide to Minimize Microbial Food Safety Hazards for Fresh Fruits and Vegetables* (Washington, DC: Center for Food Safety and Applied Nutrition, 1998).
5. AIB International, *AIB Consolidated Standards for Food Safety* (Manhattan, KS: AIB International, 1995).
6. AIB International, "HACCP Overview," In *HACCP Workshop* (Manhattan, KS: 2000).
7. W. H. Sperber, et al., "The Role of Prerequisite Programs in Managing a HACCP System," In *Dairy, Food, and Environmental Sanitation* 18, no. 7 (1998): 418–423.

8. U.S. National Advisory Committee on Microbiological Criteria for Foods (NACMCF), *Hazard Analysis and Critical Control Point Principles and Application Guidelines, Appendix A* (Washington, DC: U.S. Food and Drug Adminstration, 14 August 1997).

9. U.S. Food and Drug Administration, "Foods Adulteration Involving Hard or Sharp Foreign Objects," *FDA/ORA Compliance Guide*, Chapter 5, Subchapter 555, Section 555.425 (1999).

10. T. J. Imholte and T. Imholte-Tauscher, *Engineering for Food Safety*, Second ed. (Woodinville, WA: Technical Institute for Food Safety, 1999).

11. Baking Industry Sanitation Standards Committee (BISSC), *1998 Sanitation Standards for the Design and Construction of Bakery Equipment* (Chicago: BISSC, 1998).

12. European Committee for Standardization, *Food Processing Machinery—Basic Concepts—Part 2: Hygiene Requirements,* (British Standard EN 1672-2: 1997, Subcommittee MCE/3/5, Food Industry Machines. English version, 1997).

13

Meat and Poultry

PROCESSING CATEGORIES FOR MEAT AND POULTRY

In 1996 the United States Department of Agriculture's Food Safety and Inspection Service (USDA/FSIS) implemented the HACCP and *pathogen reduction final rule*. This rule requires all meat and poultry processors—with the exception of custom processors—to develop and implement working HACCP plans for their products. Companies are also required to develop written sanitation standard operating procedures (SSOPs) and generic *E. coli* testing programs for specific products. In addition, FSIS mandates that companies satisfy *Salmonella* testing standards set forth for various meat and poultry products.

In the final rule, FSIS also specifies certain basic requirements that meat and poultry plants must include in their HACCP plans. For example, the plans must (1) address the seven principles of HACCP, (2) identify the intended consumers of the products, and (3) flow diagram the product process. In addition, any employee who develops, modifies, or reassesses a company's HACCP plans must successfully complete a course of instruction in the application of the seven HACCP principles. This training must include sections on the development of a HACCP plan for the specific product and record review.

When developing HACCP plans for meat and poultry products, companies should first group similar products together. Examining the approved labels of the products and categorizing products according to ingredients and processing parameters (such as raw, heat-treated, ready-to-eat, and so on) normally is the easiest way to do this. FSIS requires each HACCP plan to place meat and poultry products into one of nine processing categories:

1. Slaughter—all species

2. Raw product—ground

3. Raw product—not ground (for example, meat cuts, whole or cut-up birds)

4. Thermally processed—commercially sterile (such as canned soup)

5. Not heat treated—shelf stable (such as jerky)

6. Heat treated—shelf stable (such as edible fats)

7. Fully cooked—not shelf stable (such as ham)

8. Heat treated but not fully cooked—not shelf stable (such as char-marked beef patties)

9. Product with secondary inhibitors—not shelf stable (such as fermented sausage)

Plants may develop a single HACCP plan for one processing category to cover multiple products provided that the food safety hazards, critical control points, critical limits, and processing procedures are similar. For example, a company may produce various types of hot dogs (all beef, beef and pork, and so on) under the same HACCP plan. However, a deviation in a CCP for one product may adversely affect other products under the same HACCP plan. If monitoring determines that the internal cooking temperature of the all-beef hot dogs was less than the required critical limit, other types of hot dogs produced might also be suspect.

Similarly, companies may develop a single HACCP plan to encompass more than one processing category. For example, a plant may slaughter and fabricate whole muscle cuts. Therefore, it might be more efficient to have one HACCP plan covering both processing categories ("slaughter—all species" and "raw product—not ground").

HACCP PLAN DEVELOPMENT

As discussed in chapter 2, certain preliminary tasks must be completed before the HACCP principles are applied to specific products or processes. Once the HACCP team has been assembled, meat and poultry processing plants should determine the possible number of HACCP plans to develop by dividing their products into the nine process categories. After the consumers and their intended use of the food have been identified, a detailed process flow diagram should be developed. All processing steps directly under the control of the company should be included, along with steps occurring before and after the processing stage. All ingredients and packaging material associated with the product from receiving to processing to distribution should be included in the flow diagram.

The receiving step should be detailed enough to distinguish between the receiving of dry ingredients, packaging materials, and perishable meat and non-meat items. In meat and poultry operations, a flow diagram should not just have a process step called "receiving of meat and/or poultry." It is more beneficial to break down this step into three categories: (1) receiving of refrigerated raw meat and/or poultry; (2) receiving of frozen raw meat and/or poultry; and (3) receiving of cooked meat and/or poultry (refrigerated or frozen). Potential hazards associated with the different processing categories during the receiving step are more efficiently addressed in this manner.

Once items are received they often are stored for a period of time. Meat and poultry products are frequently tempered; that is, product temperature is adjusted from a storage temperature to a processing temperature prior to the start of production. Therefore storage of all ingredients along with packaging and any tempering steps should be included in the flow diagram.

Movement of product from one processing area to another is also a critical detail in a flow diagram. An example of product movement would be opening boxed beef, portioning beef in one room, and then moving the portioned beef to another room for final packaging. A company may decide to address the potential hazards and CCPs due to movement of product in various ways. For example, if rooms in a plant are on diffeent refrigeration units, a CCP may be implemented that measures either the room or product temperature for each room.

In slaughter operations, movement of carcasses into hot coolers, aging coolers, and fabrication should be addressed along with the processing steps of edible by-products. The flow diagram for slaughter operations should specify where the process for slaughter ends if the operation also fabricates carcasses and includes grind operations. One approach may be to end the process after carcasses are chilled in the cooler for a specific period of time, or removed for fabrication.

In grinding and sausage operations, the first (coarse) and second (fine) grindings should be steps in the flow diagram along with other equipment/processes such as patty machines, choppers, emulsifiers, and stuffers. Each of these steps can potentially increase the temperature of the meat and/or poultry products and may be the best places for CCPs since further processing may increase the temperature of the final product to unacceptable levels.

As the final preliminary task in HACCP development, the flow diagram should be verified through observation of the processing steps in the plant environment. At this time additions or corrections to the process can be made. By developing a very detailed and accurate process flow diagram, the company will be better equipped to apply the seven principles of HACCP, beginning with the hazard analysis and identification of potential CCPs.

Hazard Analysis

FSIS requires that companies conduct a hazard analysis to determine potential food safety hazards that are reasonably likely to occur in the production process. This includes food safety hazards that can occur before, during, and after entry into the company's processing operations. Preventive measures for controlling the identified food safety hazards must also be determined. In reviewing a company's hazard analysis,

FSIS checks that the food safety hazards are identified, that preventive measures are listed, and that this information is in the hazard analysis section of each HACCP plan.

To determine the potential food safety hazards and possible preventive measures, the following three questions can be asked for each processing step in the flow diagram.

1. What are the potential biological, chemical, and physical hazards? In meat and poultry operations biological hazards include pathogens such as *Salmonella* spp., *Escherichia coli* O157:H7, *Listeria monocytogenes*, and *Campylobacter jejuni*. Chemical hazards include cleaners, sanitizers, lubricants, and products containing restricted ingredients such as nitrite. Buckshot, BBs, plastic, needles, metal fragments, and bone chips are physical hazards frequently associated with meat and poultry products.

A common tendency when listing potential hazards is to write "unclean equipment," "cross-contamination," "improper cooking temperature," or "excess sanitizer residue." These problems may cause biological or chemical hazards, but are not the actual hazards. At a minimum, a company should list pathogens (biological hazards), foreign objects (physical hazards), and cleaners and sanitizers (chemical hazards) that could come in contact with products. This list should be updated as new hazards are identified.

2. Are these potential hazards significant enough and likely enough to occur that they should be addressed in the HACCP plan? Once the hazards are listed, the questions of whether the risk associated with a particular hazard is significant and whether that hazard is likely enough to occur that it should be included in the HACCP plan need to be answered. Hazards that have a low incidence rate, low likelihood of occurrence, or that are controlled by an effective preventive measure at a later processing step are not normally associated with HACCP plans. In addition, if the hazard is controlled by a prerequisite program such as an SSOP or a company standard operation procedure it usually will not be included in the HACCP plan.

3. What information/method has been used to justify the decision concerning significance of a particular hazard? In slaughter operations, antibiotics and hormones are chemical hazards associated with the processing step of receiving live animals. A company may justify that this is a low incidence hazard because of USDA/FSIS or state monitoring programs. Another justification may be that the company purchases animals from a limited number of suppliers requiring a form signed by the producers to assure appropriate drug use and withdrawal times.

In processed meat and poultry operations, receiving of raw refrigerated products is a safety concern, especially if the company processes ground products. Even if the company is buying meat and poultry from another plant operating under HACCP, temperature abuse could occur during transportation. Some operations may believe that the likely occurrence of temperature abuse is low and they have monitoring devices to record temperatures while product is in transport. Others may maintain that monitoring temperatures during receiving is a preventive measure for ensuring temperature control to prevent growth of pathogens to unacceptable levels.

In ready-to-eat meat and poultry operations, a common justification during processing steps such as grinding and stuffing is that thermal processing occurs at a later step in the process. A potential biological hazard during packaging of ready-to-eat meat and poultry products is *Listeria monocytogenes* contamination from equipment. An effective SSOP program and plant program addressing personal hygiene (listed as preventive measures) or a cooking step after packaging and before consumption may be used as reasons for not addressing this biological hazard in the HACCP plan, provided the label clearly says "cook before consuming product."

In meat and poultry operations, SSOPs may be used to control chemical hazards from excess residue of cleaners, sanitizers, or biological hazards from unclean equipment. Effective company programs for sanitation, personal hygiene, receiving and storage of perishable items, and pest and rodent control may be used to address specific biological, chemical, and physical hazards. These prerequisite programs then reduce the number of possible CCPs in a HACCP plan. However, companies must ensure that these programs are effective and being maintained on a routine basis.

Critical Control Points

Once the hazard analysis has been conducted, companies must determine the CCPs for each HACCP plan. According to FSIS, all meat or poultry processes will encounter one or more food safety hazards that are deemed significant and that must be addressed in the HACCP plan. Therefore, a HACCP plan must contain at least one CCP.

In the HACCP plan, any processing step that is a significant source of hazards should be considered as a possible CCP. A CCP is any point or step where a food safety hazard can be prevented, eliminated, or reduced to acceptable levels.[1] For instance, in fabrication and grinding operations, controlling the temperature of raw product during processing only prevents pathogens from increasing to unacceptable levels. In contrast, fermentation or acidification reduces, but does not eliminate, pathogens. A thermal processing step, on the other hand, does eliminate pathogens to an acceptable level.

In slaughter operations, FSIS requires plants to have a CCP addressing "zero tolerance" of fecal contamination. The primary mode of removing contamination must first be knife trimming. Acid sprays, hot water sprays, steam vacuuming, and steam pasteurization are often used as additional methods for reducing pathogens that may be associated with fecal contamination. Plants utilizing these processes may develop a CCP that monitors the temperature of the steam or water, or the pH of the acid spray.

Critical Limits

Once a CCP has been identified a critical limit should be set to determine whether a CCP is in or out of control. Exceeding critical limits may indicate that a direct health hazard exists, a direct health hazard could develop, or that product was produced in an environment where direct health hazards may have been present. In meat and poultry operations, FSIS has many specified time and/or temperature requirements for products such as precooked ground beef, roast beef, and ham. In addition, pH and moisture-to-protein ratios are defined by FSIS for specific products such as fermented sausages, jerky, and snack sticks. At a minimum these requirements must be used by companies to determine critical limits to be used in their HACCP plans. Published and reviewed research papers also provide information on effective processing parameters for controlling pathogens in meat and poultry products.

When setting critical limits, companies need to set values that are "greater than or equal to" or "less than or equal to" and avoid ranges. For instance, it is better to specify a final internal temperature for hot dogs of $\geq 165°F$ ($\geq 74°C$) than 165°F (74°C). If this were not done and the temperature measured were 166°F (75°C) then corrective action in regulatory terms would be required even though the product is considered to be safe. In addition, a company may decide to have a higher internal temperature than required by FSIS in order to extend shelf life. However, a company may decide not to use the higher temperature as a HACCP critical limit because the FSIS lower temperature ensures a safe product. Also, if the higher temperature is set as a critical limit in the HACCP plan then this temperature will become the FSIS regulatory limit.

Monitoring

FSIS requires that meat and poultry establishments define monitoring procedures for each CCP and specify the frequency with which the procedures will be performed. A series of five questions can assist in developing detailed monitoring procedures. The questions and an example of an appropriate response for each are listed below.

1. *What will be measured?* Internal temperature of ham.

2. *Where will the critical limit be measured?* In the center of the largest ham in the smokehouse.

3. *How will the critical limit be measured?* Using a calibrated smokehouse internal thermometer with a recording chart.

4. *Who will monitor the critical limit?* Smokehouse operator (use job titles, not names of specific individuals).

5. *How often will the critical limit be measured?* Every batch.

Continuous monitoring, such as using a thermometer with a recording chart, is preferred over interval monitoring. However, continuous monitoring is not always possible. For instance, a ground beef or fresh sausage processor may monitor a product's temperature after the first grind. Depending on a company's operations, frequencies to check internal product temperature may be every half hour, every batch, or four times a day. Once the interval is set it becomes a regulatory requirement. Therefore, companies must be capable of monitoring at the set frequencies. In addition, a company must realize that if the specified critical limit is not met, all products since the last check will be in question.

Corrective Action

If monitoring indicates a deviation, corrective actions are required to ensure product safety. FSIS requires the following four action points be addressed for every corrective action:

1. The cause of the deviation is identified and eliminated

2. The CCP will be under control after the corrective action is taken

3. Measures to prevent recurrence have been established

4. No product that is injurious to health or otherwise adulterated as a result of the deviation enters commerce

One simple approach to meeting regulatory HACCP requirements for corrective actions is to state, "the plant will adhere to regulation 417.3." Meat and poultry establishments may then have a separate record sheet with the above four corrective action points and will use this sheet for documenting all corrective actions.

Other processors may decide that it is better to have a formalized approach for correcting deviations because they want their employees to follow certain guidelines when a deviation occurs. Another series of questions similar to FSIS's questions may be used; these questions and some typical responses follow.

1. *What are some possible causes of deviations?* Equipment failure; human error.

2. *How could the process be corrected?* Cook for a longer period of time; place product on hold for further analysis.

3. *How will the product be handled/disposed of?* Send product to rendering; rework product; hold and release after test results are received.

4. *What measures could be implemented to prevent recurrence?* Develop a detailed maintenance program; retrain employee.

5. *Who is responsible for implementing the corrective action?* Plant manager; supervisor.

Verification

FSIS requires plants to list verification procedures and the frequency with which they will be performed. Examples of verification activities include calibration of monitoring instruments, observation of monitoring procedures, review of records, and microbiological testing. A slaughter operation may use data from their *E. coli* testing program as a verification procedure for control of fecal contamination. A jerky operation may routinely analyze protein and moisture content to ensure that the green weight loss used during monitoring achieves a specified moisture-to-protein ratio.

Calibration of equipment is an important verification procedure in all HACCP plans. Setting the interval for calibration is also important. If a company calibrates on a daily basis and determines the next morning that the thermometer was reading higher than normal values, then all product produced the day before could be in question.

Record Keeping

Record keeping is the essential component of HACCP. FSIS requires that records contain "the actual values and observations obtained during monitoring."[2] This includes actual times, temperatures, or other quantifiable values, the calibration of instruments, corrective actions, and verification results. All records are to be signed and dated and a product code or slaughter production lot should be defined. In addition, meat and poultry establishments must review all records prior to shipment of product.

Records for slaughter establishments and companies producing refrigerated meat and poultry products must be retained for at least one year, whereas records for frozen, preserved, or shelf-stable items require two years of retention. Processors may store records off-site after six months as long as they can be retrieved within 24 hours notice by FSIS.

Processors have the flexibility to develop their own record forms. Although a plant may have four different HACCP plans, one form may be used for corrective actions and another form for calibration of instruments. If room and product temperatures are CCPs for various HACCP plans then a temperature recording log could be developed. Some companies have automated chart recorders for items such as internal temperatures of smokehouse products, room temperatures, steam pasteurization units, and acid spray cabinets. The information obtained from the chart recorder is an acceptable record for FSIS requirements as long as the plant signs, dates, and identifies the production code.

When recording data, the record should have a place for a person's signature or initials. Initials are acceptable but a company should have a file identifying the person's initials. A signature stamp is not acceptable. The time, date, and actual value and/or observation should be recorded by the person monitoring the specified CCP. It is also helpful to have a simple monitoring procedure and the critical limits for various products on the record form.

Data should be entered at the time it is collected. Data should be recorded with a pen; if an entry error occurs, a single line should be drawn through it and the mistake initialed. Since the frequency required for monitoring may be every two hours, it is also important to record any downtimes during the production shift. There should be a place for the record reviewer's signature since preshipment review of records is required by FSIS.

REFERENCES

1. U.S. National Advisory Committee on Microbiological Criteria for Foods (NACMCF), *Hazard Analysis and Critical Control Point Principles and Application Guidelines* (Washington DC: U.S. Food and Drug Administration, 14 August 1997).
2. 21 CFR 123 (123.6) "Hazard Analysis and Critical Control Point (HACCP) Plans—Fish and Fishery Products." *U.S. Code of Federal Regulations* 21, Part 123.6 (Washington, DC: U.S. Government).

14

Seafood

DESCRIPTION OF THE SEAFOOD INDUSTRY

Seafood includes all products located in the deep ocean as well as those found in freshwater rivers, streams, lakes, and estuaries. It sometimes includes products such as frog legs and alligator, depending on the jurisdiction of the agency involved. Seafood encompasses a large variety of species and product forms, making generalizations difficult. Many seafood products are cooked, some products are consumed raw, and, as in the case of oysters and clams, the flesh of the animal may even be consumed as a whole. However, even with all the variations, seafood safety issues fall into very easily defined and narrowly focused areas. The products of safety concern include: raw molluscan shellfish, species subject to the formation of histamine, cooked ready-to-eat products, and vacuum-packaged smoked fish.

Seafood is also unique in that it reacts in different ways than other meat products such as meat and poultry. First, since seafood is extremely sensitive to abuse, its quality and safety are easily compromised if handled improperly. Second, microbes associated with seafood can grow at a wide variety of temperatures, including refrigerated temperatures. Third, seafood struggle as they are caught, as often they are wild harvested. This struggling uses up the glycogen in their muscles with no corresponding drop in muscle pH. As a result, microbial growth is not discouraged. This makes it critical to control post-harvest product temperatures. Finally, the chemical composition of the fat in seafood is high in phospholipids, which break down into trimethylamine. This is the source of the "fishy" odor often associated with seafood. These fats are also highly unsaturated and are easily oxidized, resulting in additional off flavors. In general, seafood tends to deteriorate organoleptically before it becomes unsafe to eat.

SOURCES OF HAZARDS SPECIFIC TO SEAFOOD

The sources of hazards for seafood are varied and fall into three traditional categories: biological, chemical, and physical.

Biological Hazards—Bacteria

Campylobacter jejuni. Transmitted through contaminated raw clams, mussels and oysters, and contaminated water. The hazard can be controlled by thoroughly cooking seafood and by proper sanitation.

Clostridium botulinum. Found in the intestinal tracts of fish, and the gills and viscera of crabs and other shellfish. Type E is most common in fish and fishery products as it grows at temperatures as low as 38°F (3°C) and produces little evidence of spoilage. Proper thermal processes in canned seafoods, heavy salting or drying, or acidification are effective control measures.

Escherichia coli. Naturally found in the intestinal tracts of all animals. It is transferred to seafood through sewage, pollution, or by contamination after harvest through human handling. Control measures include heating sufficiently to kill the organism, holding chilled foods below 40°F (4°C), and preventing cross-contamination.

Listeria monocytogenes. Usually found through cross-contamination of cooked ready-to-eat foods by raw foods. Widespread in nature, it is controlled most effectively by good sanitation practices and thorough cooking of seafood products.

Salmonella spp. Found in the intestinal tracts of animals, but not in fish. It is typically transferred to seafood through sewage, pollution, or by contamination after harvest. The hazard can be prevented through sufficient heating, proper holding of chilled products, and prevention of cross-contamination.

Shigella spp. Naturally found in the intestinal tract of humans, it is transferred to seafood through sewage, pollution, or by contamination after harvest. The hazard can be controlled by a proper water supply and preventing ill employees from coming in contact with the food.

Staphylococcus aureus. Commonly found in the nose, throat, and hair of humans, this bacterium finds its way to the food through cross-contamination and through improper human contact with the food. Minimizing time/temperature abuse of the seafood and proper food handler hygiene are steps that can be taken to prevent the hazard.

Vibrio cholerae. Found in estuaries and brackish water, it tends to be more prevalent in the warmer months. The hazard can be prevented by thoroughly cooking the seafood and minimizing cross-contamination.

Vibrio parahaemolyticus. Naturally occurring in estuaries and coastal areas, is also more prevalent in the warmer months. The hazard can be controlled by thoroughly cooking the seafood and preventing cross-contamination.

Vibrio vulnificus. Requires salt for survival and is primarily found in the Gulf of Mexico. The hazard is more prevalent in the warmer months and can be prevented by thorough cooking of the shellfish and by preventing cross-contamination.

Yersinia enterocolitica. Naturally found in soil, water, and domesticated and wild animals. Sufficient heating, proper chilled holding, and prevention of cross-contamination are effective methods of preventing the hazard.

Biological Hazards—Viruses

Hepatitis A virus. Survives better at low temperatures and is killed at high temperatures. Raw and steamed clams, oysters, and mussels have been implicated with contamination of this virus. The hazard can be prevented by thoroughly cooking the product and prevention of cross-contamination. But since this virus seems to be more resistant to heat than other viruses, steaming mollusks only until the shells open typically will not inactivate the virus.

Norwalk virus. Considered a major cause of nonbacterial intestinal illness, it is associated with eating clams, oysters, and cockles. The hazard can be prevented by thorough cooking of the seafood and preventing cross-contamination.

Biological Hazards—Parasites

Anisakis simplex. A parasitic nematode, it is found in undercooked or raw (sushi, sashimi) fish. Parasites are only a hazard if the fish is to be consumed raw. Specific freezing processes will kill the parasite.

Pseudoterranova decipiens. Also called codworm, it is a nematode found in raw or undercooked fish. Control is the same as for *Anisakis simplex.*

Diphyllobothrium latum. A tapeworm that primarily infects freshwater fish, and is also found in salmon. Found in raw or uncooked fish, the control is as discussed above.

Chemical Hazards—Marine Biotoxins

Amnesic shellfish poisoning (ASP), diarrhetic shellfish poisoning (DSP), neurotoxic shellfish poisoning (NSP), and paralytic shellfish poisoning (PSP) have been associated in different waters with molluscan shellfish and at times small species such as herring, anchovies, and crustaceans such as crabs. The control method is typically closing and monitoring of the harvest waters, as these hazards cannot be removed from the product once present.

Ciguatera Fish Poisoning (CFP). Found in some species of tropical and subtropical fish such as red snapper. Again, the control mechanism is careful monitoring of the catch, utilizing local knowledge of the harvest area, or closing the waters.

Scombroid Toxin (Histamine). The hazard is caused by eating certain species of fin fish—including tuna, mahi-mahi, bluefish, sardines, amberjack, and mackerel—that have gone through spoilage by certain types of bacteria. The toxin is not eliminated by cooking or canning, and is typically controlled through proper chilling from harvest to process, utilizing a detailed knowledge of the temperature history.

Tetrodotoxin. A potent toxin associated with puffer fish. These fish cannot be imported into the U. S. without authorization. In other countries, such as Japan, certification of chefs preparing the fish is required.

Other chemical contaminants include aquaculture drugs, chemical contaminants (pesticides, herbicides, and so on), and food additives such as bisulfites in shrimp. These contaminants are controlled either by proper withdrawal times, as in aquaculture drugs, periodic testing and approved suppliers, as in pesticides, and monitoring and testing as in bisulfites.

Physical Hazards

Metal fragments, glass, wood, plastic, and so forth, find their way into seafood products from time to time, especially breaded fish portions, fish sticks, and breaded shrimp. Metal is the only physical hazard that is easily detected—through the use of metal detectors inline or after packaging.

HACCP REGULATIONS IN THE UNITED STATES

The U. S. Food and Drug Administration (FDA) is the primary federal agency responsible for the safety of seafood in the United States. Through the Food, Drug, and Cosmetic Act, the FDA has the responsibility to ensure that all domestic and imported seafood products are safe, wholesome, and properly labeled. In December 1997, the FDA published its final Seafood HACCP Rule, 21 CFR Part 123, defining the HACCP and sanitation requirements of seafood facilities.

The FDA has developed a highly prescriptive HACCP program for the seafood industry. The Seafood HACCP regulations require prerequisite programs. These programs must comply with: GMPs (21 CFR 110), sanitation standard operating procedures (SSOPs), monitoring and record keeping for eight areas of sanitation, and a documented HACCP plan. The FDA has identified potential hazards and critical control limits in the *Fish and Fishery Products Hazards and Controls Guide.*

The FDA may work with state regulatory agencies to ensure implementation of federal regulations. For example, in California, the FDA and the State of California Department of Health Services' Food and Drug Branch (CDHS-FDB) share jurisdiction and regulatory oversight of all seafood manufacturers and distributors. Both conduct HACCP training sessions to the industry and are standardized to a federal uniform regulatory approach. In California, the FDA and CDHA-FDB have trained more than 1,000 individuals in HACCP since 1997. Through a partnership program these agencies develop a shared work plan, have a common enforcement strategy, and conduct yearly regulatory inspections. In some instances, CDHS-FDB may exert more restrictive enforcement actions through its embargo powers. For example, a deficiency in HACCP may lead to the determination that food products are adulterated. An embargo may take place if appropriate and may be mandated in situations where illnesses have been caused by the lack of HACCP plans, lack of GMPs, or lack of SOPs. Both agencies use a proactive approach in training and education, and a reactive approach in regulatory actions to provide an effective safety net to consumers in California.

The FDA regulations require that the person developing the plan is knowledgeable and trained in the principles of HACCP. This can be done by completing a HACCP course with a curriculum that is recognized as adequate by the FDA, or through HACCP-relevant job experience.

During the initial implementation of the HACCP program in the seafood industry the FDA identified a number of problems, including the following, during inspections:

- The corrective action process did not meet the regulatory requirements, usually because (1) it did not adequately prevent adulterated product from entering the market, or (2) it did not correct the root cause of the deviation.

- The HACCP plan did not adequately distinguish who was responsible for the control of specific hazards. For example, some hazards are controlled by the companies that harvest seafood, while other hazards are controlled by the companies responsible for further processing of the seafood.

- The HACCP plan did not list specific control parameters, for example, the time and temperature parameters that must be met to prevent a food safety hazard.

- Weak linkages existed between the critical limits and monitoring procedures. For example, measuring and recording a cooler temperature is not an adequate method for monitoring product temperature unless a validation study has been conducted under a worst case scenario.

- Critical limits were set without being scientifically supported. One source of critical limits is the FDA's *Fish and Fishery Products Hazards and Controls Guide.*

In response to these problems, the FDA has developed a training program entitled "Seafood HACCP Encore Course" to help seafood processors improve their HACCP programs. This program is designed for seafood processors who have received "untitled letters" or "warning letters" from the FDA due to the inadequacy of their HACCP programs.

The National Marine Fisheries Service (NMFS) operates the National Oceanic and Atmospheric Administration Seafood Inspection Program (NOAA SIP). Through the Agricultural Marketing Act, NMFS operates this voluntary, fee-for-service inspection program. Typical services include sanitation evaluation of facilities, product inspection and certification, and reduced inspection programs such as the HACCP Quality Management Program (HACCP QMP), where a firm's adherence to the principles of HACCP and ISO 9001 are audited using internationally recognized auditing practices.

In July 1992, the NOAA SIP published a Federal Register notice announcing the availability of a new seafood inspection program based on hazard analysis critical control point (HACCP) principles. This program was an enhancement to the Integrated Quality Assurance (IQA) Program that also uses HACCP principles. Under the quality management program, the company takes on the responsibility of documenting and implementing a quality system. The NOAA SIP ensures that the quality system in place is adequate to control the processes through regular audits of the system. The HACCP Quality Management Program allows participants to apply their existing quality systems more efficiently; receive the management benefits of consistently producing safe, wholesome, and properly labeled products; and obtain the benefits of using the U.S. Department of Commerce (USDC) marketing logo associated with the program. NOAA believes that the HACCP-based service will enhance the safety, wholesomeness, economic integrity, and quality of seafood available to consumers, as well as improve seafood industry quality assurance and regulatory oversight.

Other federal agencies with jurisdiction over seafood include the U.S. Customs Service, the U.S. Environmental Protection Agency (EPA), and the U.S. Department of Agriculture (USDA). Each has some regulations associated with the labeling of seafood or the tolerances of pesticides, and so on. However, these agencies do not have specific programs designed to assure safe, wholesome, and properly labeled seafood.

Many seafood plant inspections are performed by state and local agencies that determine the compliance of the firm to both federal and state regulations. Many of these jurisdictions structure their programs to be similar to the FDA requirements and many perform these inspections at the request of the FDA.

APPLIED HACCP VERSUS QUALITY

By far the biggest controversy in seafood HACCP has been the debate over the use of quality programs to aid or oversee HACCP systems in facilities. However, many firms consider the use of HACCP systems in harmony with quality systems the best approach with regard to seafood, as seafood is generally a safe product to eat. This concept is also outlined in the Codex Alimentarius Commission HACCP Guidelines, where critical control points (CCPs) and critical limits are associated with HACCP and food safety, while defective action points (DAPs) and control limits are associated with quality and regulatory defects in the product. The development of prerequisite programs, management commitment, and employee education and training in HACCP principles are some of the factors that contribute to the success of a HACCP program.

Prerequisite Programs

For HACCP to function effectively, it must be performed in conjunction with prerequisite programs that provide a foundation of compliance for the firm. These prerequisite programs include: good manufacturing practices (GMPs) and acceptable sanitation standard operating procedures (SSOPs). The GMPs (21 CFR Part 110) are broad in focus and define measures of general hygiene along with measures the firm should take to prevent food adulteration due to unsanitary conditions. SSOPs are procedures used by the firm to define how they will accomplish adherence to the GMPs. As required by 21 CFR Part 123, the SSOPs should be written and be monitored. Some companies integrate them to become part of the firm's quality program. GMPs and SSOPs affect the overall processing environment and therefore do not lend themselves readily to a specific critical control point. Therefore, they work best in a procedural form with directions for the implementation, monitoring, and corrective action of plant and food hygiene concerns. In fact, well-defined and well-monitored SSOPs can reduce the identification and number of CCPs by controlling, for example, cross-contamination and chemical contamination. Strong SSOPs make the HACCP system more effective by allowing the system to truly concentrate on the food safety aspects of the manufacturing *process* rather than on the processing plant environment. By far, the most common reason for the failure of a HACCP system in a seafood facility is related to sanitation. The most common sanitation failure is due to employee practice. These points should be considered when auditing any seafood HACCP system.

Management Commitment

For any quality or safety system, including a HACCP plan, to work, the support of top company officials is essential. Without this support, HACCP will not become a company priority or be effectively implemented. In fact, this is noted as a common root cause for the failure of many HACCP systems in seafood facilities.

HACCP Training

Education and training are important elements in developing and implementing a HACCP program. Employees who will be responsible for the HACCP program must be adequately trained in its principles. It is also required that certain elements of the HACCP plan and its implementation be performed by properly trained personnel. Skipping this step violates the HACCP seafood regulation, and will lead the firm down a very short path to a failed audit.

HACCP AND ECONOMIC INTEGRITY

Along with product quality, economic integrity is the key to successful marketing of seafood. Quality and integrity are what buyers and consumers want. Consumers often have a limited knowledge and understanding of fish and seafood products. Consequently, their greatest concern and challenge is to purchase products that are wholesome and that have acceptable sensory appeal (such as taste, odor, texture, flavor, and appearance).

Economic integrity means that the product adheres to codes, standards, or specifications set by the producer, buyer, or regulators. In other words, the product is what it appears or is supposed to be. Certain economic integrity issues, such as species and product identity, country of origin, and short weight (net weight) are regulated by local, state, or the federal government. However, with dwindling resources, current enforcement strategies tend to place a low priority on these issues relative to food safety. Lapses in enforcement create a consumer risk of receiving mislabeled, over-breaded, overglazed, short weight, or possibly unsafe products. Such lapses are often noted by consumer groups, the media, and the seafood industry. Companies have a legal and moral obligation to provide products of high economic integrity to the buyer and consumer.

15

Dairy

SAFETY REGULATIONS IN THE DAIRY INDUSTRY

Dairy products have been an important element in human food since animals were first domesticated.[1] Originally "manufactured" within the home or on the farm, dairy products are now manufactured in small- or large-scale plants where the main goal is the production of safe, high-quality products. The food safety process for fluid milk is monitored by state and federal regulatory agencies. With less than five percent of reported food borne diseases originating from contaminated dairy products, the U.S. dairy industry has an excellent safety record—especially when the volume of dairy products manufactured is considered.[2] This record has been achieved through the efforts and actions of the National Conference on Interstate Milk Shipments (NCIMS), which has allowed the development of very prescriptive regulations for the production of Grade A milk products. Currently, the NCIMS has started an initiative to implement a voluntary HACCP program. This increasing effort to make HACCP a standard practice within the dairy industry is due to anticipation that HACCP will eventually be a mandated food safety system for the industry.[3]

Pasteurized fluid milk is a product with a very short shelf life. Federal regulations require that all milk receive a heat-treatment step (pasteurization) designed to kill all vegetative pathogenic microorganisms. If a fluid milk product is packaged under anaerobic conditions, the potential for *Clostridium botulinium* growth must be controlled either through a sterilization step that renders the product commercially sterile, or by reducing the A_w to less than 0.85.

It is imperative that dairy producers have strict controls over prerequisite programs to ensure both product safety and product quality. For example, many dairy products,

161

such as yogurt, buttermilk, and cheese, are produced using microbial cultures. The presence of therapeutic drugs may inhibit the growth of these starter cultures. Therefore, antibiotic residues must be carefully controlled for product quality reasons as well as for product safety reasons.

The process for ensuring safety is outlined here. Milk is usually received via tanker trucks and unloaded. Each tanker is checked for proper temperature and the presence of therapeutic drug residues. The temperature of the milk should be less than 45°F (7°C) and it should be held for no more than 72 hours before processing. The milk is then filtered and stored in tanks or silos. When needed, the milk is separated; the raw cream is stored or shipped elsewhere for other uses, and the remaining milk is pasteurized. The raw cream temperature should also be less than 45°F (7°C) and it should be held for no more than 72 hours. The cream is added back to the raw milk prior to homogenization and pasteurization to adjust the fat content of the milk. Vitamins may be added at the proper concentrations either before or after pasteurization. The pasteurized milk goes into a storage tank from which it is packaged, refrigerated, and placed into distribution.

TYPES OF HAZARDS

Biological, chemical, and physical contamination of dairy products is a major industry concern. Biological hazards include *Brucella, Cl. botulinum, Listeria monocytogenes, Salmonella, Escherichia coli* O157:H7, *Yersinia entercolitica, Campylobacter jejuni, Staphyloccus aureus,* natural toxins, and parasites. Chemical hazards include food additives, allergens, and unintentionally added chemicals. Potential physical hazards include metal, glass, insects, wood, plastic, and personal effects. Appendix A contains a more complete list of recognized food hazards.

Formulated dairy products such as cheese, ice cream, and yogurt may be prone to potential hazards. This can be attributed to several factors, including: (1) formulated dairy products may require extensive handling in vats, batch tanks, fruit feeders, and other equipment which potentially expose the product to the environment; (2) ingredients are often added to the milk base after the milk has been pasteurized; and (3) the final, formulated dairy product mix usually does not receive a terminal heat treatment step.

CONTROLLING RISKS THROUGH PREREQUISITE PROGRAMS

As in other food processing areas, the establishment of effective prerequisite programs will simplify any HACCP plan for the dairy industry. These guidelines assist in the day-to-day operation of a dairy plant and help ensure the manufacture of safe dairy products. Prerequisite programs may be used to reduce the likelihood of a potential hazard. If the potential hazard is reduced to the extent that it is *not* likely to occur, then a CCP is not necessary to control that specific potential hazard. However, the company needs to ensure that the prerequisite program is properly designed, operated, and maintained. This is done through inspecting, checking, and documenting the program. Questions that can be asked to ensure that the prerequisite program is operating properly include:

- Who is performing the prerequisite program?

- How were these operators trained?

- What are the specific processes used for the program?

- Where is the program being applied?

- When is the program being conducted?

- How can it be confirmed that the program is being carried out in an effective manner?

Areas covered by prerequisites may include: supplier control programs; receiving/storage programs; premises, equipment performance and maintenance programs; cleaning and sanitization of equipment and facilities; recall programs; allergen control programs; and personnel training programs. A brief overview of each of these areas as they pertain to the dairy industry follows.

Supplier Control Program

The dairy processor needs to ensure that dairy products are safe and wholesome. Milk must come from approved sources. During the formulation of a dairy product, hazards are most likely to be introduced while ingredients are being added. These ingredients may be added to a mix that contains pasteurized milk; however, the final mix may not receive a terminal pasteurization step. Therefore, these ingredients have the potential for being carriers of hazards. To reduce the potential for a food safety problem, plants may choose to purchase only from suppliers who have implemented a HACCP program.

Some companies develop control programs in partnership with suppliers to ensure understanding of and compliance with specifications. Supplier specifications and guarantees should be periodically verified. For example, periodic analyses should be run on incoming ingredients to ensure they meet specifications. Observations of the production area personnel using these ingredients should be documented.

Receiving/Storage Program

Dairy plants should have steps in place to prevent the occurrence of any product contamination. A program should be in place for storing finished product, as well as for inspecting trucks used for the shipping and receiving of products. The Code of Federal Regulations (21 CFR 110) requires inspection of incoming ingredients and packaging material.

Premises, Equipment Performance, and Maintenance Program

Dairy processing plants need to be designed in a manner that prevents any cross-contamination of product from occurring. Issues to be addressed include: proper ventilation, appropriate lighting, and adequate and accessible hand washing stations.

Plants need a written preventive maintenance program. One critical aspect is ensuring that equipment used for pasteurization or sterilization steps is operating properly and is controlled to ensure the manufacture of a safe product.

Cleaning and Sanitation Program

The plant must have a pest control program and master cleaning and sanitation program in place. Sanitation should not have any negative impact on the safety of the product being manufactured. A well-designed and operated program should reduce the likelihood of occurrence of environmental chemical and biological contaminants.

Recall Program

A recall program can be divided into three parts: traceability, recall system, and the recall initiation. A mock recall should be performed annually and a product coding system should be in place for ease of traceability.

Allergen Control Program

The plant must identify any ingredients that may contain an allergen. A written allergen-handling program should detail the control of allergens in the plant. The plant needs to work in conjunction with suppliers to determine which ingredients contain potential allergens. Allergen-containing products should be scheduled to run last on the production line to avoid cross-contamination, or sufficient time should be allowed for an allergen cleanup prior to the manufacture of a non-allergen-containing product. Some plants may treat allergens as chemical hazards in their HACCP plan.

Personnel Training Program

Documented training should occur for product handling and personal hygiene for all employees. Employee and visitor access should be controlled to avoid/prevent cross-contamination. Employees should be trained and encouraged to inform management of problems that may impact product safety.

Chapter 12 provides more detailed information about these prerequisite areas, and others, in general. As the food safety principles at the core of HACCP are applied throughout the dairy industry, the safety of an already safe product will only continue to increase.

REFERENCES

1. M. Smukowski and N. Brisk, "Dairy Products Industry," In *Encyclopaedia of Occupational Health and Safety, Vol. 3*, Fourth ed. (Geneva: International Labor Office, 1997).
2. E. C. Johnson, J. H. Nelson, and M. Johnson, "Microbiological Safety of Cheese Made from Heat-Treated Milk," *Journal of Food Protection* 53 (1990): 441–52, 519–40, 610–23.
3. Brian W. Gould, Marianne Smukowski, and J. Russell Bishop, "HACCP and the Dairy Industry: An Overview of HACCP Costs and Benefits," in *The Economics of HACCP*, L. J. Unnivehr, ed. (St. Paul, MN: Eagan Press, 2000).

16

Fruits and Vegetables

DEFINING GAPs AND GMPs

Fresh fruits and vegetables are highly perishable and, in general, their quality cannot be significantly improved after harvest. Thus, managers of fresh produce operations should focus on quality maintenance through appropriate implementation of proper production and handling practices. Since food safety hazards associated with fresh produce are difficult to correct through remedial action, prevention of hazard occurrence should be a high priority for managers. A case study of the application of HACCP principles to a fresh market tomato handling operation appears on page 173 of this chapter.

The current body of food safety literature for fresh produce makes frequent reference to the proper implementation of good agricultural practices (GAPs). However, a close examination of the literature reveals that GAP is a nebulous term that refers as much to the use of common sense as it does to science-based management protocols. No single document serves as an adequate GAP reference for all of the procedures involved in the production and handling of fresh fruits and vegetables. Recently the U.S. Food and Drug Administration (FDA) released a "guidance" document that addresses GAP implementation for reduction of microbial contamination.[1] However, the information presented is general, and the burden of identifying appropriate, effective management practices remains the responsibility of managers.

In contrast, good manufacturing practices (GMPs) are much more clearly defined in the Code of Federal Regulations.[2] Guidelines are provided for personnel, building and facilities, equipment and utensils, and production processes. GMPs as they relate to prerequisite programs in the food industry were discussed in detail in chapter 12.

HAZARDS ASSOCIATED WITH HANDLING FRESH PRODUCE

As in other areas of the food industry, potential hazards in the processing of produce can be divided into three categories: biological, chemical, and physical.

Biological

Microbial contamination (with human pathogens) has surpassed pesticide residues as the primary consumer food safety concern. Fresh fruits and vegetables differ from processed foods in that the handling of fresh produce does not entail a "kill step," such as sterilization, that renders a product commercially sterile. The consequence is that prevention of microbial hazard occurrence, as opposed to remedial treatments to eliminate hazards, is crucial during handling.[3]

Chemical

Historically, chemical (pesticide) residues represented the most significant food safety concern in consumer surveys. Agrichemical use is subject to EPA regulation with oversight (testing) by the FDA. This includes preharvest application of pesticides (fungicides, insecticides, and herbicides) as well as postharvest application of waxes, coatings, fungicides, or biocontrol agents used to prevent decay. Proper use of any agrichemical is a GAP and would not be considered a CCP in a HACCP program. Failure to meet residue tolerance will result in outright rejection of the product by regulatory authorities. In the fresh-cut industry, chemical use may include sanitizers, such as chlorine compounds, and antioxidants. Use of sanitizers generally is considered a CCP.

Physical

Physical hazards generally are not a concern for whole fruits and vegetables, where the most common types of foreign materials in a package are soil, leaves, or a piece of a broken container—all of which are precluded by GAPs. The detection of physical hazards is, however, important in the fresh-cut, minimally-processed industry, where pieces of cutting or packaging equipment can inadvertently be left in the product. Closing machines that employ wire staples or similar materials can cause problems. For example, metal package closures in fresh-cut cabbage used for coleslaw have resulted in broken teeth. X-ray analysis of packaged goods is an effective method of detection of metallic physical hazards and should be a CCP in fresh-cut processing with zero tolerance for the presence of such a hazard.

SIGNIFICANCE OF GAPs, GMPs, AND HACCP FOR THE AUDITOR

Prior to attempting to apply HACCP principles to fresh produce production and handling operations, an auditor should determine if the facilities and practices meet the minimum criteria for good agricultural practices (GAPs) and good manufacturing practices (GMPs). A systems approach, for example, a step-by-step evaluation of the production and handling system, is the proper approach for identifying potential problem areas.

Criteria addressed by GAPs or GMPs should not necessarily be included as a part of a HACCP program. For example, utilization of contaminated water for overhead irrigation or for postharvest washing is not an acceptable GAP. Therefore it would not be necessary to consider this as a CCP for a HACCP program.

Since the quality auditor's objective is to ensure that the HACCP system results in the delivery of safe food to consumers, there is little utility in attempting to distinguish between the problems associated with violation of a GAP or GMP versus a CCP in a HACCP program for fresh produce. The auditor should be acquainted, at least generally, with the recognized, critical management steps in fresh produce operations. Zagory and Hurst and the FDA offer thorough treatment of potential hazards during the production and processing of fresh produce.[4] These items, summarized below, are the items upon which auditors should focus.

Production Site

Auditors should note if fields have had applications of animal manure or municipal biosolids as fertilizers. Both are potential sources of microbial hazards, and biosolids also may contain heavy metals or other chemical hazards. Either type of fertilizer may be used in accordance with known GAPs. Residual pesticides in the soil also are of concern. If it is suspected that such hazards exist, the auditor may request that appropriate testing be performed.

Pesticide Use

The U.S. Environmental Protection Agency (EPA) regulates the use of pesticides in the agricultural sector. Pesticide users are obligated to read the chemical label, act appropriately, and keep records of those actions. In the production of fresh produce this is a GAP. In the postharvest or processing sectors this is a GMP. Failure to use agrichemicals appropriately, regardless of whether unacceptable residues exist, can result in outright rejection of the product by the FDA. Auditors who suspect that pesticide use violations exist should request appropriate residue testing.

Water

Water of inadequate quality may be a direct source of chemical or microbial hazards, or it may serve as a vehicle for spreading localized contamination at any physical location within the production and handling environments. In many fresh produce operations, water quality management may be the only legitimate CCP in a HACCP program. All other management practices are likely to be GAPs or GMPs. Discussion of water generally is divided into the following two categories.

Agricultural Water. This category includes water used for irrigation, mixing and applying pesticides and fertilizers, cooling, and frost protection. When surface groundwater (for example, that from ponds, lakes, rivers, streams, and so on) is used for agricultural operations, testing on a regular basis is appropriate to ensure that hazards are not present. In some cases risks are easily identifiable (for example, use of pond water for overhead irrigation when livestock are feeding and drinking in proximity to the pond). In other cases the risk is not so obvious, as in the documented example of outbreaks of *Cyclospora*-related illness associated with the consumption of raspberries that were sprayed with pesticide mixed from contaminated river water. Producers should also test deep wells periodically for signs of microbial or chemical contamination.

Processing Water. Postharvest uses of water include dump tanks for transferring produce from field containers or transport vehicles to the packing line, washing, rinsing, application of waxes and fungicides, cooling, and transporting product in flumes. Management of the quality of this water is essential and should be regarded as a CCP in a HACCP program for any fresh produce handling operation. Numerous sanitation treatments are approved by the EPA, but some are commodity-specific. It is the responsibility of management to read product labels to determine if a product is suitable for the intended application. Examples of such treatments include, but may not be limited to, chlorine treatment (sodium hypochlorite, calcium hypochlorite, chlorine gas, and chlorine dioxide), ozone, UV light, peroxyacetic acid, and so on. Managers should keep records of water quality, treatments utilized, frequency of treatment, testing method employed, and so forth, and make these records available to auditors.

Field Sanitation

GAPs specify that equipment used in the field should be periodically sanitized and inspected frequently for indications of gross contamination with soil or organic matter. Examples of such equipment include: containers, such as bulk bins, baskets, buckets, or picking bags; transport vehicles, including gondolas, trucks, and trailers; harvesting tools, including hand tools as well as mechanical devices; and any other field equipment. One example of a problem area is bulk bins, which may be used during the harvest season, then stored for several months. During the storage period rodents or birds may nest in the bins. Since rodents or birds may carry disease organisms, good GAPs require that bins be sanitized prior to reuse. Auditors should request that records of sanitation activities be provided.

Sanitary Facilities in the Field

Most state health departments have some requirements for the placement of portable toilets in fields. Regulations vary and compliance with regulations is a challenge. The more accessible the facilities, the more likely they are to be used by workers. Few of the fresh fruit and vegetable industries provide hand-wash stations near portable toilets. The California strawberry industry has been very progressive in making such facilities available to workers. Disposal of waste from toilets also is of concern because the waste can splash directly onto the crop or can leach into groundwater. Auditors should become familiar with regulatory policy in their particular region prior to evaluation of field operations.

Sanitary Facilities in Packinghouses and Processing Plants

The employer's responsibility of providing basic sanitary facilities (restrooms) in packinghouses or processing plants is governed by a variety of state health and business regulations. Auditors' primary concerns are cleanliness of facilities; frequency of cleaning; the use of disinfectants during cleaning; and whether the facility is properly supplied with hot water, hand soap, a sanitary hand-drying device, and so on. One practice widely implemented by the fresh-market tomato industry has been the design of restrooms that allow for privacy without the need for a door. Hand washing stations are located just outside the restroom so that managers can monitor employees' hand washing practices.

Employee Health and Hygiene

Worker hygiene is a GMP and is governed by the U.S. Code of Federal Regulations.[5] Auditors should pay special attention to employees who have any injury or illness that poses a potential risk for contamination of product—in this case, fresh fruits or vegetables. An example of such an injury is an infected cut on the hand. Likewise, any infectious disease accompanied by diarrhea or open sores is a risk. Employers should have safety training programs that address these issues with employees. Any evidence of improper personal hygiene is a reason for an auditor to recommend that the employee be sent home to correct the situation.

Packing Facility Sanitation

Fresh fruits and vegetables typically arrive at the packing facility with at least some degree of contamination with soil and organic material. Further, field-workers who may have soil on their clothes or shoes often are assigned duties in the packinghouse for a portion of the day. As much of this contamination as possible should be excluded from the packing area. Facilities should be thoroughly cleaned at least on a daily basis. Pressure cleaning, preferably with hot water and an appropriate disinfectant, is recommended for packing line machinery, floors, and all other surfaces where possible.

Workers must wash their hands thoroughly before beginning their work cycle. The FDA's *Guide to Minimize Microbial Food Safety Hazards for Fresh Fruits and Vegetables* provides an excellent treatment of this topic.

Fresh-Cut Processing Facilities

Management of a fresh-cut operation is much more intensive than that required for a normal fruit and vegetable packing operation. Fresh-cut products, sometimes called minimally processed products, are more perishable, more susceptible to microbial contamination, and more likely to contain physical hazards. Raw material receiving, inspection, and pre-cleaning, and microbiological monitoring of product and environment—all of which are optional in a standard packing operation—are essential for a fresh-cut operation where HACCP is considered a requirement.[6] Details of HACCP development and auditing for fresh-cut operations are beyond the scope of this section. Auditors of fresh-cut operations must acquaint themselves with the body of literature available on the subject.

Storage and Ripening Facilities

In storage and ripening facilities the primary concerns for auditors are cleanliness of cooling coils, walls, floors, and product containers, as well as the frequent removal of decayed product. Workers or inspectors who enter these areas should meet the requirements for personal hygiene discussed previously.

Transport of Packed Product

Transport vehicles, primarily trailers, should be inspected for condition and cleanliness prior to loading. Records of materials transported in a specific trailer should be available to auditors. Some years ago, controversy erupted when it became known that garbage had been hauled in trailers that subsequently were used for transporting food. Trailers that have physical damage, or those with ineffective cooling systems, should be removed from service.

Retailers

GMPs that apply to packing operations should be applied to retail handlers as well. Of special importance is the personal hygiene of employees who stock fresh produce.

THIRD-PARTY VERIFICATION OF GAPs, GMPs, AND HAACP IMPLEMENTATION

Within the past year, some major supermarket chains have announced that they will not accept fresh fruits and vegetables from any company that does not have third-party (independent) auditing of GAPs and GMPs. Audits may be conducted by private companies, or, in some cases, a government sponsored program may be appropriate. Such a program gives auditors an additional opportunity to examine the records of management practices for a produce handling operation. Auditors should question management regarding the existence of third-party verification and request permission to examine such records if they exist.

A CASE STUDY FOR THE IMPLEMENTATION OF A HACCP PROGRAM IN A FRESH-MARKET TOMATO HANDLING OPERATION

Outbreaks of salmonellosis were associated with consumption of fresh-market tomatoes that originated from the same packinghouse in 1990 and 1993. Analysis of environmental samples from the packinghouse did not reveal a source of *Salmonella* contamination. However, the Centers for Disease Control and cooperating industry associations and state agencies designed, implemented, and verified a HACCP program with special focus on GAP implementation that was proposed to serve as a model for this industry.[8]

All of the potential hazard criteria mentioned in chapter 16 were systematically evaluated. The following three steps in the handling system were determined to be potential problem areas: sanitation of field containers; water quality management in the dump tank; and hygiene of workers that hand-sort tomatoes on the packing line. Water quality management was the sole CCP; other factors were considered GAPs or GMPs. The packinghouse operator gave adequate attention to all GAPs and GMPs and installed automated chlorine regulating and water quality monitoring equipment at the dump tank site. CCPs for dump tank conditions were established and corrective actions were specified for instances of CCP deviations.

The packer also voluntarily implemented a sampling and testing program for the presence of *Salmonella* on his tomatoes. Since the program was begun, all samples have tested negative for *Salmonella* and no further illness has been associated with the packing operation. This serves as an example of the effectiveness of a proactive approach to a food safety problem.

REFERENCES

1. U.S. Food and Drug Administration, *Guidance for Industry: Guide to Minimize Microbial Food Safety Hazards for Fresh Fruits and Vegetables* (Washington, DC: Center for Food Safety and Applied Nutrition, 1998).
2. U.S. Food and Drug Administration, *Current Good Manufacturing Practice in Manufacturing, Packing, or Holding Food* (Code of Federal Regulations, Title 21, Volume 2, Section 110, 2000).

3. USFDA, 1998.
4. D. Zagory and W. Hurst (eds.), *Food Safety Guidelines for the Fresh-Cut Produce Industry,* Third ed. (Arlington, VA: International Fresh-Cut Produce Association, 1996; USFDA, 1998).
5. USFDA, 2000.
6. Zagory and Hurst, 1996.
7. J. W. Rushing and F. J. Angulo, "Implementation of a HACCP in a Commercial Tomato Packinghouse: A Model for the Industry," in *Dairy, Food and Environmental Sanitation* 16, no.9 (1996): 549–553.

17

Retail and Food Service

INTEGRATING HAACP IN RETAIL AND FOOD SERVICE OPERATIONS

In any retail or food service establishment the integration of HACCP principles into daily operations and management's commitment to food safety are the foundation of an effective HACCP system. Key standard operating procedures that focus on food safety should be in place for the following activities: purchasing, receiving, storage, preparation (including thawing), cooking, hot and cold holding and displaying, cooling, reheating, and serving. In retail and food service operations, the use of thermometers, prevention of contamination (for example, through water source control or cleaning and sanitizing), good employee personal hygiene, and other appropriate food handling practices are essential to the prevention of food borne illness.

HACCP PLAN DEVELOPMENT AND IMPLEMENTATION

The first step in the development and implementation of a HACCP plan is to identify and assemble a HACCP team. At a minimum, the team should include the leader or senior manager—very often the Person In Charge, the Chef, or the Executive Chef—representatives from purchasing and maintenance, the maitre d' or service manager, and the kitchen steward or sanitation manager. HACCP team members should be trained in the principles of HACCP, have a thorough understanding of their establishment's operations, and have specific accountabilities within the team. A timeline should be developed for each step or principle in the development and implementation of the HACCP plan, and sufficient resources must be provided for the training of employees and ongoing maintenance of the system.

Once the HACCP team has been identified and assembled, the company's operations and its clientele should be described to assist with hazard analysis. This allows the team to define the performance capabilities of the operation and highlight any unique requirements that the plan must address. For instance, an acceptable risk level for pathogen reduction targets would differ for an immunocompromised group, such as hospital patients, compared to an immune complete group.

Hazard Analysis

Hazard analysis in the retail or food service environment encompasses the entire food system from receiving through serving. First, menus and recipes are reviewed to identify potentially hazardous foods, whether used as an ingredient or served as a distinct item. For instance, shell eggs may be served as a breakfast item or as an ingredient in a sauce.

This may seem like a daunting task when the variety of recipes that may be encountered is considered. An approach advocated by Dr. O. P. Snyder is to group recipes into seven fundamental processes or combinations:

1. Thick, raw protein items, greater than two inches (5 cm) thick [one inch (2.5 cm) center to surface]

2. Thin, raw protein items, less than two inches (5 cm) thick

3. Stocks, sauces and brews

4. Fruits, vegetables, starches, seeds, nuts and fungi

5. Dough and batters

6. Hot combination dishes

7. Cold combination dishes[1]

Likewise, the National Restaurant Association Educational Foundation's ServSafe Approach to HACCP provides guidelines for food recipe systems categorized as:

1. Soups, stocks and stews

2. Meats and game meats

3. Poultry and feathered game

4. Seafood and shellfish

5. Fruits and vegetables

6. Stuffings, dressings, batters and breadings

7. Eggs and egg dishes

8. Salads and pre-prepared cold foods

9. Grain dishes

10. Desserts[2]

The flow of food describes the route of food from receiving through serving, and is a key element in the determination of where hazards may occur. This includes the major process operations of receiving, storing, preparing, cooking, serving and holding, transporting, and cooling or reheating. At each stage, the impact of employee handling, the environment surrounding the establishment, the physical facility and equipment, and process capability are described and assessed to identify any potential exposures or risks. Process capability assessment allows the team to clarify how much food can be safely prepared and served by the establishment. In California, food handler training is required by law for at least one manager of a retail operation, which include grocery stores, retail stores, restaurants, and food service operations at sports facilities.

The U. S. Food and Drug Administration's draft *A HACCP Principles Guide for Operators of Food Establishments at the Retail Level* recommends assignment of menu items or groups to food process flows in one of three categories for the development of food safety management systems:[3]

- *Process 1—Food process with no cook step:* ready-to-eat food that is stored, prepared, and served

- *Process 2—Food preparation for same day service:* food that is stored, prepared, cooked, and served

- *Process 3—Complex food preparation:* food that is stored, prepared, cooked, cooled, reheated, hot held, and served

Once potentially hazardous foods and their flow have been identified, the biological, chemical, and physical hazards that could be reasonably expected to occur must be determined. Specific hazards may be intrinsic to the food itself, and data is available from multiple sources, including regulatory authorities, to identify the hazards associated with certain foods and ingredients.

Next, the facility's ability to prevent, eliminate, or otherwise reduce the hazard to an acceptable level and prevent food borne illness is a consideration in estimating the risk associated with the hazard. As mentioned, the establishment's client profile should be considered, as certain population segments such as children and the elderly have lower resistance to food borne illness. However, the HACCP system must be developed to protect all customers. Size and complexity of the operation and the resulting capability to serve complex or multi-step recipes are important considerations, in some cases leading to the decision to purchase prepared items rather than deal with a recipe that may be difficult to prepare safely. Approved suppliers with well-documented safety programs should be specified for all potentially hazardous foods. Shellfish, for instance, must only be purchased from suppliers that appear on the FDA's public health service list of certified shellfish shippers or on lists of state approved sources.

Critical Control Points

Critical control points (CCPs) are specified at each step in the operation where a preventive or control measure may be applied and be effective in preventing, eliminating, or reducing the risk of a biological, chemical, or physical hazard to an acceptable level. CCPs may not be appropriate at every stage of the flow of food, although they are necessary at one or more stages for potentially hazardous foods. Controls may be defined as raw food safety certification by the supplier, washed to be safe, cooked/pasteurized to be safe, or acidified to be safe.[4]

Control points and critical control points may be distinguished for different foods and preparation methods. Using fresh raw chicken as an example, the product may contain *Salmonella.* The bacteria may be present, even if the product was received at the proper temperature of less than 41°F (5°C). However, because no action can be taken at this point to prevent, eliminate, or reduce the level of the bacteria, the receiving step is a control point. Receiving procedures are followed to measure and maintain proper temperatures and to check for visual signs of time/temperature abuse or contamination. It is at the cook step that *Salmonella* is eliminated, by cooking the chicken to a minimum temperature of 165°F (74°C) for at least fifteen seconds. Therefore, the cooking step is the CCP for this specific biological hazard.

CCPs for a cold potato salad in a food service establishment or supermarket deli would include formulating, mixing or preparation, cooling and cold storage, with acidity (pH) as well as time and temperature as critical limits. In general, CCPs for biological hazards focus on time and temperature controls during cooking, hot holding, cooling, and reheating. Employee hygiene and handling practices, and cross-contamination prevention are parts of the prerequisite programs.

Critical Limits

Critical limits are defined for each CCP to specify the times, temperatures, pH, or other parameters that must be met to achieve food safety requirements. These must be measurable, and may be a combination of time and temperature limits, or a one-sided (minimum or maximum) limit. The data that supports selection of the limit, such as the relevant Food Code requirement, state or local regulation, or other scientific research data, should be documented and maintained with the HACCP plan records. In the raw chicken example provided above, both the internal temperature of the chicken and the time maintained at this temperature are the critical limits for the cooking CCP. Critical limits should be realistic for the establishment's work environment, considering operational capabilities of the kitchen, volume of food handled, and number of employees. CCPs and critical limits should be added to each recipe and flowchart to integrate HACCP into the operational systems of the establishment.

Monitoring Procedures

The procedure by which critical limits are monitored for compliance are defined for each CCP in the HACCP plan. Each limit that will be monitored is specified, stating who will monitor, the specific method to be utilized, and the frequency with which monitoring will occur. It is essential that the monitoring plan be realistic and achievable for normal operations, and that employees are knowledgeable about the CCPs and their respective critical limits. Ideally, monitoring is performed by those people directly involved in the operation. Easy-to-use records such as time-temperature logs that are located at the workstation and clearly specify the CCP and relevant critical limits should be provided.

Corrective Actions

If it is determined during planned monitoring, or at any other time, that the critical limit for a CCP has not been met, corrective action must be taken according to the HACCP plan. The corrective actions are described in the plan, and are intended as steps to deal with the specific area of nonconformance. Again, utilizing the chicken cooking example, if the critical limit of cooking to 165°F (74°C) or higher for at least fifteen seconds is not achieved, simply continuing to cook to the specified temperature for the stated period may be the corrective action. In some cases, destruction of the product is the approved corrective action, for instance, at the hot holding CCP, cooked chicken that is held below the critical limit of 140°F (60°C) for more than four hours must be discarded.

Repeated failure to meet a critical limit may require additional employee training or even disciplinary action, or may be indicative of a need to review and verify the CCPs and critical limits of the current HACCP plan. Corrective actions, like critical limits, must be measurable, specific, and suitable for normal operations. It is extremely important that the appropriate corrective action be documented for each case of nonconformance with critical limits, to demonstrate ongoing compliance with the HACCP plan, and due diligence in the event of an investigation into a food borne illness or complaint.

Verification Procedures

Verification procedures of the HACCP plan in a retail establishment may include daily or weekly review of monitoring logs, internal or independent third-party auditing, and at a minimum, annual review of the plan. Calibration of critical limit monitoring instrumentation, such as thermometers or thermocouples, constitutes a verification step. Samples may be routinely tested to assure effectiveness of CCPs. Additionally, verification of the HACCP system should be conducted if there are changes in suppliers, menus, equipment, food flow, other changes that may introduce potential hazards, or if food is linked to a food borne illness outbreak or complaint. Employee feedback, regulatory agency alerts, supplier information, or the availability of new food safety information are also valuable tools in identifying when the HACCP system should be reviewed to ensure it is current, effective, and being followed by employees.

Record Keeping and Documentation Procedures

Record keeping and documentation should be appropriate to each element of the HACCP plan. Records that document the development of the plan and establishment of

CCPs and critical limits, and data that validates critical limits and corrective actions should be compiled and maintained in a single location by the HACCP team leader or designee. This would also apply to verification reports, purchase specifications, approved supplier documentation, and other records that may not require daily use.

Documents that are utilized to capture monitoring data should be easy to use and maintained near the point of use, such as time-temperature logs on a clipboard kept at a salad preparation area in a supermarket deli. Corrective actions and the identification of the person(s) recording the data and/or performing the corrective action should be included. These documents should be collected daily and reviewed for completeness and any necessary follow-up, and maintained in a central location by the designated HACCP team member.

MANAGEMENT AND EMPLOYEE TRAINING

A major challenge in retail and food service establishments is employee turnover. A training program for new employees should stress food safety and the establishment's approach to HACCP. Job descriptions or task analysis should include each individual's role in implementing and monitoring food safety systems. In general, it is preferable to train individual employees on those elements of food safety and the establishment's HACCP plan that are specific to their assignment, rather than an overall training program on general HACCP principles. Training should be geared to the position, as well as language and literacy level, of the employee. Training should be documented, with a written program or course outline, signed attendance record, and demonstrated proficiency in the training concepts by the employee.

Training should be ongoing, whether in response to regulatory requirements at a state or local level, or simply for continuous improvement of the operation. Positive reinforcement for compliance with food safety practices, visual aids such as hand washing signage in multiple languages, and management leadership by example are further examples of management practices that will support an effective HACCP system.

REFERENCES

1. O. P. Snyder, Jr., *HACCP-TQM Retail Food Operations Manual* (St. Paul, MN: Hospitality Institute of Technology and Management, 1999).
2. National Restaurant Association, *ServSafe© Training's A Practice Approach to HACCP* (Chicago: The Educational Foundation of The National Restaurant Association, 1998).
3. U.S. Food and Drug Administration, *Managing Food Safety: A HAACP Principles Guide for Operators of Food Establishments at the Retail Level* (Washington, DC: U.S. Public Health Service, U.S. Department of Health and Human Services, Food and Drug Administration, Center for Food Safety and Applied Nutrition, 15 April 1998).
4. Snyder, 1999.

Part V

Applying HACCP to the Medical Device Industry

18

HACCP Principles in the Design and Manufacture of Medical Devices

THE HISTORY OF HACCP IN THE MEDICAL DEVICE INDUSTRY

The medical device industry has long embraced many of the general principles of HAACP, if not specifically in name. These methods include: risk management, evaluation of design requirements, process validation, and identification of process control measures.

The U. S. Food and Drug Administration (FDA) wrote the first process validation guideline in 1987. In 1997, they published good manufacturing practices (GMP) regulations called the Quality System Regulation (QSR) in Chapter 21, Section 820 of the Code of Federal Regulations. The FDA and other regulatory agencies consider the use of techniques like HACCP, if not HACCP itself, to be essential to the manufacture of medical devices. The agency has identified six benefits resulting from the implementation of HACCP in the medical device industry:

- Quality monitoring of critical control points will decrease the likelihood of device problems

- Quality consciousness of employees will increase

- Quality items needing correction will be readily observed

- The amount of time spent on inspections will decrease

- The efficiency of inspections will increase since they will "key in" on important areas

- The consistency of inspections will increase

Table 18.1 compares the principles of HACCP to the U.S. regulatory requirements for medical devices.

Table 18.1 Comparison of HACCP principles with quality system regulation.

HACCP principle	Quality system regulation
Principle 1 Conduct hazard analysis and identify preventive measures	• 820.30(g) – Design validation shall include . . . risk analysis, where appropriate • 820.70 (a) – Where deviations from device specifications could occur as a result of the manufacturing process, the manufacturer shall establish and maintain process control procedures that describe any process control necessary to ensure conformance to specifications. Examples of preventive measures • 820.50 - Purchasing controls • 820.80 – Receiving, in-process, and finished device acceptance • 820.86 – Acceptance status • 820.70 (c) – Environmental controls • 820.70 (d) – Personnel • 920.70 (e) – Contamination control • 820.70 (g) – Equipment maintenance • 820.72 – Inspection, measuring and test equipment
Principle 2 Identify critical control points	• 820.30 (d) – Design output procedures shall contain or make reference to acceptance criteria and shall ensure that those design outputs that are essential for the proper functioning of the device are identified. • 820.70 (a) – Where deviations from device specifications could occur as a result of the manufacturing, the manufacturer shall establish and maintain process control procedures that describe any process controls necessary to ensure conformance to specifications.
Principle 3 Establish critical limits	• 820.70 (a) – Each manufacturer shall develop, conduct, control, and monitor production processes to ensure that a device conforms to its specifications.
Principle 4 Monitor each critical control point	• 820.70 (a) – Where process controls are needed they shall include: (2) Monitoring and control of process parameters and component and device characteristics during production.
Principle 5 Establish corrective action to be taken when deviation occurs	• 820.100 (a) – Each manufacturer shall establish and maintain procedures for implementing corrective and preventative action. The procedures shall include requirements for (3) Identifying the actions(s) needed for correct and prevent recurrence of nonconforming product and other quality problems.
Principle 6 Establish verification procedures	• 820.80 – Each manufacturer shall establish and maintain procedures for acceptance activities. Acceptance activities include inspection, tests, or other verification activities. • 820.100 (a) – Each manufacturer shall establish and maintain procedures for implementing corrective and preventive action. The procedures shall include requirements for: (4) Verifying or validating the corrective action to ensure that such action is effective and does not adversely affect the finished device;
Principle 7 Establish record keeping systems	• 820.70 (a) – Where process controls are needed they shall include (1) Documented instructions, standard operating procedures (SOPs) and methods that define and control the manner of production • 820.100 (h) – All activities required under this section and their results, shall be documented. • 820.181 – Device master record • 820.184 – Device history record • 820.186 – Quality system record

Source: www.fda.gov/cdrh/gmp/summary4.html

RISK MANAGEMENT

Risk management is considered to be essential to the application of regulatory requirements and to the manufacture of a medical device. A summary of those requirements requires a brief description of the regulatory requirements and references.

The FDA defines risk management as "the overall process for the control of risks." In the preamble to the QSR the FDA states its position that risk assessment is expected to be an integral part of the design process:

> *Manufacturers must also conduct such tests when they make changes in the device design or the manufacturing process that could affect safety or effectiveness as required in the original cGMP in Sec. 820.100(a)(2). The extent of testing conducted should be governed by the risk(s) the device will present if it fails. FDA considers these activities essential for ensuring that the manufacturing process does not adversely affect the device.* Federal Register/Vol. 61, No. 195/Washington DC: United States Government/ Monday Oct. 7, 1996/Rules and Regulations (p. 52620).

In the next paragraph (also p. 52620), the FDA makes it clear that risk analysis is required for medical devices:

> *FDA has deleted the term "hazard analysis" and replaced it with the term "risk analysis." FDA's involvement with ISO TC 210 made it clear that "risk analysis" is the comprehensive and appropriate term. When conducting a risk analysis, manufacturers are expected to identify possible hazards associated with the design in both normal and fault conditions. The risks associated with the hazards, including those resulting from user error, should then be calculated in both normal and fault conditions. If any risk is judged unacceptable, it should be reduced to acceptable levels by the appropriate means, for example, by redesign or warnings. An important part of risk analysis is ensuring that changes made to eliminate or minimize hazards do not introduce new hazards. Tools for conducting such analyses include Failure Mode Effect Analysis and Fault Tree Analysis, among others.*

Finally, the FDA reiterates the requirement for risk assessment by stating, "Risk analysis must be conducted for the majority of devices subject to design controls and is considered to be an essential requirement for medical devices under this regulation." (p. 52621)

From these statements it is obvious that the FDA intends for risk management and its corollaries—which include using risk assessment to identify critical control points— to be an essential process in the design and production of medical devices.

ISO 14971-1:1998, Medical Devices - Risk Management lays out the requirements for risk management in the medical device industry. The requirements specified by this standard include:

- identification of qualitative and quantitative characteristics related to medical devices

- identification of possible hazards

- estimation of risks for each hazard

- review of risks

- risk reduction

DESIGN CONTROL

Design control addresses the use of risk management techniques, as well as other techniques to effectively design a product and then transfer that product into manufacturing. Each design control section of the QSR provides similarity to HACCP techniques. QSR design planning states:

> *(b) Design and development planning. Each manufacturer shall establish and maintain plans that describe or reference the design and development activities and define responsibility for implementation. The plans shall identify and describe the interfaces with different groups or activities that provide, or result in, input to the design and development process. The plans shall be reviewed, updated, and approved as design and development evolves.*

In this design control section the FDA intends that design plans will include all those elements necessary to ensure that the device is designed and manufactured in a manner so as to reduce any risk to acceptable levels.

QSR design verification requirements state:

> *(f) Design verification. Each manufacturer shall establish and maintain procedures for verifying the device design. Design verification shall confirm that the design output meets the design input requirements. The results of the design verification, including identification of the design, method(s), the date, and the individual(s) performing the verification, shall be documented in the DHF [design history file].* U.S. Code of Federal Regulations, Title 21, Part 820.20, Quality System Regulations—Personnel (Washington, DC: U.S. Government).

Verification of device design can include items such as ensuring that manufacturing processes are capable and in control and ensuring that equipment used to manufacture medical devices is appropriate for the use.

The QSR design validation requirements state:

> *(g) Design validation. Each manufacturer shall establish and maintain procedures for validating the device design. Design validation shall be performed under defined operating conditions on initial production units, lots, or batches, or their equivalents. Design validation shall ensure that devices conform to defined user needs and intended uses and shall include testing of production units under actual or simulated use conditions. Design validation shall include software validation and risk analysis, where appropriate. The results of the design validation, including identification of the design, method(s), the date, and the individual(s) performing the validation, shall be*

documented in the DHF. U.S. Code of Federal Regulations, Title 21, Part 820.20, Quality System Regulations—Design Control (Washington, DC: U.S. Government).

The design validation section of the quality system requirement contains the first specific reference in the regulation to risk analysis. This is the latest point at which the first risk analysis work must be done. However, risk analysis generally is done at several steps of the design process prior to completing design validation.

The QSR design transfer requirements state:

(h) Design transfer. Each manufacturer shall establish and maintain procedures to ensure that the device design is correctly translated into production specifications. U.S. Code of Federal Regulations, Title 21, Part 820.20, Quality System Regulations— Design Control (Washington, DC: U.S. Government).

During design transfer activities the addition and use of techniques for evaluating processes, often called process risk assessment, comes into use. Process risk assessment includes identification of critical control points and establishment of critical limits for those control points.

MANUFACTURING PROCESSES

The following paragraphs summarize how HACCP techniques can be applied to medical devices in a general way. In actual practice, the application of HACCP techniques may be slightly different in some instances and may incorporate some or all of the items listed below.

Risk-Based Assessment

A risk-based assessment for a medical device can be done early in the design process or for existing processes and must provide the following specific results:

- A comprehensive list of customer-based quality requirements for each product.

- An assessment of each manufacturing operation with regard to the current risk it poses in achieving product quality requirements and the potential risk reduction if mitigating improvements are made. This assessment via *process failure mode and effect analysis* (PFMEA) includes identifying process validation priorities and essential control points (ECPs). (Note: ECPs for the application of HACCP in the medical device industry are the same as CCPs for the application of HACCP in the food processing industry.)

- A listing of process improvements and a process validation plan for each product line that can then be prioritized and managed. Improvements can be either short- or long-term and may be as simple as procedural changes and retraining or as complex as revised processes and new equipment.

- Improved *manufacturing process instructions* (MPIs) for current processes that include clear and complete specifications of all operating requirements consistent across all products and lines.

- A basis for general retraining of operating personnel, including management, engineers, and operators.

Inconsistencies sometimes occur which directly contribute to the inability of current manufacturing processes to deliver consistent results in meeting customer requirements. These may include:

- Procedures versus actual practices are different, perhaps subtly, with or without those performing them really recognizing the differences.

- Quality requirements are not fully defined or are not clearly specified to those who produce and/or assess products.

- Materials requirements specifications are incorporated into other documents such as procedures, bills of materials, or the like.

- Procedures describing tools and equipment are inconsistently defined, for example, start-up checks, preventive maintenance checks, confirmation of required equipment settings.

All manufacturing processes consist of a sequence of operations documented by a manufacturing process instruction (MPI). Each MPI must consist of some description (text and/or pictures) of each logical work unit in the operation, including starting and ending quality requirements and how these are assessed. The text and the illustrations must identify all steps and inspections in logical sequence and in great detail. If the MPI is followed meticulously, no additional knowledge of the process step should be necessary to perform the operation correctly, including a check that the outcome from the operation meets all requirements.

Quality Requirements

The next step is to identify the known product quality requirements for the product line (for example, in-process and final quality control specifications, and product specifications). These form the bases for defining quality requirements as they relate to the various operations in the manufacturing processes. Current product complaints, yield report defects, and so on, should be reviewed to identify any additional requirements that may not be reflected in current documents. Quality requirements are recorded in the PFMEA database on the *quality requirements* or *defect data sheet*. Where quality specifications exist as documents, the document description should be listed in lieu of individual requirements.

Develop Process Flowcharts

At this point it is important to obtain a complete process flowchart for the product line that shows each operation in the manufacturing process and its corresponding MPI. If a flowchart is not available or may not be accurate, the HACCP team should see that one is developed that properly and accurately represents the manufacturing operations, their sequence, and the current version of the MPI for each.

For each quality requirement identified, the operation(s) that initially provide that characteristic and subsequent one(s) that could likely affect it should be identified. The specific quality characteristic should be a starting *total quality control* point for the operation after the one that initially provides it and a closing TQC point for every operation that provides and could likely affect it.

Process Audits

The next step is to ensure that the process is following the procedure by performing a process audit of each operation's actual practice against its current MPI and the quality characteristics identified above, in sequence with the process flowchart. A list of the procedures audited should be maintained on a *process audit documents summary*. This is an on-site review and observation of how the operation is performed versus what the procedure states. The auditing team should observe operators, ask them to describe the steps they are performing, talk with supervisors, leads, and so forth, as needed to get a complete view of the current practice at each manufacturing step. Additionally, the auditing should verify that all needed or actual assembly steps in the procedure are clearly written "actions" listed and performed in the proper sequence.

Deviations that are observed should be documented on a *process audits observations sheet* and/or in "redline" form for further discussion and decision with the team. (Note: Extra or different "steps" may have been added correctly or incorrectly, that is, they may or may not be correct for the subject operation and product. These should be recorded so that they can be carefully assessed by engineering personnel as to whether they are acceptable and should be incorporated into the process instructions.)

Actual practices should be evaluated against MPI for the following, and observations should be noted as needed:

- TQC points—Applicable TQC points should be identified. The first step in each operation should be a TQC point to check that the outcome of the previous operation conforms to requirements. In this way defects will be detected immediately. TQC points also may be appropriate between steps in the operation. TQC points also should be indicated in the illustrations as well. The last step in each operation should also be a TQC point, where the operator checks his or her own work before passing it on to the next operation.

- Tools and equipment—All tools and equipment must be identified to the level of detail needed to ensure that there is no confusion as to the correct selection, settings, and units. Where a start-up check is needed to confirm proper operation, add it, for example, UV light sources, chemical tests, heat sources for fusing, cutting fixtures, test equipment, and so on. In some cases, a start-up check may include building, testing, and control-charting samples before beginning actual production. Also, calibration or preventive maintenance status should be checked where applicable.

- Safety—Safety-related instructions should be added for all instances where the operation poses an unusual safety hazard, for example, chemical handling, wire cutting or winding, exposed cutting or heated surfaces, electrical testing.

If any of the above aspects cannot effectively be addressed with currently available equipment, materials, process development or capability, operator skill level or otherwise, observations should be listed on the process audit observations sheet for further consideration and prioritization by the auditing team.

APPLICATION OF HACCP TO MEDICAL DEVICES

Once the process procedures and flow have been documented, the next step is to characterize the process. This generally involves using a design of experiments or other statistical technique to determine the elements that affect the process most significantly. The design of experiments also determines the center point of the process and the initial limits for the process. Process characterizations are the critical and essential first element to any medical device process validation procedure. Once this is completed, *fault tree analysis* (FTA) is performed for each component of the system, as shown in Tables 18.2 and 18.3. Next, a process failure mode and effect analysis (PFMEA) is conducted on each of the operations in the process flow, taking into account the results of

Table 18.2 Fault tree analysis.

System failure mode	Clinical effect of failure	Severity (see Table 18.3)

Source: Association of Food and Drug Officials, Medical Device HACCP Training Curriculum. (York, PA: AFDO, 1999): 3, 4, 6, 7, Appendix B.

Table 18.3 Hazard severity categories and levels.

Hazard class severity	Category (severity level)	Description
Catastrophic	I (1)	Potential for patient death or serious injury
Critical	II (2)	Potential for severe injury or requires medical or surgical intervention to prevent possible severe injury
Major	III (3)	Potential for minor injury or unanticipated surgical or medical intervention or requires physician monitoring. Potential for system or component failure. May require recall or special physician monitoring.
Minor	IV (4)	Does not meet regulatory requirements or stated performance specifications. Anticipated performance condition or adverse event covered in labeling.
Negligible	V (5)	No effect on the intended function or performance of the device.

Source: Association of Food and Drug Officials, Medical Device HACCP Training Curriculum. (York, PA: AFDO, 1999): 3, 4, 6, 7, Appendix B.

the process audits. One acceptable FMEA technique is shown in Table 18.4. A risk index such as the one shown in Table 18.5 must be used to provide the information needed to complete the PFMEA or FMEA analysis.

Mitigating actions should be initiated as identified and as appropriate per the Process FMEA, as shown in Table 18.6. Implementation priority should be on a risk-managed basis so that actions on high-risk processes yielding the greatest risk reduction should be done first, and so on.

Table 18.4 Component failure mode and effect analysis.

Component	Failure mode	Possible cause	End effect	Severity	Occurrence	Detect	Risk index (see Table 18.5)

Source: Association of Food and Drug Officials, Medical Device HACCP Training Curriculum. (York, PA: AFDO, 1999): 3, 4, 6, 7, Appendix B.

Table 18.5 Risk index for determining ECPs.

Risk index	Risk index = (S)*(O)*(D)	Risk and functionality level	Essential and nonessential design output
1–12	1 * 1 * 1 = 1 2 * 2 * 3 = 12	High and moderate risk	Identification as ECP
13–32	Combined calculated to be >12	Moderate and low risk and essential to product functionality	Components and processes essential for the safety and functionality of the device
33–125	Combined and calculated to be >32	Low risk nonessential product functionality	Identified as non-essential

S = Severity
O = Occurence
D = Detection

Source: Association of Food and Drug Officials, Medical Device HACCP Training Curriculum. (York, PA: AFDO, 1999): 3, 4, 6, 7, Appendix B.

Table 18.6 Process failure mode and effect

Component	Failure mode	Possible cause	End effect	Severity	Occurrence	Detect	Risk index (see Table 18.5)

Source: Association of Food and Drug Officials, Medical Device HACCP Training Curriculum. (York, PA: AFDO, 1999): 3, 4, 6, 7, Appendix B.

Upon completion of the Process FMEA, a team report should be developed to summarize the following data:

- Risk priority number (RPN) for each manufacturing operation prior to and after this assessment process

- Actions implemented for each manufacturing operation to achieve the RPN reduction

- Actions to be taken for each manufacturing operation to achieve the RPN reduction

Information from the PFMEA is then transferred to a hazard analysis work sheet, such as the one shown in Figure 18.1. Finally, a HACCP plan can be developed for each ECP, as shown in Figure 18.2. The ECPs and the process validation needs are evident from the Process FMEA ratings.

Periodic review of performance metrics such as yields, line defects, and product complaints can be used to monitor the production line and process. When performance issues are observed, a team should be assigned to reassess the issue via the Process FMEA and initiate action accordingly.

QSIT INSPECTION TECHNIQUES

The FDA has developed a new inspection technique called the *quality system inspection technique* (QSIT). QSIT techniques help to focus FDA inspections on four areas of the quality system: management responsibility, design control, corrective and preventive action, and production and process controls.

The QSIT manual (Guide to Inspections of Quality Systems) contains more specific information on the technique. Use of a thorough process evaluation technique such as HACCP benefits both the company and the FDA investigator as they review the Design Control and Production and Process Controls sections of the audit. HACCP techniques provide a clear description of the process and the techniques used to control it.

Firm name: _____   PMA/510(k) # _____ Class : _____

Firm address: _____   Product description: _____

_____

_____   Method of Storage and Distribution: _____

_____

_____

Prepared by ____ Date issued: _____   Intended use and consumer: _____

Approved by ____ Date: _____   Design ref. #____ Revision #____ Date_____

Effective date: ____ Revision # _____

(1) List materials/ component processing step	(2) Identify potential hazards introduced, controlled, or enhanced at this step	(3) Are any potential safety hazards significant? (yes/no)	(4) Justify your decision for column 3	(4) What preventive measure(s) can be applied to prevent the significant hazards?	(5) Is this step an essential control point? (yes/no)

Figure 18.1   Hazard analysis worksheet.

Source: United States Food and Drug Administration Center for Devices and Radiological Health.
Web site: www.fda.gov/cdrh/gmp/haccp-worksheet.pdf

Firm name: _____   PMA/510(k) # _____ Class : _____

Firm address: _____   Product description: _____

_____

_____   Method of storage and distribution: _____

_____

Prepared by _____ Date issued: _____   Intended use and consumer: _____

Approved by _____ Date: _____   Design ref. #_____ Revision #_____ Date_____

Effective date: _____ Revision # _____

(1) Essential control point (ECP)	(2) Significant hazard	(3) Essential limits for each preventive measure	(4) (6)	(5) (7) Monitoring			(8) Corrective action(s)	(9) Verification	(10) Record
			What	How	Frequency	Who			

Figure 18.2   HACCP plan form.

Source: United States Food and Drug Administration Center for Devices and Radiological Health.
Web site: www.fda.gov/cdrh/gmp/haccp-planform.pdf

Part VI

Appendices

Appendix A

Hazards in Food

Table A.1 Examples of biological hazards in food.

Pathogenic Bacteria

Aeromonas hydrophila and other ssp.	*Listeria monocytogenes*
Bacillus cereus	*Plesiomonas shigelloides*
Brucella abortis	*Salmonella* spp.
Brucella suis	*Shigella* ssp.
Campylobacter spp.	*Staphylococcus aureus*
Clostridium botulinum	*Streptococcus pyogenes*
Clostridium perfringens	*Vibrio cholerae*
Escherichia coli	*Vibrio parahaemolyticus* and other *vibrios*
E. coli O157:H7—enterohemorrhagic (EHEC)	*Vibrio vulnificus*
Escherichia coli—enteroinvasive (EIEC)	*Yersinia enterocolitica*
Escherichia coli—enteropathogenic (EPEC)	Yersinia pseudotuberculosis
Escherichia coli—enterotoxigenic (ETEC)	
Enterovirulent *Escherichia coli* Group (EEC Group)	

Viruses

Hepatitis A virus	Norwalk virus group
Hepatitis E virus	*Rotavirus*

Parasitic Protozoa and Worms

Acanthamoeba	*Giardia lamblia*
Anisakis sp. and related worms	*Nanophyetus* spp.
Ascaris lumbricoides	*Taenia solium*
Cryptosporidium parvum	*Taenia saginata*
Diphyllobothrium ssp.	*Trichinella spiralis*
Enteramoeba histolytica	*Trichuris trichiura*
Eustrongylides sp.	

Source: FDA Bad Bug Web site; Food Quality and Standards Service Food and Nutrition Division, Food and Agriculture Organization of the United Nations, *Food Quality and Safety Systems—A Training Manual on Food Hygiene and the Hazard Analysis and Critical Control Point (HACCP) System.* (Rome: Publishing Management Group, FAO Division, 1998.)

Table A.2 Examples of physical hazards in food.

Material	Injury potential	Sources
Glass	Cuts, bleeding; may require surgery to find or remove	Bottles, jars, light fixtures, utensils, gauge covers, etc.
Wood	Cuts, infection, choking; may require surgery to remove	Field sources, pallets, boxes, building materials
Stones	Choking, broken teeth	Fields, buildings
Metal	Cuts, infection; may require surgery to remove	Machinery, fields, wire, employees
Insulation	Choking; long-term if asbestos	Building materials
Bone	Choking	Improper processing
Plastic	Choking, cuts, infection; may require surgery to remove	Packaging, pallets, equipment
Personal effects	Choking, cuts, broken teeth; may require surgery to remove	Employees

Source: Food Quality and Standards Service Food and Nutrition Division, Food and Agriculture Organization of the United Nations. *Food Quality and Safety Systems—A Training Manual on Food Hygiene and the Hazard Analysis and Critical Control Point (HACCP) System.* (Rome: Publishing Management Group, FAO Information Division, 1998.)

Table A.3 Examples of chemical hazards in food.

Naturally Occurring Chemicals

Allergens	Neurotoxic shellfish poisoning (NSP)
Mycotoxins (for example, aflatoxin)	Amnesic shellfish poisoning (ASP)
Scombrotoxin (histamine)	Pyrrolizidine alkaloids
Ciguatoxin	*Phytohaemagglutinin*
Mushroom toxins	*Grayanotoxin* (Honey intoxication)
Shellfish toxins	*Phytohaemagglutinin* (Red kidney bean poisoning)
Paralytic shellfish poisoning (PSP)	Tetrodotoxin (Pufferfish)
Diarrheic shellfish poisoning (DSP)	

Added Chemicals

Polychlorinated biphenyls (PCBs)	Growth hormones
Agricultural chemicals	Prohibited substances
Pesticides	Direct
Fertilizers	Indirect
Antibiotics	

Toxic Elements and Compounds

Lead	Mercury
Zinc	Arsenic
Cadmium	Cyanide

Food Additives

Vitamins and minerals

Contaminants

Lubricants	Paints
Cleaners	Refrigerants
Sanitizers	Water or steam treatment chemicals
Coatings	Pest control chemicals

From Packaging Materials

Plasticizers	Adhesives
Vinyl chloride	Lead
Printing/coding inks	Tin

Source: Food Quality and Standards Service Food and Nutrition Division, Food and Agriculture Organization of the United Nations. *Food Quality and Safety Systems—A Training Manual on Food Hygiene and the Hazard Analysis and Critical Control Point (HACCP) System.* (Rome: Publishing Management Group, FAO Information Division, 1998.)

Appendix B

Hazards in Medical Devices

Table B.1 Examples of hazards in medical devices.

Physical Hazards	
Protrusions	Abrasions
Jagged edges	

Biological Hazards	
Microorganisms	Biocompatibility
Viruses	Pyrogens

Chemical Hazards	
Naturally occurring chemicals (for example, allergens, latex)	Unintentionally or incidentally added chemicals (for example, mold-release agents, cleaning agents, sterilizing agents)
Intentionally added chemicals (for example, stabilizers, mold inhibitors)	

Electrical Hazards	
High-energy	Electrostatic discharge
Low-energy	Electromagnetic interference

Radiation	
Overdosage	Underdosage

Explosions	
Inflammable gases	Batteries

Environmental Hazards	
Inadequate coolant or cooling capacity	Interference
Vibration	Incompatibility

Misdiagnosis or Delayed Treatment	
Stability of reagents	Electronic hardware
Performance of intravenous devices	Software algorithm
Specimen problems	Misuse or error
Electrical interference	

Other Malfunctions	
Failure to meet specifications	Device use error

Source: Medical Device HACCP Training Curriculum (York, PA: Association of Food & Drug Officials, 1999.)

Appendix C

NACMCF HACCP Guidelines

Hazard Analysis and Critical Control Point Principles and Application Guidelines

Adopted August 14, 1997

National Advisory Committee
on Microbiological Criteria for Foods

Table of Contents

EXECUTIVE SUMMARY

The National Advisory Committee on Microbiological Criteria for Foods (Committee) reconvened a Hazard Analysis and Critical Control Point (HACCP) Working Group in 1995. The primary goal was to review the Committee's November 1992 HACCP document, comparing it to current HACCP guidance prepared by the Codex Committee on Food Hygiene. Based upon its review, the Committee made the HACCP principles more concise; revised and added definitions; included sections on prerequisite programs, education and training, and implementation and maintenance of the HACCP plan; revised and provided a more detailed explanation of the application of HACCP principles; and provided an additional decision tree for identifying critical control points (CCPs).

The Committee again endorses HACCP as an effective and rational means of assuring food safety from harvest to consumption. Preventing problems from occurring is the paramount goal underlying any HACCP system. Seven basic principles are employed in the development of HACCP plans that meet the stated goal. These principles include hazard analysis, CCP identification, establishing critical limits, monitoring procedures, corrective actions, verification procedures, and record-keeping and documentation. Under such systems, if a deviation occurs indicating that control has been lost, the deviation is detected and appropriate steps are taken to reestablish control in a timely manner to assure that potentially hazardous products do not reach the consumer.

In the application of HACCP, the use of microbiological testing is seldom an effective means of monitoring CCPs because of the time required to obtain results. In most instances, monitoring of CCPs can best be accomplished through the use of physical and chemical tests, and through visual observations. Microbiological criteria do, however, play a role in verifying that the overall HACCP system is working.

The Committee believes that the HACCP principles should be standardized to provide uniformity in training and applying the HACCP system by industry and government. In accordance with the National Academy of Sciences recommendation, the HACCP system must be developed by each food establishment and tailored to its individual product, processing and distribution conditions.

In keeping with the Committee's charge to provide recommendations to its sponsoring agencies regarding microbiological food safety issues, this document focuses on this area. The Committee recognizes that in order to assure food safety, properly designed HACCP systems must also consider chemical and physical hazards in addition to other biological hazards.

For a successful HACCP program to be properly implemented, management must be committed to a HACCP approach. A commitment by management will indicate an awareness of the benefits and costs of HACCP and include education and training of employees. Benefits, in addition to enhanced assurance of food safety, are better use of resources and timely response to problems.

The Committee designed this document to guide the food industry and advise its sponsoring agencies in the implementation of HACCP systems.

DEFINITIONS

CCP Decision Tree: A sequence of questions to assist in determining whether a control point is a CCP.

Control: (a) To manage the conditions of an operation to maintain compliance with established criteria. (b) The state where correct procedures are being followed and criteria are being met.

Control Measure: Any action or activity that can be used to prevent, eliminate, or reduce a significant hazard.

Control Point: Any step at which biological, chemical, or physical factors can be controlled.

Corrective Action: Procedures followed when a deviation occurs.

Criterion: A requirement on which a judgement or decision can be based.

Critical Control Point: A step at which control can be applied and is essential to prevent or eliminate a food safety hazard or reduce it to an acceptable level.

Critical Limit: A maximum and/or minimum value to which a biological, chemical or physical parameter must be controlled at a CCP to prevent, eliminate, or reduce to an acceptable level the occurrence of a food safety hazard.

Deviation: Failure to meet a critical limit.

HACCP: A systematic approach to the identification, evaluation, and control of food safety hazards.

HACCP Plan: The written document which is based upon the principles of HACCP and which delineates the procedures to be followed.

HACCP System: The result of the implementation of the HACCP Plan.

HACCP Team: The group of people who are responsible for developing, implementing, and maintaining the HACCP system.

Hazard: A biological, chemical, or physical agent that is reasonably likely to cause illness or injury in the absence of its control.

Hazard Analysis: The process of collecting and evaluating information on hazards associated with the food under consideration to decide which are significant and must be addressed in the HACCP plan.

Monitor: To conduct a planned sequence of observations or measurements to assess whether a CCP is under control and to produce an accurate record for future use in verification.

Prerequisite Programs: Procedures, including Good Manufacturing Practices, that address operational conditions providing the foundation for the HACCP system.

Severity: The seriousness of the effect(s) of a hazard.

Step: A point, procedure, operation or stage in the food system from primary production to final consumption.

Validation: That element of verification focused on collecting and evaluating scientific and technical information to determine if the HACCP plan, when properly implemented, will effectively control the hazards.

Verification: Those activities, other than monitoring, that determine the validity of the HACCP plan and that the system is operating according to the plan.

HACCP PRINCIPLES

HACCP is a systematic approach to the identification, evaluation, and control of food safety hazards based on the following seven principles:

Principle 1: Conduct a hazard analysis.

Principle 2: Determine the critical control points (CCPs).

Principle 3: Establish critical limits.

Principle 4: Establish monitoring procedures.

Principle 5: Establish corrective actions.

Principle 6: Establish verification procedures.

Principle 7: Establish record-keeping and documentation procedures.

GUIDELINES FOR APPLICATION OF HACCP PRINCIPLES

Introduction

HACCP is a management system in which food safety is addressed through the analysis and control of biological, chemical, and physical hazards from raw material production, procurement and handling, to manufacturing, distribution, and consumption of the finished product. For successful implementation of a HACCP plan, management must be strongly committed to the HACCP concept. A firm commitment to HACCP by top management provides company employees with a sense of the importance of producing safe food.

HACCP is designed for use in all segments of the food industry from growing, harvesting, processing, manufacturing, distributing, and merchandising to preparing food for consumption. Prerequisite programs such as current Good Manufacturing Practices (cGMPs) are an essential foundation for the development and implementation of successful HACCP plans. Food safety systems based on the HACCP principles have been successfully applied in food processing plants, retail food stores, and food service operations. The seven principles of HACCP have been universally accepted by government agencies, trade associations and the food industry around the world.

The following guidelines will facilitate the development and implementation of effective HACCP plans. While the specific application of HACCP to manufacturing facilities is emphasized here, these guidelines should be applied as appropriate to each segment of the food industry under consideration.

Prerequisite Programs

The production of safe food products requires that the HACCP system be built upon a solid foundation of prerequisite programs. Examples of common prerequisite programs are listed in Appendix A. Each segment of the food industry must provide the conditions necessary to protect food while it is under their control. This has traditionally been accomplished through the application of cGMPs. These conditions and practices are now considered to be prerequisite to the development and implementation of effective HACCP plans. Prerequisite programs provide the basic environmental and operating conditions that are necessary for the production of safe, wholesome food. Many of the conditions and practices are specified in federal, state, and local regulations and guidelines (e.g., cGMPs and Food Code). The Codex Alimentarius General Principles of Food Hygiene describe the basic conditions and practices expected for foods intended for international trade. In addition to the requirements specified in regulations, industry often adopts policies and procedures that are specific to their operations. Many of these are proprietary. While prerequisite programs may impact upon the safety of a food, they also are concerned with ensuring that foods are wholesome and suitable for consumption (Appendix A). HACCP plans are narrower in scope, being limited to ensuring food is safe to consume.

The existence and effectiveness of prerequisite programs should be assessed during the design and implementation of each HACCP plan. All prerequisite programs should be documented and regularly audited. Prerequisite programs are established and managed separately from the HACCP plan. Certain aspects, however, of a prerequisite program may be incorporated into a HACCP plan. For example, many establishments have preventive maintenance procedures for processing equipment to avoid unexpected equipment failure and loss of production. During the development of a HACCP plan, the HACCP team may decide that the routine maintenance and calibration of an oven should be included in the plan as an activity of verification. This would further ensure that all the food in the oven is cooked to the minimum internal temperature that is necessary for food safety.

Education and Training

The success of a HACCP system depends on educating and training management and employees in the importance of their role in producing safe foods. This should also include information on the control of foodborne hazards related to all stages of the food chain. It is important to recognize that employees must first understand what HACCP is and then learn the skills necessary to make it function properly. Specific training activities should include working instructions and procedures that outline the tasks of employees monitoring each CCP.

Management must provide adequate time for thorough education and training. Personnel must be given the materials and equipment necessary to perform these tasks. Effective training is an important prerequisite to successful implementation of a HACCP plan.

Developing a HACCP Plan

The format of HACCP plans will vary. In many cases the plans will be product and process specific. However, some plans may use a unit operations approach. Generic HACCP plans can serve as useful guides in the development of process and product HACCP plans; however, it is essential that the unique conditions within each facility be considered during the development of all components of the HACCP plan.

In the development of a HACCP plan, five preliminary tasks need to be accomplished before the application of the HACCP principles to a specific product and process. The five preliminary tasks are given in Figure C.1.

Assemble the HACCP Team

The first task in developing a HACCP plan is to assemble a HACCP team consisting of individuals who have specific knowledge and expertise appropriate to the product and process. It is the team's responsibility to develop the HACCP plan. The team should be multi disciplinary and include individuals from areas such as engineering, production,

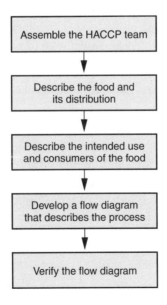

Figure C.1 Preliminary tasks in the development of the HACCP plan.

sanitation, quality assurance, and food microbiology. The team should also include local personnel who are involved in the operation as they are more familiar with the variability and limitations of the operation. In addition, this fosters a sense of ownership among those who must implement the plan. The HACCP team may need assistance from outside experts who are knowledgeable in the potential biological, chemical and/or physical hazards associated with the product and the process. However, a plan which is developed totally by outside sources may be erroneous, incomplete, and lacking in support at the local level.

Due to the technical nature of the information required for hazard analysis, it is recommended that experts who are knowledgeable in the food process should either participate in or verify the completeness of the hazard analysis and the HACCP plan. Such individuals should have the knowledge and experience to correctly: (a) conduct a hazard analysis; (b) identify potential hazards, (c) identify hazards which must be controlled; (d) recommend controls, critical limits, and procedures for monitoring and verification; (e) recommend appropriate corrective actions when a deviation occurs; (f) recommend research related to the HACCP plan if important information is not known; and (g) validate the HACCP plan.

Describe the Food and Its Distribution

The HACCP team first describes the food. This consists of a general description of the food, ingredients, and processing methods. The method of distribution should be described along with information on whether the food is to be distributed frozen, refrigerated, or at ambient temperature.

Describe the Intended Use and Consumers of the Food

Describe the normal expected use of the food. The intended consumers may be the general public or a particular segment of the population (e.g., infants, immunocompromised individuals, the elderly, etc.).

Develop a Flow Diagram Which Describes the Process

The purpose of a flow diagram is to provide a clear, simple outline of the steps involved in the process. The scope of the flow diagram must cover all the steps in the process which are directly under the control of the establishment. In addition, the flow diagram can include steps in the food chain which are before and after the processing that occurs in the establishment. The flow diagram need not be as complex as engineering drawings. A block type flow diagram is sufficiently descriptive (see Appendix C.B). Also, a simple schematic of the facility is often useful in understanding and evaluating product and process flow.

Verify the Flow Diagram

The HACCP team should perform an on-site review of the operation to verify the accuracy and completeness of the flow diagram. Modifications should be made to the flow diagram as necessary and documented.

After these five preliminary tasks have been completed, the seven principles of HACCP are applied.

Conduct a Hazard Analysis (Principle 1)

After addressing the preliminary tasks discussed above, the HACCP team conducts a hazard analysis and identifies appropriate control measures. The purpose of the hazard analysis is to develop a list of hazards which are of such significance that they are reasonably likely to cause injury or illness if not effectively controlled. Hazards that are not reasonably likely to occur would not require further consideration within a HACCP plan. It is important to consider in the hazard analysis the ingredients and raw materials, each step in the process, product storage and distribution, and final preparation and use by the consumer. When conducting a hazard analysis, safety concerns must be differentiated from quality concerns. A hazard is defined as a biological, chemical or physical agent that is reasonably likely to cause illness or injury in the absence of its control. Thus, the word hazard as used in this document is limited to safety.

A thorough hazard analysis is the key to preparing an effective HACCP plan. If the hazard analysis is not done correctly and the hazards warranting control within the HACCP system are not identified, the plan will not be effective regardless of how well it is followed.

The hazard analysis and identification of associated control measures accomplish three objectives: Those hazards and associated control measures are identified. The analysis may identify needed modifications to a process or product so that product safety is further assured or improved. The analysis provides a basis for determining CCPs in Principle 2.

The process of conducting a hazard analysis involves two stages. The first, hazard identification, can be regarded as a brain storming session. During this stage, the HACCP team reviews the ingredients used in the product, the activities conducted at each step in the process and the equipment used, the final product and its method of storage and distribution, and the intended use and consumers of the product. Based on this review, the team develops a list of potential biological, chemical or physical hazards which may be introduced, increased, or controlled at each step in the production process. Appendix C.C lists examples of questions that may be helpful to consider when identifying potential hazards. Hazard identification focuses on developing a list of potential hazards associated with each process step under direct control of the food operation. A knowledge of any adverse health-related events historically associated with the product will be of value in this exercise.

After the list of potential hazards is assembled, stage two, the hazard evaluation, is conducted. In stage two of the hazard analysis, the HACCP team decides which potential hazards must be addressed in the HACCP plan. During this stage, each potential hazard is evaluated based on the severity of the potential hazard and its likely occurrence. Severity is the seriousness of the consequences of exposure to the hazard. Considerations of severity (e.g., impact of sequelae, and magnitude and duration of illness or injury) can be helpful in understanding the public health impact of the hazard.

Consideration of the likely occurrence is usually based upon a combination of experience, epidemiological data, and information in the technical literature. When conducting the hazard evaluation, it is helpful to consider the likelihood of exposure and severity of the potential consequences if the hazard is not properly controlled. In addition, consideration should be given to the effects of short term as well as long term exposure to the potential hazard. Such considerations do not include common dietary choices which lie outside of HACCP. During the evaluation of each potential hazard, the food, its method of preparation, transportation, storage and persons likely to consume the product should be considered to determine how each of these factors may influence the likely occurrence and severity of the hazard being controlled. The team must consider the influence of likely procedures for food preparation and storage and whether the intended consumers are susceptible to a potential hazard. However, there may be differences of opinion, even among experts, as to the likely occurrence and severity of a hazard. The HACCP team may have to rely upon the opinion of experts who assist in the development of the HACCP plan.

Hazards identified in one operation or facility may not be significant in another operation producing the same or a similar product. For example, due to differences in equipment and/or an effective maintenance program, the probability of metal contamination may be significant in one facility but not in another. A summary of the HACCP team deliberations and the rationale developed during the hazard analysis should be kept for future reference. This information will be useful during future reviews and updates of the hazard analysis and the HACCP plan.

Appendix C.D gives three examples of using a logic sequence in conducting a hazard analysis. While these examples relate to biological hazards, chemical and physical hazards are equally important to consider. Appendix C.D is for illustration purposes to further explain the stages of hazard analysis for identifying hazards. Hazard identification and evaluation as outlined in Appendix C.D may eventually be assisted by biological risk assessments as they become available. While the process and output of a risk assessment (NACMCF, 1997)[1] is significantly different from a hazard analysis, the identification of hazards of concern and the hazard evaluation may be facilitated by information from risk assessments. Thus, as risk assessments addressing specific hazards or control factors become available, the HACCP team should take these into consideration.

Upon completion of the hazard analysis, the hazards associated with each step in the production of the food should be listed along with any measure(s) that are used to control the hazard(s). The term control measure is used because not all hazards can be prevented, but virtually all can be controlled. More than one control measure may be required for a specific hazard. On the other hand, more than one hazard may be addressed by a specific control measure (e.g. pasteurization of milk).

For example, if a HACCP team were to conduct a hazard analysis for the production of frozen cooked beef patties (Appendices B and D), enteric pathogens (e.g., *Salmonella* and verotoxin-producing *Escherichia coli*) in the raw meat would be identified as hazards. Cooking is a control measure which can be used to eliminate these hazards. The following is an excerpt from a hazard analysis summary table for this product.

Step	Potential hazard(s)	Justification	Hazard to be addressed in plan? Y/N	Control measure(s)
5. Cooking	Enteric pathogens: e.g., *Salmonella*, verotoxigenic-*E. coli*	Enteric pathogens have been associated with outbreaks of foodborne illness from undercooked ground beef	Y	Cooking

The hazard analysis summary could be presented in several different ways. One format is a table such as the one given above. Another could be a narrative summary of the HACCP team's hazard analysis considerations and a summary table listing only the hazards and associated control measures.

Determine Critical Control Points (CCPs) (Principle 2)

A critical control point is defined as a step at which control can be applied and is essential to prevent or eliminate a food safety hazard or reduce it to an acceptable level. The potential hazards that are reasonably likely to cause illness or injury in the absence of their control must be addressed in determining CCPs.

Complete and accurate identification of CCPs is fundamental to controlling food safety hazards. The information developed during the hazard analysis is essential for the HACCP team in identifying which steps in the process are CCPs. One strategy to facilitate the identification of each CCP is the use of a CCP decision tree (Examples of decision trees are given in Appendices C.E and C.F). Although application of the CCP decision tree can be useful in determining if a particular step is a CCP for a previously identified hazard, it is merely a tool and not a mandatory element of HACCP. A CCP decision tree is not a substitute for expert knowledge.

Critical control points are located at any step where hazards can be either prevented, eliminated, or reduced to acceptable levels. Examples of CCPs may include: thermal processing, chilling, testing ingredients for chemical residues, product formulation control, and testing product for metal contaminants. CCPs must be carefully developed and documented. In addition, they must be used only for purposes of product safety. For example, a specified heat process, at a given time and temperature designed to destroy a specific microbiological pathogen, could be a CCP. Likewise, refrigeration of a pre-cooked food to prevent hazardous microorganisms from multiplying, or the adjustment of a food to a pH necessary to prevent toxin formation could also be CCPs. Different facilities preparing similar food items can differ in the hazards identified and the steps which are CCPs. This can be due to differences in each facility's layout, equipment, selection of ingredients, processes employed, etc.

Establish Critical Limits (Principle 3)

A critical limit is a maximum and/or minimum value to which a biological, chemical or physical parameter must be controlled at a CCP to prevent, eliminate, or reduce to an acceptable level the occurrence of a food safety hazard. A critical limit is used to distinguish between safe and unsafe operating conditions at a CCP. Critical limits should not be confused with operational limits which are established for reasons other than food safety.

Each CCP will have one or more control measures to assure that the identified hazards are prevented, eliminated, or reduced to acceptable levels. Each control measure has one or more associated critical limits. Critical limits may be based upon factors such as: temperature, time, physical dimensions, humidity, moisture level, water activity (aw), pH, titratable acidity, salt concentration, available chlorine, viscosity, preservatives, or sensory information such as aroma and visual appearance. Critical limits must be scientifically based. For each CCP, there is at least one criterion for food safety that is to be met. An example of a criterion is a specific lethality of a cooking process such as a 5D reduction in *Salmonella*. The critical limits and criteria for food safety may be derived from sources such as regulatory standards and guidelines, literature surveys, experimental results, and experts.

An example is the cooking of beef patties (Appendix C.B). The process should be designed to ensure the production of a safe product. The hazard analysis for cooked meat patties identified enteric pathogens (e.g., verotoxigenic *E. coli* such as *E. coli* O157:H7, and salmonellae) as significant biological hazards. Furthermore, cooking is the step in the process at which control can be applied to reduce the enteric pathogens to an acceptable level. To ensure that an acceptable level is consistently achieved, accurate information is needed on the probable number of the pathogens in the raw patties, their heat resistance, the factors that influence the heating of the patties, and the area of the patty which heats the slowest. Collectively, this information forms the scientific basis for the critical limits that are established. Some of the factors that may affect the thermal destruction of enteric pathogens are listed in the following table. In this example, the HACCP team concluded that a thermal process equivalent to 155°F for 16 seconds would be necessary to assure the safety of this product. To ensure that this time and temperature are attained, the HACCP team for one facility determined that it would be necessary to establish critical limits for the oven temperature and humidity, belt speed (time in oven), patty thickness and composition (e.g., all beef, beef and other ingredients). Control of these factors enables the facility to produce a wide variety of cooked patties, all of which will be processed to a minimum internal temperature of 155°F for 16 seconds. In another facility, the HACCP team may conclude that the best approach is to use the internal patty temperature of 155°F and hold for 16 seconds as critical limits. In this second facility the internal temperature and hold time of the patties are monitored at a frequency to ensure that the critical limits are constantly met as they exit the oven. The example given below applies to the first facility.

Process step	CCP	Critical limits
5. Cooking	YES	Oven temperature: ___ F Time; rate of heating and cooling (belt speed in ft/min): ___ ft/min Patty thickness: ___ in. Patty composition: e.g. all beef Oven humidity: ___ % RH

Establish Monitoring Procedures (Principle 4)

Monitoring is a planned sequence of observations or measurements to assess whether a CCP is under control and to produce an accurate record for future use in verification. Monitoring serves three main purposes. First, monitoring is essential to food safety management in that it facilitates tracking of the operation. If monitoring indicates that there is a trend towards loss of control, then action can be taken to bring the process back into control before a deviation from a critical limit occurs. Second, monitoring is used to determine when there is loss of control and a deviation occurs at a CCP, i.e., exceeding or not meeting a critical limit. When a deviation occurs, an appropriate corrective action must be taken. Third, it provides written documentation for use in verification.

An unsafe food may result if a process is not properly controlled and a deviation occurs. Because of the potentially serious consequences of a critical limit deviation, monitoring procedures must be effective. Ideally, monitoring should be continuous, which is possible with many types of physical and chemical methods. For example, the temperature and time for the scheduled thermal process of low-acid canned foods is recorded continuously on temperature recording charts. If the temperature falls below the scheduled temperature or the time is insufficient, as recorded on the chart, the product from the retort is retained and the disposition determined as in Principle 5. Likewise, pH measurement may be performed continually in fluids or by testing each batch before processing. There are many ways to monitor critical limits on a continuous or batch basis and record the data on charts. Continuous monitoring is always preferred when feasible. Monitoring equipment must be carefully calibrated for accuracy.

Assignment of the responsibility for monitoring is an important consideration for each CCP. Specific assignments will depend on the number of CCPs and control measures and the complexity of monitoring. Personnel who monitor CCPs are often associated with production (e.g., line supervisors, selected line workers, and maintenance personnel) and, as required, quality control personnel. Those individuals must be trained in the monitoring technique for which they are responsible, fully understand the purpose and importance of monitoring, be unbiased in monitoring and reporting, and accurately report the results of monitoring. In addition, employees should be trained in procedures to follow when there is a trend towards loss of control so that adjustments can be made in a timely manner to assure that the process remains under control. The person responsible for monitoring must also immediately report a process or product that does not meet critical limits.

All records and documents associated with CCP monitoring should be dated and signed or initialed by the person doing the monitoring.

When it is not possible to monitor a CCP on a continuous basis, it is necessary to establish a monitoring frequency and procedure that will be reliable enough to indicate that the CCP is under control. Statistically designed data collection or sampling systems lend themselves to this purpose.

Most monitoring procedures need to be rapid because they relate to on-line, "real-time" processes and there will not be time for lengthy analytical testing. Examples of monitoring activities include: visual observations and measurement of temperature, time, pH, and moisture level.

Microbiological tests are seldom effective for monitoring due to their time-consuming nature and problems with assuring detection of contaminants. Physical and chemical measurements are often preferred because they are rapid and usually more effective for assuring control of microbiological hazards. For example, the safety of pasteurized milk is based upon measurements of time and temperature of heating rather than testing the heated milk to assure the absence of surviving pathogens.

With certain foods, processes, ingredients, or imports, there may be no alternative to microbiological testing. However, it is important to recognize that a sampling protocol that is adequate to reliably detect low levels of pathogens is seldom possible because of the large number of samples needed. This sampling limitation could result in a false sense of security by those who use an inadequate sampling protocol. In addition, there are technical limitations in many laboratory procedures for detecting and quantitating pathogens and/or their toxins.

Establish Corrective Actions (Principle 5)

The HACCP system for food safety management is designed to identify health hazards and to establish strategies to prevent, eliminate, or reduce their occurrence. However, ideal circumstances do not always prevail and deviations from established processes may occur. An important purpose of corrective actions is to prevent foods which may be hazardous from reaching consumers. Where there is a deviation from established critical limits, corrective actions are necessary. Therefore, corrective actions should include the following elements: (a) determine and correct the cause of non-compliance; (b) determine the disposition of non-compliant product and (c) record the corrective actions that have been taken. Specific corrective actions should be developed in advance for each CCP and included in the HACCP plan. As a minimum, the HACCP plan should specify what is done when a deviation occurs, who is responsible for implementing the corrective actions, and that a record will be developed and maintained of the actions taken. Individuals who have a thorough understanding of the process, product and HACCP plan should be assigned the responsibility for oversight of corrective actions. As appropriate, experts may be consulted to review the information available and to assist in determining disposition of non-compliant product.

Establish Verification Procedures (Principle 6)

Verification is defined as those activities, other than monitoring, that determine the validity of the HACCP plan and that the system is operating according to the plan. The NAS (1985)[2] pointed out that the major infusion of science in a HACCP system centers on proper identification of the hazards, critical control points, critical limits, and instituting proper verification procedures. These processes should take place during the development and implementation of the HACCP plans and maintenance of the HACCP system. An example of a verification schedule is given in Table C.1.

One aspect of verification is evaluating whether the facility's HACCP system is functioning according to the HACCP plan. An effective HACCP system requires little

Table C.1 Example of a company established HACCP verification schedule.

Activity	Frequency	Responsibility	Reviewer
Verification activities scheduling	Yearly or upon HACCP system change	HACCP coordinator	Plant manager
Initial validation of HACCP plan	Prior to and during initial implementation of plan	Independent expert(s)[a]	HACCP team
Subsequent validation of HACCP plan	When critical limits changed, significant changes in process, equipment changed, after system failure, etc.	Independent expert(s)[a]	HACCP team
Verification of CCP monitoring as described in the plan (e.g., monitoring of patty cooking temperature)	According to HACCP plan (e.g., once per shift)	According to HACCP plan (e.g., line supervisor)	According to HACCP plan (e.g., quality control)
Review of monitoring, corrective action records to show compliance with the plan	Monthly	Quality assurance	HACCP team
Comprehensive HACCP system verification	Yearly	Independent expert(s)[a]	Plant manager

[a] Done by others than the team writing and implementing the plan. May require additional technical expertise as well as laboratory and plant test studies.

end-product testing, since sufficient validated safeguards are built in early in the process. Therefore, rather than relying on end-product testing, firms should rely on frequent reviews of their HACCP plan, verification that the HACCP plan is being correctly followed, and review of CCP monitoring and corrective action records.

Another important aspect of verification is the initial validation of the HACCP plan to determine that the plan is scientifically and technically sound, that all hazards have been identified and that if the HACCP plan is properly implemented these hazards will be effectively controlled. Information needed to validate the HACCP plan often include (1) expert advice and scientific studies and (2) in-plant observations, measurements, and evaluations. For example, validation of the cooking process for beef patties should include the scientific justification of the heating times and temperatures needed to obtain an appropriate destruction of pathogenic microorganisms (i.e., enteric pathogens) and studies to confirm that the conditions of cooking will deliver the required time and temperature to each beef patty.

Subsequent validations are performed and documented by a HACCP team or an independent expert as needed. For example, validations are conducted when there is an unexplained system failure; a significant product, process or packaging change occurs; or new hazards are recognized.

In addition, a periodic comprehensive verification of the HACCP system should be conducted by an unbiased, independent authority. Such authorities can be internal or external to the food operation. This should include a technical evaluation of the hazard analysis and each element of the HACCP plan as well as on-site review of all flow diagrams and appropriate records from operation of the plan. A comprehensive verification is independent of other verification procedures and must be performed to ensure that the HACCP plan is resulting in the control of the hazards. If the results of the comprehensive verification identifies deficiencies, the HACCP team modifies the HACCP plan as necessary.

Verification activities are carried out by individuals within a company, third party experts, and regulatory agencies. It is important that individuals doing verification have appropriate technical expertise to perform this function. The role of regulatory and industry in HACCP was further described by the NACMCF (1994)[3].

Examples of verification activities are included as Appendix C.G.

Establish Record-Keeping and Documentation Procedures (Principle 7)

Generally, the records maintained for the HACCP System should include the following:

1. A summary of the hazard analysis, including the rationale for determining hazards and control measures.

2. The HACCP Plan

    Listing of the HACCP team and assigned responsibilities.
    Description of the food, its distribution, intended use, and consumer.
    Verified flow diagram.
    HACCP Plan Summary Table that includes information for:
        Steps in the process that are CCPs
        The hazard(s) of concern
        Critical limits
        Monitoring*
        Corrective actions*
        Verification procedures and schedule*
        Record-keeping procedures*

    * A brief summary of position responsible for performing the activity and the procedures and frequency should be provided

The following is an example of a HACCP plan summary table:

CCP	Hazards	Critical limit(s)	Monitoring	Corrective actions	Verification	Records

3. Support documentation such as validation records.

4. Records that are generated during the operation of the plan.

Examples of HACCP records are given in Appendix H.

IMPLEMENTATION AND MAINTENANCE OF THE HACCP PLAN

The successful implementation of a HACCP plan is facilitated by commitment from top management. The next step is to establish a plan that describes the individuals responsible for developing, implementing, and maintaining the HACCP system. Initially, the HACCP coordinator and team are selected and trained as necessary. The team is then responsible for developing the initial plan and coordinating its implementation. Product teams can be appointed to develop HACCP plans for specific products. An important aspect in developing these teams is to assure that they have appropriate training. The workers who will be responsible for monitoring need to be adequately trained. Upon completion of the HACCP plan, operator procedures, forms and procedures for monitoring and corrective action are developed. Often it is a good idea to develop a timeline for the activities involved in the initial implementation of the HACCP plan. Implementation of the HACCP system involves the continual application of the monitoring, record-keeping, corrective action procedures and other activities as described in the HACCP plan.

Maintaining an effective HACCP system depends largely on regularly scheduled verification activities. The HACCP plan should be updated and revised as needed. An important aspect of maintaining the HACCP system is to assure that all individuals involved are properly trained so they understand their role and can effectively fulfill their responsibilities.

REFERENCES

1. National Advisory Committee on Microbiological Criteria for Foods. *The Principles of Risk Assessment for Illness Caused by Foodborne Biological Agents.* Adopted April 4, 1997.
2. National Academy of Sciences, *An Evaluation of the Role of Microbiological Criteria for Foods and Food Ingredients* (Washington, DC: National Academy Press, 1985).
3. National Advisory Committee on Microbiological Criteria for Foods. "The role of Regulatory Agencies and Industry in HACCP," *Int. J. Food Microbiol.* 21 (1994): 187–195.

APPENDIX C.A

Examples of Common Prerequisite Programs

The production of safe food products requires that the HACCP system be built upon a solid foundation of prerequisite programs. Each segment of the food industry must provide the conditions necessary to protect food while it is under their control. This has traditionally been accomplished through the application of cGMPs. These conditions and practices are now considered to be prerequisite to the development and implementation of effective HACCP plans. Prerequisite programs provide the basic environmental and operating conditions that are necessary for the production of safe, wholesome food. Common prerequisite programs may include, but are not limited to:

Facilities. The establishment should be located, constructed and maintained according to sanitary design principles. There should be linear product flow and traffic control to minimize cross-contamination from raw to cooked materials.

Supplier Control. Each facility should assure that its suppliers have in place effective GMP and food safety programs. These may be the subject of continuing supplier guarantee and supplier HACCP system verification.

Specifications. There should be written specifications for all ingredients, products, and packaging materials.

Production Equipment. All equipment should be constructed and installed according to sanitary design principles. Preventive maintenance and calibration schedules should be established and documented.

Cleaning and Sanitation. All procedures for cleaning and sanitation of the equipment and the facility should be written and followed. A master sanitation schedule should be in place.

Personal Hygiene. All employees and other persons who enter the manufacturing plant should follow the requirements for personal hygiene.

Training. All employees should receive documented training in personal hygiene, GMP, cleaning and sanitation procedures, personal safety, and their role in the HACCP program.

Chemical Control. Documented procedures must be in place to assure the segregation and proper use of non-food chemicals in the plant. These include cleaning chemicals, fumigants, and pesticides or baits used in or around the plant.

Receiving, Storage, and Shipping. All raw materials and products should be stored under sanitary conditions and the proper environmental conditions such as temperature and humidity to assure their safety and wholesomeness.

Traceability and Recall. All raw materials and products should be lot-coded and a recall system in place so that rapid and complete traces and recalls can be done when a product retrieval is necessary.

Pest Control. Effective pest control programs should be in place.

Other examples of prerequisite programs might include quality assurance procedures; standard operating procedures for sanitation, processes, product formulations and recipes; glass control; procedures for receiving, storage and shipping; labeling; and employee food and ingredient handling practices.

APPENDIX C.B

Example of a Flow Diagram for the Production of Frozen Cooked Beef Patties

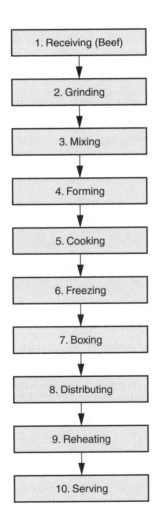

APPENDIX C.C

Examples of Questions to Be Considered When Conducting a Hazard Analysis

The hazard analysis consists of asking a series of questions which are appropriate to the process under consideration. The purpose of the questions is to assist in identifying potential hazards.

A. Ingredients

1. Does the food contain any sensitive ingredients that may present microbiological hazards (e.g., *Salmonella*, *Staphylococcus aureus*); chemical hazards (e.g., aflatoxin, antibiotic or pesticide residues); or physical hazards (stones, glass, metal)?

2. Are potable water, ice, and steam used in formulating or in handling the food?

3. What are the sources (e.g., geographical region, specific supplier)

B. Intrinsic Factors—Physical characteristics and composition (e.g., pH, type of acidulants, fermentable carbohydrate, water activity, preservatives) of the food during and after processing.

1. What hazards may result if the food composition is not controlled?

2. Does the food permit survival or multiplication of pathogens and/or toxin formation in the food during processing?

3. Will the food permit survival or multiplication of pathogens and/or toxin formation during subsequent steps in the food chain?

4. Are there other similar products in the market place? What has been the safety record for these products? What hazards have been associated with the products?

C. Procedures used for processing

1. Does the process include a controllable processing step that destroys pathogens? If so, which pathogens? Consider both vegetative cells and spores.

2. If the product is subject to recontamination between processing (e.g., cooking, pasteurizing) and packaging which biological, chemical or physical hazards are likely to occur?

D. Microbial content of the food

1. What is the normal microbial content of the food?

2. Does the microbial population change during the normal time the food is stored prior to consumption?

3. Does the subsequent change in microbial population alter the safety of the food?

4. Do the answers to the above questions indicate a high likelihood of certain biological hazards?

E. Facility design

1. Does the layout of the facility provide an adequate separation of raw materials from ready-to-eat (RTE) foods if this is important to food safety? If not, what hazards should be considered as possible contaminants of the RTE products?

2. Is positive air pressure maintained in product packaging areas? Is this essential for product safety?

3. Is the traffic pattern for people and moving equipment a significant source of contamination?

F. Equipment design and use

1. Will the equipment provide the time-temperature control that is necessary for safe food?

2. Is the equipment properly sized for the volume of food that will be processed?

3. Can the equipment be sufficiently controlled so that the variation in performance will be within the tolerances required to produce a safe food?

4. Is the equipment reliable or is it prone to frequent breakdowns?

5. Is the equipment designed so that it can be easily cleaned and sanitized?

6. Is there a chance for product contamination with hazardous substances; e.g., glass?

7. What product safety devices are used to enhance consumer safety?
   • metal detectors
   • magnets
   • sifters
   • filters
   • screens
   • hermometers
   • bone removal devices
   • dud detectors

8. To what degree will normal equipment wear affect the likely occurrence of a physical hazard (e.g., metal) in the product?

9. Are allergen protocols needed in using equipment for different products?

G. Packaging

1. Does the method of packaging affect the multiplication of microbial pathogens and/or the formation of toxins?

2. Is the package clearly labeled "Keep Refrigerated" if this is required for safety?

3. Does the package include instructions for the safe handling and preparation of the food by the end user?

4. Is the packaging material resistant to damage thereby preventing the entrance of microbial contamination?

5. Are tamper-evident packaging features used?

6. Is each package and case legibly and accurately coded?

7. Does each package contain the proper label?

8. Are potential allergens in the ingredients included in the list of ingredients on the label?

H. Sanitation

1. Can sanitation have an impact upon the safety of the food that is being processed?

2. Can the facility and equipment be easily cleaned and sanitized to permit the safe handling of food?

3. Is it possible to provide sanitary conditions consistently and adequately to assure safe foods?

I. Employee health, hygiene, and education

1. Can employee health or personal hygiene practices impact upon the safety of the food being processed?

2. Do the employees understand the process and the factors they must control to assure the preparation of safe foods?

3. Will the employees inform management of a problem which could impact upon safety of food?

J. Conditions of storage between packaging and the end user

1. What is the likelihood that the food will be improperly stored at the wrong temperature?

2. Would an error in improper storage lead to a microbiologically unsafe food?

K. Intended use

1. Will the food be heated by the consumer?

2. Will there likely be leftovers?

L. Intended consumer

1. Is the food intended for the general public?

2. Is the food intended for consumption by a population with increased susceptibility to illness (e.g., infants, the aged, the infirmed, immunocompromised individuals)?

3. Is the food to be used for institutional feeding or the home?

APPENDIX C.D

Examples of How the Stages of Hazard Analysis are used to Identify and Evaluate Hazards*

Hazard analysis stage	Frozen cooked beef patties produced in a manufacturing plant	Product containing eggs prepared for foodservice	Commercial frozen pre-cooked, boned chicken for further processing
Stage 1: Hazard identification Determine potential hazards associated with product	Enteric pathogens (i.e., *E. coli* 0157:H7 and *Salmonella*)	*Salmonella* in finished product	*Staphylococcus aureus* in finished product
Stage 2: Hazard evaluation Assess severity of health consequences if potential hazard is not properly controlled.	Epidemiological evidence indicates that these pathogens cause severe health effects including death among children and elderly. Undercooked beef patties have been linked to disease from these pathogens.	Salmonellosis is a food borne infection causing a moderate to severe illness that can be caused by ingestion of only a few cells of *Salmonella*.	Certain strains of *S. aureus* produce an enterotoxin which can cause a moderate foodborne illness.
Determine likelihood of occurrence of potential hazard if not properly controlled.	*E. coli* 0157:H7 is of very low probability and salmonellae is of moderate probability in raw meat.	Product is made with liquid eggs which have been associated with past outbreaks of salmonellosis. Recent problems with *Salmonella* serotype Enteritidis in eggs cause increased concern. Probability of *Salmonella* in raw eggs cannot be ruled out. If not effectively controlled, some consumers are likely to be exposed to *Salmonella* from this food.	Product may be contaminated with *S. aureus* due to human handling during boning of cooked chicken. Enterotoxin capable of causing illness will only occur as *S. aureus* multiplies to about 1,000,000/g. Operating procedures during boning and subsequent freezing prevent growth of *S. aureus*, thus the potential for enterotoxin formation is very low.
Using information above, determine if this potential hazard is to be addressed in the HACCP plan.	The HACCP team decides that enteric pathogens are hazards for this product.	HACCP team determines that if the potential hazard is not properly controlled, consumption of product is likely to result in an unacceptable health risk.	The HACCP team determines that the potential for enterotoxin formation is very low. However, it is still desirable to keep the initial number of *S. aureus* organisms low. Employee practices that minimize contamination, rapid carbon dioxide freezing and handling instructions have been adequate to control this potential hazard.
	Hazards must be addressed in the plan.	**Hazard must be addressed in the plan.**	**Potential hazard does not need to be addressed in plan.**

* For illustrative purposes only. The potential hazards identified may not be the only hazards associated with the products listed. The responses may be different for different establishments.

APPENDIX C.E

Example I of a CCP Decision Tree

Important considerations when using the decision tree:

The decision tree is used after the hazard analysis.

The decision tree then is used at the steps where a hazard that must be addressed in the HACCP plan has been identified.

A subsequent step in the process may be more effective for controlling a hazard and may be the preferred CCP.

More than one step in a process may be involved in controlling a hazard.

More than one hazard may be controlled by a specific control measure.

Q1.   Does this step involve a hazard of sufficient likelihood of occurrence and severity to warrant its control?

Q2.   Does a control measure for the hazard exist at this step?

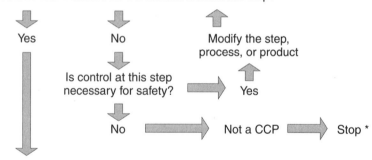

Q3.   Is control at this step necessary to prevent, eliminate, or reduce the risk of the hazard to consumers?

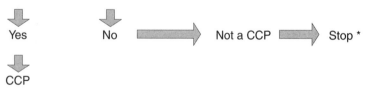

* Proceed to next step in the process

APPENDIX C.F

Example II of a CCP Decision Tree

Q1. Do control measure(s) exist for the identified hazard?

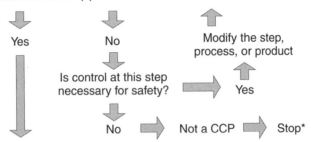

Q2. Does this step eliminate or reduce the likely occurrence of a hazard to an acceptable level?

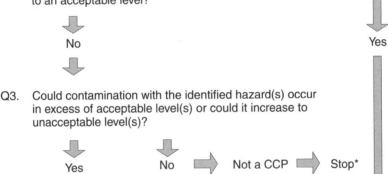

Q3. Could contamination with the identified hazard(s) occur in excess of acceptable level(s) or could it increase to unacceptable level(s)?

Q4. Will a subsequent step eliminate the identified hazard(s) or reduce its likely occurrence to an acceptable level?

Critical control point

* Proceed to next step in the process

APPENDIX C.G

Examples of Verification Activities

A. Verification procedures may include:

1. Establishment of appropriate verification schedules.

2. Review of the HACCP plan for completeness.

3. Confirmation of the accuracy of the flow diagram.

4. Review of the HACCP system to determine if the facility is operating according to the HACCP plan.

5. Review of CCP monitoring records.

6. Review of records for deviations and corrective actions.

7. Validation of critical limits to confirm that they are adequate to control significant hazards.

8. Validation of HACCP plan, including on-site review.

9. Review of modifications of the HACCP plan.

10. Sampling and testing to verify CCPs.

B. Verification should be conducted:

1. Routinely, or on an unannounced basis, to assure CCPs are under control.

2. When there are emerging concerns about the safety of the product.

3. When foods have been implicated as a vehicle of foodborne disease.

4. To confirm that changes have been implemented correctly after a HACCP plan has been modified.

5. To assess whether a HACCP plan should be modified due to a change in the process, equipment, ingredients, etc.

C. Verification reports may include information on the presence and adequacy of:

1. The HACCP plan and the person(s) responsible for administering and updating the HACCP plan.

2. The records associated with CCP monitoring.

3. Direct recording of monitoring data of the CCP while in operation.

4. Certification that monitoring equipment is properly calibrated and in working order.

5. Corrective actions for deviations.

6. Sampling and testing methods used to verify that CCPs are under control.

7. Modifications to the HACCP plan.

8. Training and knowledge of individuals responsible for monitoring CCPs.

9. Validation activities.

APPENDIX C.H

Examples of HACCP Records

A. Ingredients for which critical limits have been established.

1. Supplier certification records documenting compliance of an ingredient with a critical limit.

2. Processor audit records verifying supplier compliance.

3. Storage records (e.g., time, temperature) for when ingredient storage is a CCP.

B. Processing, storage, and distribution records

1. Information that establishes the efficacy of a CCP to maintain product safety.

2. Data establishing the safe shelf life of the product; if age of product can affect safety.

3. Records indicating compliance with critical limits when packaging materials, labeling or sealing specifications are necessary for Food safety.

4. Monitoring records.

5. Verification records.

C. Deviation and corrective action records.

D. Employee training records that are pertinent to CCPs and the HACCP plan.

E. Documentation of the adequacy of the HACCP plan from a knowledgeable HACCP expert.

Appendix D

Codex HACCP Guidelines

GUIDELINES FOR THE APPLICATION
OF THE HACCP SYSTEM

Prior to application of HACCP to any sector of the food chain, that sector should be operating according to the Codex General Principles of Food Hygiene, the appropriate Codex Codes of Practice, and appropriate food safety legislation. Management commitment is necessary for implementation of an effective HACCP system. During hazard identification, evaluation, and subsequent operations in designing and applying HACCP systems, consideration must be given to the impact of raw materials, ingredients, food manufacturing practices, role of manufacturing processes to control hazards, likely end-use of the product, categories of consumers of concern, and epidemiological evidence relative to food safety.

The intent of the HACCP system is to focus control at CCPs. Redesign of the operation should be considered if a hazard which must be controlled is identified but no CCPs are found.

HACCP should be applied to each specific operation separately. CCPs identified in any given example in any Codex Code of Hygienic Practice might not be the only ones identified for a specific application or might be of a different nature.

The HACCP application should be reviewed and necessary changes made when any modification is made in the product, process, or any step.

It is important when applying HACCP to be flexible where appropriate, given the context of the application taking into account the nature and the size of the operation.

Application

The application of HACCP principles consists of the following tasks as identified in the Logic Sequence for Application of HACCP (Figure D.1).

    1. *Assemble HACCP team.* The food operation should assure that the appropriate product specific knowledge and expertise is available for the development of an effective HACCP plan. Optimally, this may be accomplished by assembling a multidisciplinary team. Where such expertise is not available on site, expert advice should be

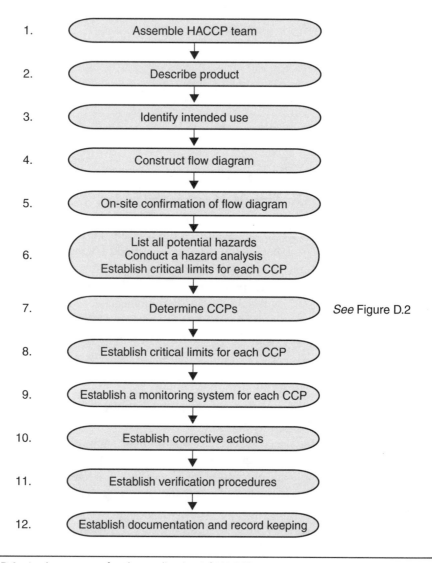

Figure D.1   Logic sequence for the application of HACCP.

obtained from other sources. The scope of the HACCP plan should be identified. The scope should describe which segment of the food chain is involved and the general classes of hazards to be addressed (e.g. does it cover all classes of hazards or only selected classes).

2. *Describe product.* A full description of the product should be drawn up, including relevant safety information such as: composition, physical/chemical structure (including A_w, pH, etc.), microcidal/static treatments (heat-treatment, freezing, brining, smoking, etc.), packaging, durability and storage conditions and method of distribution.

3. *Identify intended use.* The intended use should be based on the expected uses of the product by the end user or consumer. In specific cases, vulnerable groups of the population, e.g. institutional feeding, may have to be considered.

4. *Construct flow diagram.* The flow diagram should be constructed by the HACCP team. The flow diagram should cover all steps in the operation. When applying HACCP to a given operation, consideration should be given to steps preceding and following the specified operation.

5. *On-site confirmation of flow diagram.* The HACCP team should confirm the processing operation against the flow diagram during all stages and hours of operation and amend the flow diagram where appropriate.

6. *List all potential hazards associated with each step, conduct a hazard analysis, and consider any measures to control identified hazards* (see Principle 1). The HACCP team should list all of the hazards that may be reasonably expected to occur at each step from primary production, processing, manufacture, and distribution until the point of consumption.

The HACCP team should next conduct a hazard analysis to identify for the HACCP plan which hazards are of such a nature that their elimination or reduction to acceptable levels is essential to the production of a safe food.

In conducting the hazard analysis, wherever possible the following should be included:

- the likely occurrence of hazards and severity of their adverse health effects

- the qualitative and/or quantitative evaluation of the presence of hazards

- survival or multiplication of microorganisms of concern

- production or persistence in foods of toxins, chemicals or physical agents

- conditions leading to the above

The HACCP team must then consider what control measures, if any, exist which can be applied for each hazard.

More than one control measure may be required to control a specific hazard(s) and more than one hazard may be controlled by a specified control measure.

(answer questions in sequence)

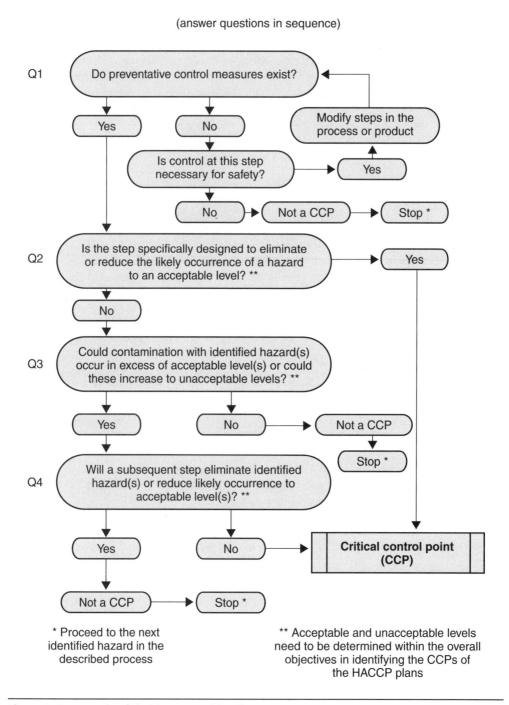

* Proceed to the next
identified hazard in the
described process

** Acceptable and unacceptable levels
need to be determined within the overall
objectives in identifying the CCPs of
the HACCP plans

Figure D.2 Example of decision tree to identify CCPs.

7. *Determine Critical Control Points* (see Principle 2).[1] There may be more than one CCP at which control is applied to address the same hazard. The determination of a CCP in the HACCP system can be facilitated by the application of a decision tree (e.g. Figure D.2), which indicates a logic reasoning approach. Application of a decision tree should be flexible, given whether the operation is for production, slaughter, processing, storage, distribution or other. It should be used for guidance when determining CCPs. This example of a decision tree may not be applicable to all situations. Other approaches may be used. Training in the application of the decision tree is recommended.

If a hazard has been identified at a step where control is necessary for safety, and no control measure exists at that step, or any other, then the product or process should be modified at that step, or at any earlier or later stage, to include a control measure.

8. *Establish critical limits for each CCP* (see Principle 3). Critical limits must be specified and validated if possible for each Critical Control Point. In some cases more than one critical limit will be elaborated at a particular step. Criteria often used include measurements of temperature, time, moisture level, pH, A_w, available chlorine, and sensory parameters such as visual appearance and texture.

9. *Establish a monitoring system for each CCP* (see Principle 4). Monitoring is the scheduled measurement or observation of a CCP relative to its critical limits. The monitoring procedures must be able to detect loss of control at the CCP. Further, monitoring should ideally provide this information in time to make adjustments to ensure control of the process to prevent violating the critical limits. Where possible, process adjustments should be made when monitoring results indicate a trend towards loss of control at a CCP. The adjustments should be taken before a deviation occurs. Data derived from monitoring must be evaluated by a designated person with knowledge and authority to carry out corrective actions when indicated. If monitoring is not continuous, then the amount or frequency of monitoring must be sufficient to guarantee the CCP is in control. Most monitoring procedures for CCPs will need to be done rapidly because they relate to on-line processes and there will not be time for lengthy analytical testing. Physical and chemical measurements are often preferred to microbiological testing because they may be done rapidly and can often indicate the microbiological control of the product. All records and documents associated with monitoring CCPs must be signed by the person(s) doing the monitoring and by a responsible reviewing official(s) of the company.

---

[1]Since the publication of the decision tree by Codex, its use has been implemented many times for training purposes. In many instances, while this tree has been useful to explain the logic and depth of understanding needed to determine CCPs, it is not specific to all food operations, e.g. slaughter, and therefore it should be used in conjunction with professional judgement, and modified in some cases.

10. *Establish corrective actions* (see Principle 5). Specific corrective actions must be developed for each CCP in the HACCP system in order to deal with deviations when they occur.

The actions must ensure that the CCP has been brought under control. Actions taken must also include proper disposition of the affected product. Deviation and product disposition procedures must be documented in the HACCP record keeping.

11. *Establish verification procedures* (see Principle 6). Establish procedures for verification. Verification and auditing methods, procedures and tests, including random sampling and analysis, can be used to determine if the HACCP system is working correctly. The frequency of verification should be sufficient to confirm that the HACCP system is working effectively. Examples of verification activities include:

- Review of the HACCP system and its records;

- Review of deviations and product dispositions;

- Confirmation that CCPs are kept under control.

Where possible, validation activities should include actions to confirm the efficacy of all elements of the HACCP plan.

12. *Establish Documentation and Record Keeping* (see Principle 7). Efficient and accurate record keeping is essential to the application of a HACCP system. HACCP procedures should be documented. Documentation and record keeping should be appropriate to the nature and size of the operation. Documentation examples are:

- Hazard analysis

- CCP determination

- Critical limit determination

Record examples are:

- CCP monitoring activities

- Deviations and associated corrective actions

- Modifications to the HACCP system

An example of a HACCP worksheet is attached as Figure D.3.

Training

Training of personnel in industry, government, and academia in HACCP principles and applications, and increasing awareness of consumers are essential elements for

Figure D.3 Example of a HACCP worksheet.

the effective implementation of HACCP. As an aid in developing specific training to support a HACCP plan, working instructions and procedures should be developed which define the tasks of the operating personnel to be stationed at each Critical Control Point.

Cooperation between primary producer, industry, trade groups, consumer organizations, and responsible authorities is of vital importance. Opportunities should be provided for the joint training of industry and control authorities to encourage and maintain a continuous dialogue and create a climate of understanding in the practical application of HACCP.

Appendix E

Body of Knowledge for the Hazard Analysis and Critical Control Point (HACCP) Examination

I. HACCP Overview (10 questions)

  A. History

    1. NASA, Pillsbury, U.S. Army Natick Laboratories

    2. Low-acid canned food (LACF) regulations

    3. National Academy of Sciences 1985 Report

    4. National Advisory Committee on Microbiological Criteria for Foods (NACMCF)

    5. Expansion of HACCP

      a. Medical devices

      b. Market-driven HACCP

      c. Regulatory-driven HACCP

      d. Integrated product safety system (e.g. "farm-to-table;" "concept-to-end-use")

      e. International acceptance

        • Codex Alimentarius

        • Ag Canada

        • Trade equivalence

B. Scope

    1. Product safety management system

    2. Relationship of HACCP to other systems (e.g., quality management, risk management, non-safety regulatory requirements, customer specifications)

C. Benefits of HACCP

    1. Primary benefit: product safety

    2. Secondary benefits (e.g., improved quality, economics, customer/consumer confidence, and inspection time)

D. Management Responsibility

    1. Commitment to HACCP

    2. Moving HACCP beyond regulatory compliance

    3. Education/training needs

    4. Commitment to prerequisite programs

    5. Continuous improvement of management systems

    6. Knowledge of current and emerging regulations, hazards, and technology

E. HACCP Terminology

II. Prerequisite Programs (18 questions)

A. Foundation for HACCP System

    1. Control of operational conditions

    2. Control of environmental conditions

B. Examples of Prerequisite Programs (e.g., GMPs, SSOPs, GAPs, GLPs)

    1. Facilities (adjacent properties, building exterior/interior)

    2. Raw materials controls (e.g., specifications, supplier approval, receipt and storage, testing)

    3. Sanitation and personal hygiene (e.g., master schedule, pest control, environmental surveillance, chemical control, housekeeping, cleaning: routine, personal, health, and hygiene)

    4. Training and education

    5. Production equipment (e.g., sanitary design/installation, cleaning/sanitation, preventive maintenance, calibration)

    6. Production controls (e.g., product zone controls, foreign material control, metal protection program, allergen control, glass control)

7. Storage and distribution (e.g., temperature and humidity control; transport vehicle cleaning and inspection)

8. Product controls/traceability (e.g., labeling; complaint investigation)

9. Hazardous materials handling

10. Product recall

III. HACCP Plan Development (47 questions)

    A. Preliminary Tasks

        1. Assemble the HACCP team

        2. Describe the product and its distribution

        3. Describe the intended use and end-user, consumer, patient

        4. Develop a process flow diagram

        5. Verify the process flow diagram

    B. HACCP Principles

        1. Conduct a hazard analysis (specific to plant, process, product)

           a. Identify hazards

           b. Evaluate hazards

              • Severity (seriousness of consequences of exposure to hazard)

              • Likelihood of occurrence

           c. Identify control measures for each hazard that is identified as reasonably likely to occur

        2. Determine the critical control points (CCPs)

           a. Control points

           b. Critical control points

           c. CCP decision trees

        3. Establish critical limits

           a. HACCP-related concepts

              • Critical limits

              • Specification limits, operating limits, and process control limits

           b. Sources of information for establishing limits

        4. Establish monitoring procedures

           a. Continuous monitoring vs. sampling and testing

b. Specified procedures

- Methods

- Frequency

- Responsibility

5. Establish corrective actions

a. Adjustment vs. corrective action

b. Corrective action procedures

- Identify cause of derivation

- Determine product disposition

- Record corrective actions

- Implement preventive action

- Reevaluate HACCP plan

6. Establish verification procedures

a. Documentation and record review

b. Calibration

c. Testing and analysis

d. Validation

7. Establish record keeping and documentation procedures

a. The HACCP plan and the support documentation used to develop the plan

b. Records of CCP monitoring

c. Records of corrective action

d. Records of verification activities

e. Document control

IV. Implementation and Maintenance of HACCP System (25 questions)

A. Prerequisite programs

B. Training and education

C. Initiate the system (operational qualification)

D. Validation and reassessment

E. Verification of the HACCP System

   1. Types and roles of HACCP Audits

      a. Internal

      b. Third-party

      c. Regulatory

   2. Review CCP records (e.g., monitoring records, corrective action records, calibration records; including frequency, responsibilities, trend analysis, record keeping procedures)

   3. Direct observations of system procedures

TOTAL = 100 questions

Bibliography

"A State-of-the-Art Approach to Food Safety." *FDA Backgrounder.* U.S. Food and Drug Administration, August 1999.

AIB International. *AIB Consolidated Standards for Food Safety.* Manhattan, KS: AIB International, 1995.

AIB International. "HACCP Overview," presented in HACCP Workshop. Manhattan, KS: AIB International, 2000.

American National Standard, ANSI/ASQC Q10011-1, Q10011-2, Q10011-3. *Guidelines for Auditing Quality Systems.* Milwaukee: American Society for Quality Control, 1994.

Association of Food and Drug Officials. *Medical Device HACCP Training Curriculum.* Draft Edition. York, PA: AFDO, 1999.

Association of Food and Drug Officials. *Seafood HACCP Training Curriculum.* 3rd ed. York, PA: AFDO, 1999.

ASQ CQA Brochure.

Baking Industry Sanitation Standards Committee. *1998 Sanitation Standards for the Design and Construction of Bakery Equipment.* Chicago: BISSC, 1998.

Bennet, William L., and Leonard L. Steed. "An Integrated Approach to Food Safety." *Quality Progress* (February, 1999): 37–42.

Boyle, Elizabeth A. E., and Kelly J. K. Getty. *Developing and Implementing HACCP in Meat Plants.* A workshop notebook compiled by Boyle and Getty at Kansas State University, Manhattan, KS, 1998.

Burson, Dennis and Mindy Brashears. *Implementing Your Company's HACCP Plan: Meat Slaughter and Processing.* A workshop notebook compiled by Burson and Brashears at the University of Nebraska, Lincoln, NE, 1998.

Campden and Chorleywood. *HACCP: A Practical Guide.* Second ed. Technical Manual No. 38. Food and Drink Research Association, 1997.

Canadian Food Inspection Agency. *Food Safety Enhancement Program Implementation Manual,* Vol. II. (Ottawa, Canada: Government of Canada, 1995).

Codex Commission on Food Hygiene. *Guidelines for the Application of the Hazard Analysis and Critical Control Point (HACCP) System.* Adopted by the Joint FAO/WHO Codex Commission, 20th Session, 1993. 1991.

Codex. *Hazard Analysis and Critical Control Point (HACCP) System and Guidelines for its Application.* Alinorm 97/13A. Rome: Codex Alimentarius Committee on Food Hygiene, 1997.

Corlett, Donald A., Jr. *HACCP User's Manual.* Gaithersburg, MD: Aspen, 1998.

Dillon, Mike and Chris Griffith. *How to HACCP.* U.K.: MD Associates, 1996.

Doyle, M. P., L. R. Beuchat, and T. J. Montville. *Food Microbiology: Fundamentals and Frontiers.* Washington, DC: ASM Press, 1997.

European Committee for Standardization. *Food Processing Machinery—Basic Concepts—Part 2: Hygiene requirements.* British Standard EN 1672-2: 1997, Subcommittee MCE/3/5, Food Industry Machines. English version, 1997.

European Standard, EN 1441, Medical Devices—Risk Analysis.

Food and Agricultural Organization of the United Nations (FAO), Food Quality Standards Service Food and Nutrition Division. *Food Quality and Safety Systems—A Training Manual on Food Hygiene and the Hazard Analysis and Critical Control Point (HACCP) System.* Rome: Publishing Management Group, FAO Information Division, 1998.

Food and Agricultural Organization of the United Nations. *The Use of Hazard Analysis Critical Control Point (HACCP) Principles in Food Control.* Rome: FAO, 1995.

Gould, Brian W., Marianne Smukowski, and J. Russell Bishop. "HACCP and the Dairy Industry: An Overview of HACCP Costs and Benefits," in *The Economics of HACCP,* L. J. Unnivehr, ed. St. Paul, MN: Eagon Press, 2000.

Imholte, Thomas J., and Tammy Imholte-Tauscher. *Engineering for Food Safety.* Second ed. Woodinville, WA: Technical Institute for Food Safety, 1999.

International Commission for the Microbiological Specifications for Food (ICMFS), 1988.

International Standard ISO 14971, Medical Devices—Risk Management—Part 1: Application of Risk Analysis.

International Standard IEC 601-1-4, Medical Electrical Equipment, Part 1: General Requirements for Safety.

Johnson, E. C., J. H. Nelson, and M. Johnson. "Microbiological Safety of Cheese Made from Heat-Treated Milk," *Journal of Food Protection* 53, 1990.

Kraft Foods, Inc. *Supplier/Comanufacturer HACCP Standard.* Northfield, IL: Kraft Foods, Inc., 24 February 1997.

Lee, J. S., and K. S. Hilderbrand, Jr. *Hazard Analysis and Critical Control Point Application to the Seafood Industry.* ORESU-H-92-01. OR: Oregon Sea Grant, Oregon State University, 1992.

Lund, B. M., T. C. Baird-Parker, and G. W. Gould. *The Microbiological Safety and Quality of Food, Vol. 1.* Gaithersburg, MD: Aspen Publishers, 2000.

———. *The Microbiological Safety and Quality of Food, Vol. 2.* Gaithersburg, MD: Aspen Publishers, 2000.

Mihalic, Michael W. and Dennis Edwards. *Rich Products Corporation QA/Sanitation Conference Manuals.* Buffalo, NY: Rich Products Corporation, 2000.

Mortimore, Sara, and Carol Wallace. *HACCP: A Practical Approach.* Second ed. New York: Chapman and Hall, 1995.

Mortimore, Sara, and Carol Wallace. *HACCP: A Practical Approach.* Third ed. Gaithersburg, MD: Aspen, 1998.

National Academy of Sciences. *An Evaluation of the Role of Microbiological Criteria for Foods and Food Ingredients.* Washington, DC: National Academy Press, 1985.

National Restaurant Association. *ServSafe© Training's a Practical Approach to HACCP.* Chicago: The Educational Foundation of The National Restaurant Association, 1998.

National Seafood HACCP Alliance for Training and Education. "Chapter 11: Record-Keeping Procedures," in *HACCP: Hazard Analysis and Critical Control Point Training Curriculum* (1997): 111–126.

Pierson, Merle D. and Donald A. Corlett, Jr. *HACCP Principles and Applications.* New York: Van Norstrand Reinhold, 1992.

Process Validation Guidance, Global Harmonization Task Force, Study Group 3, June 1, 1998.

Puri, Subhash C. *Statistical Methods for Food Quality Management.* Ottawa, Canada: Agriculture Canada Publication, 1989.

Rushing, James W. and Frederick J. Angulo. "Implementation of a HACCP in a Commercial Tomato Packinghouse: A Model for the Industry," in *Dairy, Food and Environmental Sanitation* 16, no. 9 (1996): 549–553.

Russell, J. P. (ed.). *The Quality Audit Handbook.* Milwaukee: ASQC Quality Press, 1997.

Smukowski, M. and N. Brisk. "Dairy Products Industry," *Encyclopaedia of Occupation Health and Safety* 3. Fourth ed. Geneva: International Labor Office, 1997.

Snyder, O. Peter, Jr., Ph.D. *HACCP-TQM Retail Food Operations Manual.* St. Paul, MN: Hospitality Institute of Technology and Management, 1999.

Sperber, William H., et al. "The Role of Prerequisite Programs in Managing a HACCP System," in *Dairy, Food, and Environmental Sanitation* 18, no. 7 (1998): 418–423.

Stevenson, Kenneth E. and Dane T. Bernard. *HACCP—A Systematic Approach to Food Safety.* Third ed. Washington, DC: The National Food Processors Institute, 1999.

U.S. National Advisory Committee on Microbiological Criteria for Foods (NACMCF). *Guidelines for Application of HACCP Principles.* Washington, DC: U.S. Food and Drug Administration, 14 August 1997.

U.S. National Advisory Committee on Microbiological Criteria for Foods (NACMCF). *Hazard Analysis and Critical Control Point Principles and Application Guidelines.* J. Food Protection 61 (1998): 762.

U.S. National Advisory Committee on Microbiological Criteria for Foods (NACMCF). *Hazard Analysis and Critical Control Point Principles and Application Guidelines, Appendix A.* Washington, DC: U.S. Food and Drug Administration, 14 August 1997.

U.S. Public Health Service, U.S. Department of Health and Human Services. "Annex 5: HACCP Guidelines," in *1999 Food Code.* Washington, DC: U. S. Food and Drug Administration, 1999.

U.S. Department of Health and Human Services, U.S. Public Health Service, U.S. Food and Drug Administration, Center for Food Safety and Applied Nutrition and Office of Seafood. *Fish & Fisheries Products Hazards & Control Guide.* Second ed. (1998): 232, 234.

U.S. Food and Drug Administration. *Hazards and Controls Guide for Fish and Fishery Products.* Second ed. USFDA, 1999.

U.S. Food and Drug Administration. *Guidelines on General Principles of Process Validation.* May 11, 1987.

U.S. Food and Drug Administration. *Guide to Inspections of Quality Systems (QSIT).* August 1999.

U.S. Food and Drug Administration. *Current Good Manufacturing Practice in Manufacturing, Packing, or Holding Human Food.* Title 21 Code of Federal Regulations Part 110, 1986.

U.S. Food and Drug Administration. *Current Good Manufacturing Practice in Manufacturing, Packing, or Holding Food.* Code of Federal Regulations, Title 21, Volume 2, Section 110, 2000. http://www.fda.gov

U.S. Food and Drug Administration. *Procedures for the Safe and Sanitary Processing and Importing of Fish and Fishery Products* (Seafood HACCP Regulation). Title 21 Code of Federal Regulations Part 123, 1995.

U.S. Department of Agriculture. *Hazard Analysis and Critical Control Point (HACCP) Systems* (Meat and Poultry HACCP Regulation). Title 9 Code of Federal Regulations Parts 416 and 417, 1996.

U.S. Food and Drug Administration. *Guidance for Industry: Guide to Minimize Microbial Food Safety Hazards for Fresh Fruits and Vegetables.* Washington, DC: Center for Food Safety and Applied Nutrition, 1998. http://www.fda.gov

U.S. Food and Drug Administration. "Foods Adulteration Involving Hard or Sharp Foreign Objects." *FDA/ORA Compliance Guide*, Chapter 5, Subchapter 555, Section 555.425, 1999.

USDA/FSIS. "Appendix A: Compliance Guidelines for Meeting the Lethality Conformance Standards for Certain Meat and Poultry Products." 1999. http://www.fsis.usda.gov.\oa\fr\95033f-b.htm

USDA/FSIS. "Appendix B: Compliance Guidelines for Cooling Heat-Treated Meat and Poultry Products (Stabilization)." 1999. http://www.fsisusda.gov.\oa\fr\95033f-b/htm

USDA/FSIS. *Code of Federal Regulations—Animal and Animal Products.* 9 CFR Ch. III. Part 417-Hazard Analysis and Critical Control Point (HACCP) Systems. 2000. http://www.fsis.usda.gov /oa/haccp/imphaccp.htm

U.S. Public Health Service, U.S. Department of Health and Human Services, U.S. Food and Drug Administration. *Managing Food Safety: A HACCP Principles Guide for Operators of Food Establishments at the Retail Level,* Draft. Washington, DC: Center for Food Safety and Applied Nutrition, 15 April 1998.

U.S. Food and Drug Administration. A Quality System Regulation, Title 21, Section 820.

U.S. Department of Agriculture. Qualified through Verification (QTV) Program for the Fresh-Cut Produce Industry. Washington, DC: Agricultural Marketing Service, Processed Products Branch, 1999. http://www.usda.gov

Zagory, Devon and William C. Hurst (eds.). *Food Safety Guidelines for the Fresh-Cut Produce Industry.* Third Ed. Arlington, VA: International Fresh-Cut Produce Association, 1996.

Glossary

AFDO—Association of Food and Drug Officials

Audit—A planned, systematic, independent, and documented examination and review to determine whether activities and related results comply with planned arrangements and whether these arrangements are implemented effectively and suitable to achieve the objectives[1]*

CAC—Codex Alimentarius Commission, an agency of FAO and WHO

Calibration—The comparison of a measurement instrument or system of unverified accuracy to a measurement instrument of known accuracy to detect any variation from the true value[1]

CCP—*See* critical control point

CFIA—Canadian Food Inspection Agency

CFR—Code of Federal Regulations

cGMP—Current Good Manufacturing Practices

CIP—Clean-in-place

CL—*See* critical limit

Cleaning—The removal of soil, food residue, dirt, grease and other objectionable material[2]

COA—Certificate of Analysis

Codex—An abbreviation for CAC

---

*Indicates that the definition has been adapted from the definition as cited in the original source.

Contaminate—The introduction or occurrence of a contaminant in food or a food environment[2]

Control—(a) To manage the conditions of an operation to maintain compliance with established criteria; (b) The state where correct procedures are being followed and the criteria are being met[3]

Control measure—Any action or activity that can be used to prevent, eliminate, or reduce a significant hazard[3]

Control point—Any step at which biological, chemical, or physical factors can be controlled[3]; medical device definition—Any step at which a specification or quality factor(s) can be controlled[4]*

COP—Clean out-of-place

CP—*See* control point

Critical control point—Any step at which control can be applied to prevent, eliminate the occurrence of, or reduce to an acceptable level a product safety hazard[3]*

Critical limit—A maximum and or minimum value to which a biological, chemical, or physical parameter must be controlled at a CCP to prevent, eliminate, or reduce to an acceptable level the occurrence of a food safety hazard[3]

Cross-functional team—A group consisting of members from more than one department that is organized to accomplish a project[1]

Customer—Recipient of a product or service provided by a supplier[1]

Deviation—Failure to meet a critical limit[3]

Dry labbing—Recording a value in the absence of an observation

ECP—*See* essential control point

EL—*See* essential limit

Essential control point—A term used for medical device HACCP that is similar to a CCP—a point, step, or procedure at which control can be applied and is essential to prevent, eliminate, or reduce a hazard to an acceptable level[4]

Essential limit—A term used for medical device HACCP that is similar to a CL—a maximum and/or minimum value to which a product, process, or quality parameter must be controlled at an ECP to prevent, eliminate or reduce to an acceptable level the occurrence of a device hazard[4]

FAO—Food and Agriculture Organization, an agency of the United Nations

FDA—United States Food and Drug Administration, an agency of the Department of Health and Human Services

FR—Federal Register

FSIS—Food Safety Inspection Service, an agency of USDA

---

*Indicates that the definition has been adapted from the definition as cited in the original source.

GAP—Good agricultural practices

GMP—Good manufacturing practices

HACCP—Hazard analysis critical control point; a systematic approach to the identification, evaluation, and control of product safety hazards[3]

Hazard—A biological, chemical, or physical agent that is reasonably likely to cause illness or injury in the absence of its control[3]

Hazard analysis—The process of collecting and evaluating information on hazards associated with food under consideration to decide which are significant and must be addressed in the HACCP plan[3]

HVAC—Heating, ventilation, and air conditioning

ISO—International Organization for Standardization

MSDS—Material safety data sheet

NACMCF—National Advisory Committee on Microbiological Criteria for Foods

Pathological—Being able to develop a disease state

PC—Pest control

PO—Purchase order

Prerequisite program—Procedures including good manufacturing practices that address operational conditions providing the foundation for the HACCP system[3]

Principles of HACCP[3]

    Principle 1—Conduct a hazard analysis

    Principle 2—Determine the critical control points (CCPs)

    Principle 3—Establish critical limits

    Principle 4—Establish monitoring procedures

    Principle 5—Establish corrective actions

    Principle 6—Establish verification procedures

    Principle 7—Establish record keeping and documentation procedures

Process—A set of interrelated resources and activities which transform inputs into outputs[5]

Product safety system—The organization structure, procedures, processes, and resources needed to implement product safety management

Record—Document or electronic medium which furnishes objective evidence of activities performed or results achieved[1]

Sanitation—The reduction by means of chemical agents or physical methods of the number of microorganisms in the environment to a level that does not compromise food safety or suitability[2]*

---

*Indicates that the definition has been adapted from the definition as cited in the original source.

Severity—The seriousness of the effect(s) of a hazard[3]

SSOP—Standard sanitation operating procedures

Supplier—Any provider whose goods and services may be used at any stage in the production, design, delivery, and use of another company's products and services[1]

Training—Refers to the skills that employees need to learn to perform or improve the performance of their current job or tasks, or the process of providing those skills[1]

TC—Technical Committee of ISO

TQM—Total quality management

USDA—United States Department of Agriculture

Validation—That element of verification focused on collecting and evaluating scientific and technical information to determine if the HACCP plan, when properly implemented, will effectively control the hazards[3]

Verification—Those activities, other than monitoring, that determine the validity of the HACCP plan and if the system is operating according to the plan[3]

WHO—World Health Organization, an agency of the United Nations

SOURCES:

1. Duke Okes and Russell T. Westcott (eds.), *The Certified Quality Manager Handbook*, 2nd ed (Milwaukee: ASQ Quality Press, 2001).
2. Codex. *Hazard Analysis and Critical Control Point (HACCP) System and Guidelines for its Application*. Alinorm 97/13A. Rome: Codex Alimentarius Committee on Food Hygiene, 1997.
3. NACMCF
4. AFDO Medical Device Manual
5. ANSI/ISO/ASQC A8402-1994, *Quality Management and Quality Assurance—Vocabulary* (Milwaukee: American Society for Quality Control, 1994).

Index